SHAKESPEARE'S LATE STYLE

When Shakespeare gave up tragedy around 1607 and turned to the new form we call romance or tragicomedy, he created a distinctive poetic idiom that has often bewildered audiences and readers. The plays of this period – *Pericles, Cymbeline, The Winter's Tale, The Tempest,* and Shakespeare's contributions to the collaborative *Henry VIII* and *The Two Noble Kinsmen* – exhibit a challenging verse style: verbally condensed, metrically and syntactically sophisticated, both conversational and highly wrought. In *Shakespeare's Late Style,* McDonald anatomizes the components of this late style, illustrating in a series of topically organized chapters the contribution of such features as ellipsis, syntax, grammatical suspension, and multiple forms of repetition. Resisting the sentimentality that frequently attends discussion of an artist's "late" period, *Shakespeare's Late Style* shows how the poetry of the last plays reveals their creator's ambivalent attitude toward art, language, men and women, the theatre, and his own professional career.

RUSS MCDONALD is Reader in Renaissance Literature at Goldsmiths College, University of London. He is the author of *The Bedford Companion to Shakespeare, Shakespeare and the Arts of Language,* and, most recently, *"Look to the Lady": Sarah Siddons, Ellen Terry, and Judi Dench on the Shakespearean Stage*; he has edited a number of Shakespeare plays, including *A Midsummer Night's Dream* and *Othello,* as well as an anthology entitled *Shakespeare: An Anthology of Criticism and Theory.* Having taught Shakespeare in five American universities, he is the recipient of several teaching awards, including North Carolina Professor of the Year, 2003.

D1331217

SHAKESPEARE'S LATE STYLE

RUSS McDONALD

CAMBRIDGE
UNIVERSITY PRESS

CAMBRIDGE UNIVERSITY PRESS
Cambridge, New York, Melbourne, Madrid, Cape Town, Singapore,
São Paulo, Delhi, Dubai, Tokyo

Cambridge University Press
The Edinburgh Building, Cambridge CB2 8RU, UK

Published in the United States of America by Cambridge University Press, New York

www.cambridge.org
Information on this title: www.cambridge.org/9780521129626

First published 2006
Reprinted 2008
This digitally printed version 2009

A catalogue record for this publication is available from the British Library

ISBN 978-0-521-82068-4 Hardback
ISBN 978-0-521-12962-6 Paperback

There has been no subject less accurately investigated than that of English prosody. And however some may imagine it a trivial affair, and an enquiry about little things; there are others we trust to whom it will appear, that no grand and heroic achievement was ever performed by him that neglected little things.

Anonymous review (1784) of Edward Capell's *Notes and Various Readings*, *The English Review*, May 1784

Contents

Acknowledgements

This book began to take shape so long ago that a proper list of people who deserve thanks is not merely impracticable but impossible. Among the many who helped bring it into being, I recall with special gratitude the encouragement and criticism of Anne Barton, Thomas Berger, Stephen Booth, A. R. Braunmuller, the late Inga-Stina Ewbank, Clare Kinney, James Longenbach, Catherine Loomis, Gordon McMullan, Ruth Morse, Michael Neill, Stanley Wells, and George T. Wright. Sarah Stanton, my editor at Cambridge University Press, has lived up to her reputation for critical intelligence, honesty, and patience. My warmest gratitude is due to Gail and Jack McDonald.

Portions of several chapters were presented, formally and informally, at meetings of the Shakespeare Association of America, the International Conference at the Shakespeare Institute of the University of Birmingham, the Folger Shakespeare Library Teaching Shakespeare Institute, and to various audiences at the following institutions: Nazareth College, the Ohio State University, the University of Rochester, the University of North Carolina at Greensboro, St. Lawrence University, the University of California at Berkeley, the University of Alabama. I am indebted to many who on those occasions responded with criticism, advice, suggestions, doubts, and kindness.

Staff members at the following libraries have been much more helpful than they needed to be, and I thank them: the Furness Library at the University of Pennsylvania, Rush Rhees Library of the University of Rochester, Jackson Library of the University of North Carolina at Greensboro, the Folger Shakespeare Library, and the British Library. Having worked on this book over more than one sabbatical leave, I am grateful for the support of numerous deans and chairs at the University of Rochester and the University of North Carolina at Greensboro. I also wish to thank my colleagues in the English Departments of both those universities.

Some material has been reworked extensively from articles that appeared in *Shakespeare Quarterly* and *Shakespeare Survey*, and I appreciate the editors' permission to reprint.

Introduction

"In all of Shakespeare's development," write C. L. Barber and Richard Wheeler, "there is no change in dramatic style so striking as that between the final tragedies and the late romances."[1] Barber and Wheeler use the term "dramatic style" loosely, referring chiefly to the theatrical sub-genre and the point of view that selects and informs it. But the sentence is true in a strict sense as well, when "style" is taken to mean syntax, meter, diction, repetition, figurative language, and other such verbal and poetic properties. Around 1607, Shakespeare was drawn to a new kind of story and, at the same time, gave his characters a new kind of poetry to speak. At the beginning of this phase, having completed *Macbeth* and begun and perhaps finished *Coriolanus* or *Antony and Cleopatra* (or perhaps both), he contributed to the completion of *Pericles*, collaborating with George Wilkins or possibly finishing a play that Wilkins had begun; at the end of this phase, from about 1611 to 1613, he collaborated with John Fletcher on three plays, *Henry VIII*, *The Two Noble Kinsmen*, and *Cardenio*; between 1608 and 1611 he wrote three unaided plays, *Cymbeline*, *The Winter's Tale*, and *The Tempest*. Modern scholarship cannot decide what to call these seven plays, indeed can scarcely agree on what to call any one of them: comedy? romance? pastoral? tragicomedy? Whatever the designation, Shakespeare's shift from tragedy to the new form coincided with and is related – both as cause and effect – to his development of a poetic style like nothing he (or anybody else) had composed before: it is audacious, irregular, ostentatious, playful, and difficult. This book undertakes a detailed examination of that late style.

The plays of this period have resisted most critical efforts to account for their attraction and theatrical power. This is not merely the conventional claim of one who seeks to justify a critical project by decrying the

---

[1] C. L. Barber and Richard Wheeler, *The Whole Journey: Shakespeare's Power of Development* (Berkeley: University of California Press, 1986), p. 298.

inadequacy of previous efforts. From G. Wilson Knight in the 1930s to Philip Edwards in the 1950s to Howard Felperin in the 1970s, it was generally agreed that criticism had failed to take the measure of these extraordinary works, and even the abundant attention of the past quarter century has not altered that perception. Kiernan Ryan, summarizing twentieth-century scholarship in 1999, acknowledges the perceived inadequacy of most recent efforts. He also identifies a potentially helpful way of proceeding:

It is to the deliberate detail of their language and form that we must look, if the last plays are to be released from both the retrospection of old and new historicism and the abstractions of the allegorists. For it is by dislocating the dramatic narrative and contorting conventional poetic discourse that Shakespearean romance articulates its alienation from its own age and its commerce with futurity. What makes these plays still strike us as enigmatic and elusive is neither their engrossment in recondite topical allusions nor their veiled subscription to the perennial mysteries of myth and religion. It is the fact that we have not yet mastered their formal grammar and poetic idiom, and so have not yet learned how to read them.[2]

None of the other major phases of Shakespeare's career nor any of the other dramatic kinds – comedy, history, tragedy – has seemed so needy.

One possible explanation for this perceived critical failure is that most commentators begin broadly, exploring indisputably central themes such as forgiveness and redemption or attempting to define and contextualize the plays' distinctive dramatic form. My study takes the opposite point of departure, beginning with microscopic units such as syllables and lines and moving outward. It is a response to Ryan's challenge that we take seriously the "formal grammar and poetic idiom" of these plays. But my aim is not merely to redress the neglect of the late style. The chapters that follow not only define its principal properties but also explore the relation of that style to the dramatic forms it was devised to serve. The remarkable stylistic and formal developments both signify and derive from Shakespeare's revised understanding of the world, his refreshed sense of the positive capacities of language, and his reconceived faith in the power of the theatre and the role of the artist. These affirmations seem not to be sustained wholeheartedly through the entire group of plays, however. Much attention has been paid to Shakespeare's last thoughts, chiefly by the allegory hunters of the nineteenth century and their twentieth-century descendants and detractors; considerable notice has been given to the

---

[2] Kiernan Ryan, *Shakespeare: The Last Plays* (London: Longman, 1999), p. 18.

generic problems posed by the late plays; but relatively little has been written about the late verse. Ideas, genre, poetry – these three areas of critical thought have not been successfully triangulated. By beginning with particulars and furnishing a genuine poetics of the late works, I hope to offer a more specific and thus a more persuasive account of Shakespeare's final period.

This preliminary chapter moves eventually to a statement of purpose and method, but it opens by introducing certain critical problems that require elucidation before stylistic analysis can begin. First comes the question of textual authority, the status of the play-texts available to us. The fact of collaboration also demands a brief comment, especially as it affects stylistic analysis. Next is "lateness," an abiding and enormously influential notion in discussions of the plays from *Pericles* on. That problem leads conveniently to a brief critical history of the last plays in general, a survey glancing at some of the major approaches and important names. It is followed by a summary of the comparatively little work done on the late style, and then by a consideration of dramatic kind: what nomenclature best suits these works? Since one of my aims is to identify the points of correspondence between poetics and dramatic mode, this last critical question is uncommonly significant, more significant, in fact, than the answer. Finally, after referring to certain critical models I have found helpful, I set forth my argument in moderate detail. Given that the taxonomy I shall construct is (once again) literal, in these pages the phrase "the late style" means, for the most part, dramatic verse. The stylistic changes that become audible around 1607 are most easily discerned in the poetry, although many of the traits that make the verse challenging also complicate the prose, and some prose passages will be cited and discussed. In both its manifestations, prose and verse, Shakespeare's late style is difficult – difficult to listen to, difficult to read, difficult to understand, and difficult to talk about.

THE TOPIC OF TEXTS

Any treatment of stylistic particulars must acknowledge the distinctive textual circumstances of this group of plays. Each one considered here, unlike many of the earlier works, exists in only one version, all later texts deriving from the first printing. *Macbeth, Coriolanus, Antony and Cleopatra, The Tempest, The Winter's Tale, Henry VIII,* and *Cymbeline* were published initially in the 1623 Folio; *Pericles* appeared in 1609 in an unsatisfactory quarto, from which the five subsequent quartos were reproduced; *The Two Noble Kinsmen,* advertised as the work of Shakespeare and Fletcher, finally saw print in a quarto of 1634 and again in the second Beaumont and Fletcher Folio (1679); no text of *Cardenio* has survived. Scholarship has so far failed to learn why so few of the plays from the second half of Shakespeare's career found their way into print: between 1594 and 1600, thirteen of his plays were published, whereas between 1601 and 1616, only five appeared. This discrepancy suggests a changed attitude towards publication on the part of the author (or authors) or of the owners of those texts, the King's Men, and a number of explanations for this reduction have been proposed, from company prosperity (no need to sell) to a glutted market (too many books being sold) to a decline in Shakespeare's popularity.

Recently two additional possibilities have been advanced: first, that the company's involvement with the aristocracy, especially the Earls of Pembroke and Montgomery, "might have prompted Shakespeare and his fellows to change their publication strategy from print for a relatively wide readership to manuscript presentation copies for a small group of influential patrons"; and second, that Shakespeare and his fellows withheld the playbooks because even at this early date they had begun to entertain the possibility of a collected edition of his plays.[3] After publication of the second quarto of *Hamlet* in 1604, perhaps a defensive response to the faulty Q1 of 1603, none of Shakespeare's plays appeared in quarto for the first time except *King Lear* and *Pericles,* the latter in the unsatisfactory version of 1609. Thorpe's quarto version of the Sonnets also appeared in 1609, of course, but its origins, especially whether it was published with the poet's permission, are debatable. Whatever the cause or causes, the texts of many of the plays we rank among Shakespeare's greatest achievements were not available to the reading public until after his death.

This dearth of textual choices limits the close reader, of course – "limits," but does not disable. The increased complexity of the style, particularly the syntax, as Chapters 3 and 4 will demonstrate, yields a relatively high quotient of confusing sentences or phrases, but editors lack an alternative text that might help them clarify or emend a difficult or manifestly corrupt passage. Naturally such textual instability affects the work of the stylistic critic, whose conclusions about minute poetic or

---

[3] The quotation is from Lukas Erne, *Shakespeare as Literary Dramatist* (Cambridge: Cambridge University Press, 2003), p. 112. Erne considers both these possibilities in some detail (pp. 108–14) and makes a persuasive, if not a knockdown, argument.

syntactic effects might seem dubious or unreliable. While it would of course be desirable to have better texts, versions reflecting greater fidelity to the words that Shakespeare wrote or that the King's Men performed – especially in the case of *Pericles* – the existing copies nevertheless offer thousands of comprehensible and more or less authoritative lines and sentences, plenty of territory for noticing poetic choices and linguistic properties. As Coburn Freer remarks about the problem of textual instability, "if such objections vitiate the study of the poetry in Renaissance drama, they also invalidate every other kind of criticism, except the study of the text and the facts connected with its generation and transmission."[4]

An irreducible fact about the poetry treated in this book is its status as dramatic verse. Much will be made of Shakespeare's metrical disposition, his increasingly elliptical approach to expression, the tangled structure of much of the poetic syntax, the insistent repetitions audible in the verse, and other such formal features. These technical properties combine to produce poetry initially delivered from the stage, and this theatrical origin has shaped, and thus needs to be borne in mind throughout, the ensuing analysis. How audience members perceive the distinctive verse of the late plays determines how they respond to the dramatic narrative, how they react intellectually and emotionally, how they comprehend the meaning of the story enacted before them. In other words, what they hear is as important as what they see, and in fact what they hear to some extent determines what they see. Recognizing the theatrical status of the medium is one of the ways in which the analysis performed in this book differs from what some detractors of poetics deride as "New Criticism." The kind of poetic analysis conducted fifty years ago would not normally have insisted on the relevance of the dramatic context, would have been more likely to address the play as poem and contented itself with certain favored critical topics, notably metaphor, tension, paradox, and irony. As we have learned, a just appraisal of almost any aspect of Shakespeare's style must include an awareness of its theatrical provenance.[5]

---

[4] Coburn Freer, *The Poetics of Jacobean Drama* (Baltimore: Johns Hopkins University Press, 1981), p. 11.

[5] The patriarch of this insistence on the theatrical was J. L. Styan, *The Shakespeare Revolution* (Cambridge: Cambridge University Press, 1975); more recent exponents of performance criticism include James L. Bulman, *Shakespeare, Theory, and Performance* (London: Routledge, 1996), Barbara Hodgdon, *The Shakespeare Trade: Performances and Appropriations* (Philadelphia: University of Pennsylvania Press, 1996), and William B. Worthen, *Shakespeare and the Authority of Performance* (Cambridge: Cambridge University Press, 1997) and *Shakespeare and the Force of Modern Performance* (Cambridge: Cambridge University Press, 2003).

To acknowledge that origin is not, however, to insist that it constitutes the only legitimate context: Lukas Erne has argued convincingly that "Shakespeare did not only expect that at some point in the future people would 'read – and reread' his plays. He could not help knowing that his plays were being read and reread, printed and reprinted, excerpted and anthologized as he was writing more plays."[6] Moreover, although Erne himself eschews detailed analysis of verbal properties, he acknowledges that his argument "does go some way toward justifying such an approach, suggesting that a close, 'readerly,' attention to the play's text is not a modern aberration."[7] Much of the analysis undertaken herein depends upon the leisure needed to reflect on the verse, to read and re-read, to notice its patterns and other effects. And yet we must remain conscious that these verbal configurations are acting upon the ear of the audience and affecting their perception of the semantic content of the poetry, even though the operation of those effects may be extremely subtle or even subliminal. Hence, the discussion that follows is not predicated exclusively on one or the other conception of textual ontology.

COLLABORATION

The problems of what was written are complicated by some uncertainty about who wrote what. According to MacDonald Jackson, with reference to *Pericles*, "The very gateway to the final period of Shakespeare's play-wrighting career is . . . obstructed by thorny problems of text and authorship."[8] So, it might be added, is the exit ramp. Even if we tidy up the end of the career, placing *Pericles* after *Antony and Cleopatra* and *Coriolanus* and thus treating the plays from *Pericles* through *Cardenio* as a discrete group, we cannot avoid the inconvenient fact that four of the seven were written by Shakespeare and somebody else. As will become clear in the next section, nineteenth-century suspicions about the presence of another hand in *The Two Noble Kinsmen* and *Henry VIII* helped to

---

[6] *Shakespeare as Literary Dramatist*, p. 25. Erne has thoroughly documented what a number of scholars have been arguing for some time. Even before the Styan-led revolution of performance criticism in the 1970s, Sigurd Burckhardt insisted that "to be understood [Shakespeare] must be *read* – with attention to sometimes minute detail. There is an odd superstition abroad that nothing can be part of Shakespeare's intention that cannot be communicated directly across the footlights." *Shakespearean Meanings* (Princeton: Princeton University Press, 1968), p. vii. See also Harry Berger, *Imaginary Audition: Shakespeare on Stage and Page* (Berkeley: University of California Press, 1989).

[7] Erne, *Shakespeare as Literary Dramatist*, p. 22.

[8] MacDonald Jackson, *Defining Shakespeare: 'Pericles' as Test Case* (Oxford: Oxford University Press, 2004), p. 11.

stimulate interest in the last plays as a group. Those early concerns, although based on a non-systematic impressionism, have been validated by stylometric and other kinds of tests developed by twentieth-century scholarship, especially the meticulous labors of Cyrus Hoy in the 1950s.[9] Recent scholarship has returned attention to the practice of collaboration. Brian Vickers's *Shakespeare, Co-Author*, focusing on the investigations of such scholars as Jonathan Hope, David Lake, and MacDonald Jackson, offers an exhaustive account of the current state of attribution studies.[10]

Scholars agree on the following general conclusions: that Shakespeare both began and ended his career writing with other people, and probably did so in the middle of it as well; that *Pericles* was a collaborative effort with George Wilkins, even though we can't be sure by whom the product was conceived or how the partnership functioned; and that *Henry VIII*, *The Two Noble Kinsmen*, and *Cardenio* were all joint productions with John Fletcher, although questions remain about the nature of this final collaborative relationship, such as who plotted the plays? Did the two authors work together or separately? Did Fletcher touch up certain scenes first written by Shakespeare? Might a third playwright have contributed? Other questions that used to receive attention, such as the nineteenth-century belief that Shakespeare couldn't have written the scene depicting the descent of Jupiter in Act 5 of *Cymbeline*, have mostly disappeared from the critical discourse. While specialists still quibble over certain scenes and decline to speculate on some small samples, such as prologues and epilogues, we can say that Shakespeare is probably responsible for the following sections of the collaborative plays. *Pericles*: Acts 3, 4, and 5, with Wilkins having written Acts 1 and 2 (although there may be some Shakespeare in the first two acts and some Wilkins in the last three); *Henry VIII*: 1.1, 1.2, 2.3, 2.4, 3.2.1–203, and 5.1; *The Two Noble Kinsmen*: 1.1 through 2.1, 3.1, 3.2, and 5 (but not 5.1.1–33 or 5.2).[11]

---

[9] Hoy's conclusions appear in a series of articles entitled "The Shares of Fletcher and his Collaborators in the Beaumont and Fletcher Canon (I-VII)," published in *Studies in Bibliography* between 1956 and 1962. Some of his conclusions have been modified by later work, such as that of Jonathan Hope, *The Authorship of Shakespeare's Plays: A Socio-Linguistic Study* (Cambridge: Cambridge University Press, 1994), although in general Hoy's attribution of scenes and passages in the Shakespeare–Fletcher collaborations has remained the starting point for most analysts. See also Jackson, *Defining Shakespeare*.

[10] Brian Vickers, *Shakespeare, Co-Author* (Oxford: Oxford University Press, 2002). Vickers's second chapter, "Identifying Co-Authors" (pp. 44–134), surveys the history of attribution studies by describing the various kinds of tests employed. Chapter 5 (pp. 291–332) considers the evidence for the joint authorship of *Pericles*, chapter 6 (pp. 333–432) for *Henry VIII* and *The Two Noble Kinsmen*.

[11] In addition to Vickers, who is interested in the methods of distinction, see *William Shakespeare: A Textual Companion*, ed. Stanley Wells and Gary Taylor, with John Jowett and William Montgomery (Oxford: Oxford University Press, 1988); Hope, *The Authorship of Shakespeare's*

Accepting these conclusions about division of labor, I should acknowledge their significance for the present study. Although I sometimes write of one or another of these collaborative works as if it were entirely Shakespeare's, such reference is largely a critical convenience. The phrase "the style of *Henry VIII*," for example, denotes those scenes or parts of scenes that most scholars have assigned to Shakespeare. A similar assumption obtains when *Henry VIII* is referred to loosely as one of the "romances," although it should probably be called a history play. The reader should consider such phrases a kind of shorthand, with the assurance that all stylistic illustrations are taken from Shakespearean scenes. For purposes of clarity I have evaded other potential complications. Although Shakespeare is generally assigned the last three acts of *Pericles*, "it is nevertheless true," as Frank Kermode points out, "that the first scenes also occasionally have lines that sound like idiosyncratic Shakespeare," in support of which claim he cites the image of the "blind mole" and the "poor worm" (1.1.100–2).[12] While remaining aware that such possibly Shakespearean lines exist here and there, I have mostly resisted the diversion that entering into such controversies would entail.

That collaboration renders parts of certain plays unavailable for stylistic analysis may be taken less as a hindrance than as a benefit. Having the presence of another poetic hand – Fletcher's much more than Wilkins's, of course – is most instructive in the attempt to establish Shakespeare's stylistic profile after 1607–8. The audible differences between two distinct styles of verse initially set scholars to investigating the details of composition and led them eventually to establish the order of the canon. And the differences between Fletcher's and Shakespeare's verse are marked: respectively, smooth versus choppy, heavily versus subtly patterned, delicate versus rough. According to Charles Lamb, Fletcher "lays line upon line, making up one after the other; adding image to image so deliberately that we see where they join: Shakespeare mingles every thing, he runs line into line, embarrasses sentences and metaphors; before one idea has burst its shell another is hatched and

Plays, and Jackson, *Defining Shakespeare*, as well as the following editions: Suzanne Gossett, ed., *Pericles* (London: Thomson Learning, 2004); Gordon McMullan, ed., *Henry VIII, or All is True* (London: Thomas Nelson, 2000); Eugene Waith, ed., *The Two Noble Kinsmen* (Oxford: Oxford University Press, 1989); Lois Potter, ed., *The Two Noble Kinsmen* (London: Thomas Nelson, 1997). Jeffrey Masten, *Textual Intercourse* (Cambridge: Cambridge University Press, 1997) is interested especially in the gender politics of collaboration and in the political history of modern attribution studies.
[12] Frank Kermode, *Shakespeare's Language* (London: Penguin, 2000), pp. 255–56.

clamorous for disclosure.["13] This is one of the most insightful stylistic analyses ever written, and without pausing now to illustrate its accuracy, I will have occasion throughout the book to refer to Lamb's distinctions as a way of sharpening the definition of Shakespeare's particular style.

LATENESS

Shakespeare's style, like everything connected with the last plays, is inevitably associated with the idea of "lateness," Shakespeare's "last" productions, his "final period," even his "swan song." An implausibly large number of critics find themselves unable to write about the last phase of Shakespeare's career without invoking the late years of Ibsen, Michelangelo or, invariably, Beethoven. The composer represents "an ideal example of the final achievement of a great artist, when he seems to acquire a new profundity, a new understanding, in making a last attempt to solve the enigma of life" – Kenneth Muir's sentence is typical of this critical position.[14] A variation on the theme is found in Adorno's interpretive reversal of the terms, so that "the antiharmonistic postures of Michelangelo, of the mature Rembrandt and Beethoven are all attributable to the inner development of the concept of harmony and in the last analysis to its insufficiency."[15] Such rhetoric is difficult to escape, based as it is on perception of a distinctive voice in a recognizable phase of an artist's career. Still, throughout this book the phrase "Shakespeare's late style" is meant to function chiefly as a chronological pointer: a term designating the dramatic verse Shakespeare composed between 1607 and 1613, a sign divested, insofar as possible, of emotional or teleological connotations. Logically, of course, the use of the adjective "late" implies a way of thinking about the style, acknowledges a category separating it from the expressive forms discernible in earlier plays, but such groupings need not be sentimentalized, nor must the style be considered necessarily superior, the plays regarded as wiser.[16]

[13] *The Works of Charles and Mary Lamb*, ed. E. V. Lucas (London: 1904), IV, 341–42. Lamb also remarks of Fletcher's style that "its motion is circular, not progressive. Each line revolves on itself in a sort of separate orbit. They do not join into one another like a running hand" (p. 329).

[14] Kenneth Muir, *Last Periods of Shakespeare, Racine, and Ibsen* (Liverpool: Liverpool University Press, 1961), p. 3.

[15] Theodor Adorno, *Aesthetic Theory* (London: Routledge and Kegan Paul, 1984), p. 161.

[16] Another figure whose late work is sometimes compared to that of Shakespeare is Henry James. This comparison can be more fruitful than some of the others, based as it is on the specific resemblances between two styles of writing (albeit that one is verse, the other prose). See John Porter Houston, *Shakespearean Sentences: A Study in Style and Syntax* (Baton Rouge: Louisiana State University Press, 1988), pp. 200–5.

Owing to the overexposure of such comparisons with other major artists, "lateness" is an idea that has recently come under attack, and it is worth scrutinizing the critical history of this concept and noting some of its ramifications for the study of style.[17] The santification of the late plays, and indeed our capacity for talking about "late plays" at all, is a function, interestingly enough, of very close reading. In the nineteenth century such scholars as William Spalding, the German G. G. Gervinus, and above all F. J. Furnivall, the prodigiously energetic editor and founder of the New Shakespeare Society – these scholars and others, mostly working independently of one another, set out to determine which parts of certain disputed texts were written by William Shakespeare.[18] This goal required that they establish Shakespeare's poetic identity, a task they undertook by means of detailed prosodic investigations. Thus they were able to determine that, broadly speaking, Shakespeare liberalized his blank verse as he matured, writing a progressively less regular line as he moved from histories and comedies to the tragedies and beyond: such relaxation of the line, they discovered, entailed the poet's admission of multiple forms of variation, particularly enjambment and light endings, along with an increasing tolerance for lineal disruption. Knowledge of this progression then allowed scholars to determine with considerable certainty the order in which the plays were composed.[19]

"Of these tests," A. C. Bradley concluded, "that of rhyme and that of feminine endings, discreetly employed, are of use in broadly distinguishing Shakespeare's plays into two groups, earlier and later, and also in marking out the very latest dramas."[20] Bradley is cautious, as well he

---

[17] Suzanne Gossett, in her Introduction to the Arden3 edition of *Pericles*, enumerates the obstacles to considering it a "late" play: "the 'lateness' paradigm is inadequate to describe a play which is not entirely by Shakespeare; on which Shakespeare worked when he was not yet forty-four years old; which reworks a plot that had already served as a frame for one of his earliest comedies; and which he may have been writing simultaneously with or shortly before *Coriolanus*, a play with ties to an entirely different section of Shakespeare's *oeuvre*" (p. 54). The most thorough treatment of this topic promises to be Gordon McMullan's *Shakespeare and the Idea of Late Writing: Authorship, Biography, Reception* (Cambridge University Press, forthcoming).

[18] See William Spalding, *A Letter on Shakespere's Authorship of "The Two Noble Kinsmen,"* ed. J. H. Burton (London: New Shakespeare Society, 1876). For a detailed survey of some of these tests and their results, see Vickers, *Shakespeare, Co-Author*, especially pp. 44–134, and *passim*.

[19] See Barbara A. Mowat, "'What's In A Name?': Tragicomedy, Romance, or Late Comedy?" in *A Companion to Shakespeare*, ed. Jean Howard and Richard Dutton, 4 vols. (Oxford: Blackwell, 2003), IV, 129–53. For an overview of the changes in verse style through the course of the career, see Russ McDonald, *Shakespeare and the Arts of Language* (Oxford: Oxford University Press, 2001), chapter 5.

[20] A. C. Bradley, *Shakespearean Tragedy: Lectures on "Hamlet," "Othello," "King Lear" and "Macbeth," With a New Introduction by John Russell Brown* (London: Macmillan, 1972), pp. 405–6.

might have been. In evaluating the conclusions derived from prosodic comparisons, we need to keep in mind the sometimes slippery nature of the evidence: as Lois Potter has reminded us, "nineteenth-century attempts to compare the frequency with which dramatists used feminine endings and run-on lines were often vitiated by their use of texts in which editors had already tampered with the metre."[21] The "discreet" use of these quasi-scientific studies had an immense impact on scholarship because it helped to foster a relatively firm and persuasive chronology of composition. In the seventeenth century, for example, Dryden and his contemporaries believed that *Pericles*, on the basis of its (intentional) naive effects and (unintentional) textual corruption, must have been a very early play, one that perhaps Shakespeare the apprentice had been given to salvage.[22] Such error was dispelled by nineteenth-century metrical scholars, who were able not only to calculate approximately when *Pericles* was written but also to ascertain that only part of it was Shakespeare's. Finally, knowing that *Pericles* was composed late allowed literary critics to discern its affinities with those other plays that seem to have been composed near the end of the career.

Enter Edward Dowden, poet and Professor of English Literature in Trinity College, Dublin. Alert to the scholarly advances of his recent predecessors and colleagues, the poet and critic set forth for the Victorian reader the ramifications of the newly established phases of Shakespeare's career.[23] The subtitle of Dowden's most important book, published in 1875, is telling: *Shakspere: A Critical Study of His Mind and Art.*[24] There he famously introduced, or at least articulated most eloquently, the theory that the tones of Shakespeare's plays correspond directly to the states of Shakespeare's mind. According to this correspondence of mood and mode, the dramatic–poetic metamorphosis that manifestly occurs in the late work bespeaks a spiritual passage from despair to serenity, an artist no longer "in the depths," but "on the heights." Here is the relevant passage from the version published two years later, in which the argument is distilled:

---

[21] Introduction to Lois Potter's Arden edition of *The Two Noble Kinsmen*, p. 20.

[22] See Howard Felperin, *Shakespearean Romance* (Princeton: Princeton University Press, 1972), pp. 291–92.

[23] "Reader" is the appropriate noun: although many nineteenth- and early twentieth-century critics did remember the theatrical origins of the texts, Dowden very clearly thought of the plays chiefly as dramatic poems, as works to be read.

[24] (London, 1875).

The impression left upon the reader by Shakspere's last plays is that, whatever his trials and sorrows and errors may have been, he had come forth from them wise, large-hearted, calm-souled. He seems to have learned the secret of life, and while taking his share in it, to be yet disengaged from it; he looks down upon life, its joys, its griefs, its errors, with a grave tenderness, which is almost pity. The spirit of these last plays is that of serenity which results from fortitude, and the recognition of human frailty; all of them express a deep sense of the need of repentance and the duty of forgiveness . . . And it will be felt that the name which I have given to this last period – Shakspere having ascended out of the turmoil and trouble of action, out of the darkness and tragic mystery, the places haunted by terror and crime, and by love contending with these, to a pure and serene elevation – it will be felt that the name, on the heights, is neither inappropriate nor fanciful.[25]

Overheated though the rhetoric may be, Dowden's romantic, idealized narrative has had a potent, lasting influence on twentieth- and even twenty-first century criticism.

Our story continues with the intervention of Lytton Strachey, who at the beginning of the twentieth century belittled Dowden's romantic account of Shakespeare's spiritual progress. Recasting Dowden's "serenity" as disengagement and boredom, Strachey famously denigrated the late work on the grounds of artistic ennui:

It is hard to resist the conclusion that he was getting bored himself. Bored with people, bored with real life, bored with drama, bored, in fact, with anything except poetical dreams. He is no longer interested, one often feels, in what happens, or who says what, so long as he can find place for a faultless lyric, or a new, unimagined rhythmical effect, or a grand and mystic speech. In this mood he must have written his share in *The Two Noble Kinsmen*, leaving the plot and characters to Fletcher to deal with as he pleased, and reserving to himself only the opportunities for pompous verse. In this mood he must have broken off half-way through the tedious history of *Henry VIII*; and in this mood he must have completed, with all the resources of his rhetoric, the miserable archaic fragment of *Pericles*.[26]

This is the notorious passage, usually cited so that the critic can ridicule and dismiss it.[27] But it is worth considering the possibility that, up to a point and in a way he did not intend, Strachey may be right. If we overlook momentarily the cause he superciliously proposes – "boredom" – we may

[25] Edward Dowden, *Shakspere* (London: Macmillan, 1877), p. 60.
[26] Lytton Strachey, "Shakespeare's Final Period," *Independent Review*, 3 (August, 1904), 414–15.
[27] An exception to the automatic dismissal of Strachey's argument is James Sutherland, who softens the rhetoric slightly to speak of Shakespeare's artistic "fatigue." See "The Language of the Last Plays," in *More Talking of Shakespeare*, ed. John Garrett (London: Longmans, 1959), pp. 144–58.

notice that Strachey has perceptively identified some cardinal features of Shakespeare's late work: the comparative unimportance of character ("bored with people"), the fabulous plots and fairy-tale atmosphere ("bored with real life"), the episodic and putatively undramatic structure of romance ("bored with drama"), the relative lack of differentiation among speakers ("no longer interested . . . in . . . who says what"). Moreover, the claim that the aging Shakespeare was interested in nothing but poetical dreams reflects the high degree of fantasy in the late work – the magic of the masque in *The Tempest*, for instance, and the importance of the oneiric throughout. It also acknowledges that this dreaminess has made its way into the texture of the verse.

Publishing "Shakespeare's Final Period" in 1904 in *The Independent Review*, Strachey was writing as a self-fashioned modernist, a twentieth-century scientific critic obliged to expose and remedy the sentimental excesses of Victorian bardolatry.[28] He was also writing as a young man – he was twenty-four – impatient with the supposed spiritual wisdom of palsied eld. Although his iconoclasm did not succeed in dislodging the late plays from their exalted status, he won a convert or two: down through the twentieth-century, doubt was now and then expressed about the reverence with which the late phase of the career was regarded. Strachey's valuable contribution was to deplore the error of reading a career backwards: "For some reason or another, the end of a man's life seems naturally to afford the light by which the rest of it should be read; last thoughts do appear in some strange way to be really best and truest; and this is particularly the case when they fit in nicely with the rest of the story, and are, perhaps, just what one likes to think of oneself."[29] More recently, Gordon McMullan has complained about such retrospective reading of moments in an artistic career, showing that our knowledge of what came late in an artistic oeuvre, whether music or painting or drama, can shape – or, more to the point, distort – our understanding of how that work emerged.[30]

[28] There is confusion over the date of the essay, chiefly because the reprint in Strachey's *Books and Characters: French and English* (London: Chatto and Windus, 1922) gives an erroneous date (1906) for the original publication. It first appeared in August of 1904.

[29] Strachey, "Shakespeare's Final Period," p. 415.

[30] See Gordon McMullan's forthcoming essay, "'The Technique of it is Mature': Inventing the Late Plays in Print and in Performance," in *From Stage to Print in Early Modern England*, ed. Peter Holland and Stephen Orgel (Basingstoke: Palgrave Macmillan); and book, *Shakespeare and the Idea of Late Writing*. We might, however, remember the words of T. S. Eliot on the career of James Joyce: "As with Shakespeare, his later work must be understood through the earlier, and the first through the last; it is the whole journey, not any one stage of it, that assures him his place among the great." Cited in Barber and Wheeler, *The Whole Journey*, p. vii.

The romantic schema and the reaction to it had an especially pernicious effect on the collaborative plays, *Pericles* to some extent, but most particularly *Henry VIII* and *The Two Noble Kinsmen*. Failing as they do, for different reasons, to conform to the transcendental paradigm laid out by Dowden, they were mostly ignored through the first half of the twentieth century. Occasionally, however, a censorious voice would sound, condescending to or even mocking the contribution of the aging Shakespeare. Witness Theodore Spencer's acerbic conclusions about *The Two Noble Kinsmen*: perhaps impishly, Spencer encourages the reader to "wonder whether his retirement was entirely voluntary . . . One can even imagine a deputation calling on Shakespeare – it is not an agreeable thought – to suggest that, all things considered, it would be wise to go home and write no more."[31] Spencer's critical objections are largely stylistic:

The Fletcherian parts of the play are first-rate theater; their contrasts and conflicts make an immediate and successful impression. The Shakespearean parts, on the other hand, are static and, though with splendor, stiff. They are slow, dense, compared with Fletcher's easy liquescence. They have a deliberate yet vague grandeur, a remote and half-exhausted exaltation; they are expressed through a clotted rhetoric that is the poetry of an old man who has finished with action. Their style is the style of old age, and the imagery is an old man's imagery.[32]

Although the stylistic distinctions are unexceptionable, the conclusions about "old age" seem tendentious and exaggerated for effect. Fifty years after Spencer, Anthony Dawson revived his idea: "What is wrong with imagining Shakespeare's career trailing off, going from bad to worse, from *The Tempest* to *Cymbeline* and parts of *Henry VIII*, before being judiciously terminated by his worried partners in the King's Men, who perhaps asked young Fletcher to do what he could to make the old master's new texts acceptable to their increasingly perplexed audiences?"[33]

However courageous and amusing their polemics may be, Strachey, Spencer, and Dawson are mavericks. For the most part the late plays are admired, but admiration does not usually extend much beyond *The Tempest*. Even though we know that the collaborations belong in the picture, even though we recognize the extravagance of Dowden's rhetoric,

---

[31] Theodore Spencer, "*The Two Noble Kinsmen*," *Modern Philology*, 36 (1939), 257.
[32] *Ibid.*, 276.
[33] Anthony Dawson, "*Tempest* in a Teapot: Critics, Evaluation, Ideology," in *Bad Shakespeare: Revaluations of the Shakespeare Canon*, ed. Maurice Charney (Rutherford, NJ: Fairleigh-Dickinson University Press, 1988), pp. 62–63.

even though we have come to admit Shakespeare's close connection to Fletcher and the fashions of the London stage at the time, even though post-structuralism and its critical offshoots have amplified the anti-romantic strain – despite all these contra-indications, our view of the plays composed from about 1608 still owes much to Dowden and his conception of "late" serenity and transcendence. Consider the following sentence from Stephen Greenblatt's *Will in the World* (2004): "the greatest of these late plays, *The Winter's Tale* and *The Tempest*, both have a distinctly autumnal, retrospective tone. Shakespeare seems to be self-consciously reflecting upon what he has accomplished in his professional life and coming to terms with what it might mean to leave it behind."[34]

It is not inappropriate that knowledge of Shakespeare's earlier work should be allowed to inform efforts to understand the late, but we must be aware that to do so is often to subscribe implicitly to a myth of progress; and thus we must be careful not to allow such comparisons automatically to privilege the later plays as more accomplished, more sincere, or – the most common error – wiser than those that have come before. A defense against such sentimentality is Philip Edwards's directive that we ought to "wonder what criticism would have made of these plays, or any one of them, if all Shakespeare's other plays had been lost."[35]

CRITICAL HISTORY: PLAYS

The passage just cited prefaces Edwards's helpful synopsis of commentary on the late plays published in the first half of the twentieth century. In that survey Edwards identifies five principal approaches: (1) "The Poet Himself," the views of the allegorists and their critics; (2) "Conditioned Art," the practical studies of influence and stagecraft by A. H. Thorndike and G. E. Bentley; (3) "Myth, Symbol, Allegory," the theories of G. Wilson Knight, D. G. James, and Derek Traversi; (4) "The Pattern of Tragedy, and a Christian Interpretation," dominated by E. M. W. Tillyard and S. L. Bethell; and (5) "The Shape and Meaning of Romance," the investigations of the romance and pastoral traditions contributed by J. M. Nosworthy, J. F. Danby, and Frank Kermode. When Edwards, looking to the future, concludes that "criticism might for the moment

---

[34] Stephen Greenblatt, *Will in the World: How Shakespeare Became Shakespeare* (New York: Norton, 2004), p. 370.

[35] Philip Edwards, "Shakespeare's Romances: 1900–1957," *Shakespeare Survey 11* (1958), 2. A similar caution is developed by Anthony Dawson, "*Tempest* in a Teapot."

ignore the illumination and the universality in the last plays," he attests to the dominance of schools of criticism concerned largely with what he calls "symbolic patterns," "mankind's spiritual pilgrimage," and "man's apprehension of the mystery of salvation and immortality."[36] His survey was published in 1958, and the wide-angle approaches he describes were sustained over the next decade, encouraged partly by the critical sovereignty of Northrop Frye.

In 1972 Howard Felperin prefaced his *Shakespearean Romance* with the claim that "Many of the problems that have beset modern reinterpretation and revaluation of these plays remain to be solved."[37] Other critics agreed, and Felperin's book was part of an outpouring of critical work on the last phase, analysis representing the viewpoints identified by Edwards and more besides. Some of these books include *Shakespeare's Tragicomic Vision* (1972), in which Joan Hartwig promotes "tragicomedy," not "romance," as the proper descriptive term; Barbara A. Mowat's *The Dramaturgy of Shakespeare's Romances* (1976), an analysis of the self-conscious, metadramatic qualities of the texts; *Shakespeare's Romances Reconsidered* (1978), a collection of essays deriving from a symposium held at the University of Alabama in 1975; and Frances A. Yates's *Shakespeare's Last Plays* (1975), a learned topical interpretation with particular attention to Jacobean Protestantism.[38]

With the eventual exhaustion of myth criticism and the emergence of new methodologies, interest in reconciliation and "mankind's spiritual pilgrimage" came to be supplanted by a radical skepticism about the putative harmonies of the final period. Ruth Nevo's *Shakespeare's Other Language* (1987) and the concluding chapter of Janet Adelman's *Suffocating Mothers: Fantasies of Maternal Origin in Shakespeare's Plays, "Hamlet" to "The Tempest"* (1991) represent one version of this backlash, offering what might be called a "post-Freudian" approach. According to Alison Thorne, whose recent critical survey concentrates on psychoanalytic and feminist readings, these critics have "set about excavating the dark subtext that lurks within their versions of the Shakespearean family romance."[39]

[36] Edwards, "Shakespeare's Romances," p. 18.

[37] *Shakespearean Romance*, p. 4.

[38] Joan Hartwig, *Shakespeare's Tragicomic Vision* (Baton Rouge: Louisiana State University Press, 1972); Barbara A. Mowat, *The Dramaturgy of Shakespeare's Romances* (Athens: University of Georgia Press, 1976); Henry Jacobs and Carol McGinnis Kay, eds., *Shakespeare's Romances Reconsidered* (Lincoln: University of Nebraska Press, 1978); Frances A. Yates, *Shakespeare's Last Plays: A New Approach* (London: Routledge & Kegan Paul, 1975).

[39] Introduction to *Shakespeare's Romances*, ed. Alison Thorne (New York: Palgrave Macmillan, 2003), p. 18. Ruth Nevo, *Shakespeare's Other Language* (London: Methuen, 1987); Janet Adelman,

With the rise of new historicism and cultural materialism after about 1980, *The Tempest* began to monopolize the critical scene, particularly the text's "imbrication into [the] discourse of colonialism,"[40] and only recently has its hegemony begun to diminish. Some critics have attempted topical, political readings of other texts, especially *Cymbeline*; of this work, Constance Jordan's learned and subtle political interpretations are the most persuasive.[41] Offering another fresh angle of vision, feminist critics have contributed a "reassessment of attitudes to female agency and sexuality": "Do the female characters exist solely as the projection of the male protagonists' (or their creators') primal wishes and fears? Or are they given scope to inscribe their own subjectivity and alternative feminine values, however tentatively, outside the confines of the diseased masculine imagination?"[42] Such questions are still in the air.

Towards the end of the 1990s, as critics began to look retrospectively at critical conclusions as well as at possible new directions, a sense of disappointment was still prevalent. Echoing Kiernan Ryan's remark about our not yet knowing how to read the romances, cited above, Simon Palfrey has complained that "the modern academic tradition has lost access to something of the plays' keenness and vim."[43] In other words, there is a sense that criticism is going around in circles and that the various approaches, from the mythic to the topical, have not produced a wholly satisfactory way of approaching the late work. This is one explanation,

---

Suffocating Mothers: Fantasies of Maternal Origin in Shakespeare's Plays, "Hamlet" to "The Tempest" (London: Routledge, 1991).

[40] The quotation is from Francis Barker and Peter Hulme, "Nymphs and Reapers Heavily Vanish: The Discursive Con-texts of *The Tempest*," in *Alternative Shakespeares*, ed. John Drakakis (London: Methuen, 1985), p. 198.

[41] See Constance Jordan, *Shakespeare's Monarchies* (Ithaca: Cornell University Press, 1995). David Bergeron, in *Shakespeare's Romances and the Royal Family* (Lawrence: University of Kansas Press, 1985), attempts a detailed topical reading of the late plays along the lines that his title suggests, but the book seems not to have convinced most readers, and its influence has not been great. Early examples of this approach include Emrys Jones's "Stuart Cymbeline," *Essays in Criticism*, 11 (1961), 84–99, and Bernard Harris's "'What's Past is Prologue': *Cymbeline* and *Henry VIII*," in *Later Shakespeare*, Stratford-upon-Avon Studies 8, ed. John Russell Brown and Bernard Harris (London: Edward Arnold, 1966), pp. 203–33; see also Leah Marcus, *Puzzling Shakespeare* (Berkeley: University of California Press, 1989), and, most recently, Ros King, *"Cymbeline": Constructions of Britain* (London: Ashgate, 2005).

[42] Thorne, Introduction to *Shakespeare's Romances*, p. 20. See, among many others, Adelman, *Suffocating Mothers*; Helen Wilcox, "'If I Prove Honey-Mouthed, Let my Tongue Blister': Women's Language in Shakespeare's Tragicomedies," *Shakespeare Jahrbuch*, 134 (1998), 97–107; Stephen Orgel, "Prospero's Wife," *Representations*, 8 (1984), 1–13; Susan Snyder, "Mamillius and Gender Polarization in *The Winter's Tale*," *Shakespeare Quarterly*, 50 (1999), 1–9.

[43] Simon Palfrey, *Late Shakespeare: A New World of Words* (Oxford: Oxford University Press, 1997), p. 2.

I think, for the renewed attention to textual problems, the possibility of revision, and the significance of collaboration. Without making extravagant claims, I would hope that the attention to stylistic detail proposed in this book may serve as one means of relieving the critical frustration still attending the late plays.

CRITICAL HISTORY: STYLE

Despite the abundance of books and articles devoted to Shakespeare's last period, detailed analysis of the verse is relatively rare. This neglect is hardly surprising: most twentieth-century critics seeking "universals" and "symbolic patterns" had little time for the minutiae of poetics, although it is only fair to point out that some of those mentioned above, especially G. Wilson Knight and Frank Kermode, were atypical in their ability to read both poetic and mythic patterns. It would seem that the dominance of the New Critics might have generated some important attempts at explication, especially since the late verse was sometimes thought to be affiliated with the "metaphysical" style. In fact, however, New Criticism took little notice of the late plays, perhaps because their discontinuities and sprawling structures made them unlike lyric poems and thus inhospitable to the demonstration of the unity characteristic of the verbal icon.

In those decades in the middle of the twentieth century when stylistic criticism was reputable, if rare, most work in this area fell, according to Maurice Charney, into two categories: "admiration" or "computation."[44] Thereafter, from about 1975, stylistic scrutiny tended to diminish as much contextual criticism generated an atmosphere unsympathetic and sometimes even hostile to poetics, an antipathy that increased noticeably in the 1980s. First, concentration on broad contexts for the drama mostly diverted attention from the close study of language: critics devoted to such topics as power politics and history, gender roles and sexuality, social marginality, race, ethnicity, and nationhood exhibited little interest in poetics. The fast-growing sub-discipline of performance criticism also posed a challenge, usually unspoken but sometimes explicit, to the value of stylistic or any other kind of "literary" criticism. The prominence of the word "discourse" in the work of this period would seem to imply a connection to stylistic matters, but the emphasis invariably fell not on that noun but on the prepositional phrase following it: "discourse of

---

[44] Maurice Charney, *Style in Hamlet* (Princeton: Princeton University Press, 1967), p. xvii.

power," "of class," "of gender," "of race," "of the body." A recent critic has summarized this period as given over to "modes of analysis that for all their methodological sophistication tend to interpret Renaissance works as bundles of historical or cultural content, without much attention to the ways that their meanings are shaped and enabled by the possibilities of form."[45] Such assumptions offered little help to the reader struggling with the obliquities of the late style.

Those twentieth-century critics who did address themselves to the topic of Shakespeare and language rarely had much to say about late developments, a neglect that seems attributable partly to fatigue: however comprehensive their stated intentions, most of them begin to flag as they near the finish line.[46] In *The Language of Shakespeare's Plays*, Ifor Evans cannot conceal his impatience with the late work, developing an especially invidious comparison between Leontes' "There may be in the cup / A spider steep'd" (2.1.39ff.), and Othello's "What sense had I of her stolen hours of lust?" (3.3.338ff.), to the detriment of Sicilia. Evans gives up on *The Winter's Tale* midway into the play, as soon as the proto-tragic mood is dispelled: "It is as if [Shakespeare] had tried in the early scenes to work his way back from the unstrenuous and artificial beauty of *Cymbeline* and now he had given up the attempt."[47] F. E. Halliday concludes *The Poetry of Shakespeare's Plays* with an Epilogue, on *Henry VIII* and *The Two Noble Kinsmen*, in which he spends several pages whipping Fletcher on Shakespeare's behalf ("Fletcher rarely ris[es] above the level of a smutty and sentimental mediocrity, while Shakespeare writes some of his noblest poetry").[48] Finally, the peculiarities of the late style have generated some genuinely bizarre suggestions. James Sutherland, in a modified, more decorous version of Strachey's position, asserts that a kind of artistic weariness or disengagement affected the mature poet's habits of composition. Thus, he says, when the Queen in *Cymbeline* berates Pisanio for

---

[45] Mark David Rasmussen, *Renaissance Literature and its Formal Engagements* (New York: Palgrave, 2002), p. 3.

[46] I am thinking of books such as F. E. Halliday's *The Poetry of Shakespeare's Plays* (London: House of Stratus, 2001; originally published 1964); Ifor Evans's *The Language of Shakespeare's Plays* (London: Methuen, 1952); and Frank Kermode's *Shakespeare's Language* (London: Penguin, 2000).

[47] *The Language of Shakespeare's Plays*, p. 207. Unless otherwise noted, all quotations from Shakespeare's plays are from *The Riverside Shakespeare*, ed. G. B. Evans (Boston: Houghton-Mifflin, 1974).

[48] *The Poetry of Shakespeare's Plays*, p. 250. In fairness, it should be pointed out that Halliday in his Introduction presents an exceptionally acute prosodic contrast between the verse of *The Comedy of Errors* and that of *The Tempest*, employing comparable passages to enumerate the distinct characteristics of each style.

being "a depender on a thing that leans" (for his service to the banished and therefore tottering Posthmus), the woolgathering Shakespeare "was wondering what should follow, his eye wandered idly over his manuscript, and he saw the words that he had written for Pisanio's entrance – 'Enter *Pisa*.' – and the leaning tower came into his head."[49] Probably this fanciful scenario should be allowed to pass without further comment.

Significant exceptions to these charges of critical neglect and distaste may not abound, but they do exist. Editors, having lived with a text for years and feeling an obligation to help readers, have been more apt than most scholars and critics to pay close attention to the mechanics of Shakespearean verse. Those scholars who prepared the second series of Arden texts, for example, offer useful observations that will appear later in this Introduction and in subsequent chapters.[50] Their solicitude is shared by some of their successors, notably Lois Potter, whose edition of *The Two Noble Kinsmen* contains an exceptionally thorough look at the stylistic problems of the late plays and at the difficulties attendant on collaboration. Some of those critics who have confronted the problems of attribution have taught us much about Shakespeare's distinctive voice, particularly Marco Mincoff and MacDonald Jackson.[51] Sutherland's "The Language of the Last Plays" (despite its excursion to Pisa) provides sound generalizations, while John Porter Houston's *Shakespearean Sentences* charts variations in the construction of the verse sentence, especially in *Cymbeline*.[52] Stephen Orgel, most amply in the Introduction to his edition of *The Winter's Tale*, addresses directly the problem of comprehensibility, suggesting that perhaps early modern audiences didn't understand the extremely convoluted passages any better than we do.[53] Anne Barton's articles and introductions have brilliantly illuminated some characteristic turns in the workings of the late verse,[54] and Inga-Stina Ewbank, C. L. Barber, Roger Warren, Stanley Cavell, and some others

---

[49] Sutherland, "The Language of the Last Plays," p. 155.

[50] See J. M. Nosworthy's *Cymbeline* (London: Methuen, 1955), J. H. P. Pafford's *The Winter's Tale* (London: Methuen, 1963), and Frank Kermode's *The Tempest* (London: Methuen, 1954).

[51] For Mincoff, see "The Authorship of *The Two Noble Kinsmen*," *English Studies*, 33 (1952), 97–115 and "*Henry VIII* and Fletcher," *Shakespeare Quarterly*, 12 (1961), 239–60. Jackson's most accessible work is *Defining Shakespeare: "Pericles" as Test Case*.

[52] Houston, *Shakespearean Sentences*, especially pp. 198–221.

[53] *The Winter's Tale* (Oxford: Oxford University Press, 1996), and *The Tempest* (Oxford: Oxford University Press, 1987). The specific discussion I mention is found near the beginning of the Introduction to *The Winter's Tale*, pp. 11–12.

[54] Anne Barton, "Leontes and the Spider: Language and Speaker in Shakespeare's Last Plays," in *Essays, Mainly Shakespearean* (Cambridge: Cambridge University Press, 1994), pp. 161–81, originally published in *Shakespeare's Styles*, ed. Philip Edwards, Inga-Stina Ewbank, and G. K. Hunter

have written memorably about the contribution of language to particular plays.[55] Certain other stylistic critics, while not concentrating on the late verse, have taught us how to listen to these texts: I am thinking in particular of George T. Wright, first in the indispensable *Shakespeare's Metrical Art* and then in *Hearing the Measures*; of Patricia Parker on wordplay and rhetoric, particularly in *Literary Fat Ladies* and *Shakespeare from the Margins*; and of Stephen Booth, especially in his Yale edition of the Sonnets, the unjustly neglected *An Essay on Shakespeare's Sonnets*, and his more recent work on wordplay.[56]

The one important book concerned strictly with the language of the late plays is Simon Palfrey's *Late Shakespeare: A New World of Words*. His method of addressing Shakespeare's adoption of the new theatrical mode is (more or less) deconstructive, and therefore it is not surprising that metaphor is usually the focus of the inquiry. For Palfrey,

the critical challenge is how best to reconstruct Renaissance discourse, engaged as it is with recovering, revamping, and at times challenging ancient models: in order to thus build up, however, one's readings must first break things down a little. Shakespeare's intellectual world is kinetic, disjunctive, swiftly alive to contradictory possibilities. Above all, it is this fact of a world in process, unfinished, clamorous and turbulent, which must be respected and, through rigorous attention to the plays' mnemonic and metaphoric multiplicity, retrieved.[57]

Other features related to poetics present themselves as his analysis unfolds – vocabulary, of course, formal travesty, rhythms (although not usually in the metrical sense), and the borders between verse and prose. With the benefit of considerable learning and microscopic attention to verbal

---

(Cambridge: Cambridge University Press, 1980), pp. 131–50; her Introductions to the editions of *Hamlet* (Harmondsworth: Penguin, 1980) and especially *The Tempest* (Harmondsworth: Penguin, 1968); and other essays collected in *Essays, Mainly Shakespearean*.

[55] Inga-Stina Ewbank, "'My Name is Marina': The Language of Recognition," in *Shakespeare's Styles*, pp. 111–30; C. L. Barber, "'Thou that Beget'st Him That did Thee Beget': Transformation in *Pericles* and *The Winter's Tale*," *Shakespeare Survey* 22 (1969), 59–67; Roger Warren, "Theatrical Virtuosity and Poetic Complexity in *Cymbeline*," *Shakespeare Survey* 29 (1976), 41–49; Stanley Cavell, "Recounting Gains, Showing Losses: Reading *The Winter's Tale*," in *Disowning Knowledge in Six Plays of Shakespeare* (Cambridge: Cambridge University Press, 1987), pp. 193–222.

[56] George T. Wright, *Shakespeare's Metrical Art* (Berkeley: University of California Press, 1988) and *Hearing the Measures* (Madison: University of Wisconsin Press, 1998); Patricia Parker, *Literary Fat Ladies: Rhetoric, Gender, Property* (London: Methuen, 1987) and *Shakespeare from the Margins: Language, Culture, Context* (Chicago: University of Chicago Press, 1996); Stephen Booth, *An Essay on Shakespeare's Sonnets* (New Haven: Yale University Press, 1969), his edition of *Shakespeare's Sonnets* (New Haven: Yale University Press, 1977), "Shakespeare's Language and the Language of Shakespeare's Time," *Shakespeare Survey* 50 (1997), 1–17, and *Precious Nonsense* (Berkeley: University of California Press, 1998).

[57] *Late Shakespeare: A New World of Words*, p. 78.

texture, Palfrey searches out the political ramifications of Shakespearean romance, a generic term he conditionally accepts. Thus he tends to favor registers of language inflected by class and ideology, particularly those that magnify the anti-romantic energies of the romance form. As the quoted excerpt will have suggested, Palfrey's interests are contiguous to rather than congruent with the topics considered here.

GENRE

Modern criticism has rejected the Victorian biographical-symbolic reading of the late plays: Prospero as Shakespeare, the ingénues as his beloved daughters, the absent mothers (a refraction of his relationship with Anne) darkening the picture slightly, but forgiveness and reconciliation all around. Nevertheless, one of Dowden's major tenets retains its sovereignty even today:

> There is a romantic element about these plays. In all there is the same romantic incident of lost children recovered by those to whom they are dear – the daughters of Pericles and Leontes, the sons of Cymbeline and Alonso. In all there is a beautiful romantic background of sea or mountain. The dramas have a grave beauty, a sweet serenity, which seem to render the name "comedies" inappropriate; we may smile tenderly, but we never laugh loudly, as we read them. Let us, then, name this group consisting of four plays . . . Romances.[58]

In proposing such a designation, Dowden was developing a suggestion Coleridge had made decades earlier, when he spoke of *The Tempest* as a romance; Hazlitt, also, had referred to *Cymbeline* as "a dramatic romance."[59]

Since *Pericles, Cymbeline, The Winter's Tale*, and *The Tempest* undeniably resembled one another and differed from the rest of the canon, the decision to group them into one category and interpret them as the culmination of an artistic career – of *the* artistic career – struck a cultural chord, harmonizing with Victorian ideas of struggle and triumph, sin and redemption. Moreover, the ease with which "romance" took hold and its persistence in the thinking of scholars, teachers, and producers indicate that the term has met a lasting taxonomic need, for the category satisfied most (though not all) critics and editors for over a century. In 1916, for

---

[58] *Shakspere*, pp. 55–56.
[59] Coleridge in 1811 or 1812 refers to *The Tempest* as both "a specimen of the romantic drama" and as a "romance." See *Coleridge on Shakespeare*, ed. Terence Hawkes (Harmondsworth: Penguin, 1969), p. 224; and William Hazlitt, *Characters of Shakespear's Plays* (London: C. H. Reynell, 1817), p. 1.

example, H. B. Charlton introduced his edition of *The Winter's Tale* (1916) by enumerating common motifs and narrative staples and concluding that "all these are of the essence of Shakespearian romance . . . "[60] By the middle of the century "romance" had become the default term, and many editors of complete Shakespeare editions divided the plays into four categories, *Romances* being the last.[61]

Readers of the Folio of 1623 were offered no such group, of course. *The Tempest* appeared as the first of the comedies, *The Winter's Tale* as the last; *Cymbeline* stood last among the tragedies, the final play in the volume; *Henry VIII* was printed with the other histories; and for reasons unknown, *Pericles* and *The Two Noble Kinsmen* were not included. The presence of three generic divisions in the Folio does not mean, however, that Shakespeare's contemporaries were unable to conceive of other dramatic forms and names, as we know from the list recited by Polonius, to cite only one authority. Pastoral plays appeared and reappeared on the London stage in the 1590s and beyond, and just as Shakespeare was giving up tragedy, "tragicomedy" was attracting much interest in London theatrical circles. Although it had the advantage of classical sanction – Plautus's *Amphitruo* was the Roman model for tragicomedy – Fletcher and Beaumont set about to market a new, improved version of the form, that commended by the Italian Giambatista Guarini in *Il Pastor Fido*, the basis for Fletcher's *The Faithful Shepherdess*. Shakespeare was aware of these currents as he wrote his last plays, but at their first appearance, as far as we know, none of his efforts was described as a tragicomedy.

Nor was any described as a romance, and more than a few critics have expressed discomfort with Dowden's ahistorical category, some rejecting it altogether. In 1910 A. H. Thorndike, partial to the narrative of Shakespeare's professional connection to Beaumont and Fletcher,

---

[60] (London: D. C. Heath, 1916), pp. xii-xiii. The entire quotation runs as follows: "The mingling of the tragic and the idyllic, the sharp contrast of maniacal jealousy and tenderest love; the unnatural events and happy coincidences; the creation of an unhistorical history and an ungeographical geography; elaborate stage displays, trial scenes, statues stepping into life; unexpected catastrophes and a more unexpected denouement; above all the *motif* of the oracle: all these are of the essence of Shakespearian romance, and in the very spirit of Greek romance and of *Pandosto*."

[61] In complete editions such as *The Riverside Shakespeare* and David Bevington's for Harper-Collins, *Pericles, Cymbeline, The Winter's Tale,* and *The Tempest* are supplemented by *The Two Noble Kinsmen*, with *Henry VIII* included among the histories. Peter Alexander (1951), G. B. Harrison (1952), and Alfred Harbage (1969) did not include *The Two Noble Kinsmen. The Oxford Shakespeare* (1986), ed. Stanley Wells and Gary Taylor, chooses a chronological sequence, ignoring generic groups, and *The Norton Shakespeare* (1997), ed. Stephen Greenblatt *et al.*, based on Oxford, also organizes chronologically but provides a "Table of Contents by Genre," which includes the category "Romances."

dismissed "romance" in favor of "tragicomedy."[62] Some fifty years later G. E. Bentley also emphasized the physical conditions of the Jacobean theatre scene when he explained Shakespeare's shift practically, as a creative response to the King's Men's occupation of the Blackfriars Playhouse.[63] Joan Hartwig, declaring her bias in the title of *Shakespeare's Tragicomic Vision*, believes that the romance tradition, particularly what she calls its "puppet characters," limits our understanding of what the dramatist was trying to achieve in the last plays.[64] An eloquent objector to "romance" as the appropriate generic term is Stephen Orgel: "The new genre . . . has proved as obfuscatory as it has been enlightening; various attempts to move beyond the circularity of the definition, refine its terms, establish the genre with a tradition, have revealed a good deal about the history of romance, but perhaps nothing so much as its ultimate inadequacy as a critical category for Shakespearean drama."[65] Orgel himself seems slightly to prefer "tragicomedy," but he has moved the discussion forward by contesting our attachment to such prescriptive designations. Having lamented the anachronism and limitations of the term "romance" for works of drama, he goes on: "What this means is not that we can now comfortably declare the play a tragicomedy, rather than a romance, but that we can see how fluid the concept of genre was for Shakespeare's age."[66]

This modification of the dispute is developed by Barbara Mowat, who urges us to look beyond the competing labels to "family resemblances," a term she borrows from Alastair Fowler and Ludwig Wittgenstein. Speaking mainly of *Pericles, Cymbeline, The Winter's Tale,* and *The Tempest,* she categorizes them with "the subgenre of Fletcherian tragicomedy and with that of non-dramatic romances" but believes that "the family of works with which the plays share the most numerous and most intriguing connections is that set of dramas that trace back to the English miracle

---

[62] A. H. Thorndike, *The Influence of Shakespeare on Beaumont and Fletcher* (Worcester, Mass.: Wood, 1901).

[63] G. E. Bentley, "Shakespeare and the Blackfriars Theatre," *Shakespeare Survey* 1 (1948), 1–15.

[64] See chapter 1, especially pp. 13–22.

[65] Introduction to *The Winter's Tale*, p. 3. Orgel's doubts about logical circularity are anticipated by Philip Edwards, who reminds us that "there is some danger of errors in critical logic when Shakespeare's motives, inferred from the nature of the Romances, are used to aid enquiry into the nature of the Romances" ("Shakespeare's Romances: 1900–1957," p. 2).

[66] Orgel, Introduction to *The Winter's Tale*, p. 5. For a more thorough discussion of early modern ideas of genre, see also "Shakespeare and the Kinds of Drama," *Critical Inquiry*, 6 (1979), 107–23. Looking at the same problem from another point of view, Northrop Frye makes a similar suggestion: "Once we have learned to distinguish the modes, however, we must then learn to recombine them." *Anatomy of Criticism* (Princeton: Princeton University Press, 1957), pp. 50–51.

plays and then forward through the dramatic romances from *Clyomon and Clamydes* through *Mucedorus.*"[67] Almost all recent discussions of literary kinds display this non-prescriptive, familial emphasis, reflecting an agreement that critical boxes are not very useful because writers pay very little attention to them.[68] This is not to say that there should be no discussion of generic categories, which often become helpful guides to artistic practice, merely that with many works of art, especially Shakespeare's late plays, we need more than one category.

Mowat ends her essay on the problem of generic nomenclature by referring to "these creakily old-fashioned, deeply resonant, Shakespearean *tragicomic romances*" (emphasis added), and I intend to follow her lead.[69] In other words, during the course of this book I will use several terms to describe this group of plays: "romances," "tragicomedies," "late plays," "last plays," "final plays," and sometimes other nouns and other combinations as well. As Mowat demonstrates, both "romance" and "tragicomedy" survive alongside one another because both are necessary, each pointing to certain essential features that the other does not comprise, and the same is true for the other descriptive terms. For my purposes, Dowden's "romance" is probably the most frequently applicable, pointing as it does to the correspondences between narrative structures and stylistic predilections I shall be considering. But at certain points "tragicomedy" casts valuable light on a critical problem and thus ought to remain available for use where necessary.

It must be acknowledged, however, that whatever the category is called, *Henry VIII* and *The Two Noble Kinsmen* don't fit it very well. *Henry VIII* has enough in common with the four major romances to warrant consideration along with them, as commentators since Coleridge have recognized: he referred to it as "a sort of historical masque or show play." But it

---

[67] "'What's in a Name?'" p. 135. In pursuing this set of connections, Mowat extends a genealogical argument offered earlier by Howard Felperin and, perhaps less specifically, by Northrop Frye. See Felperin's *Shakespearean Romance*, pp. 12–34, and Frye's *A Natural Perspective: The Development of Shakespearean Comedy and Romance* (New York: Columbia University Press, 1965), and *The Secular Scripture: A Study of the Structure of Romance* (Cambridge, Mass.: Harvard University Press, 1976).

[68] This loose kind of grouping based on the principles of Fowler and Wittgenstein is also prominent in the argument of Helen Cooper, writing at almost exactly the same time as Mowat. Cooper's discussion concerns romance generally: "The romance genre – any genre, indeed – is best thought of as a lineage or a family of texts rather than as a series of incarnations or clones of a single Platonic Idea. A family changes over time as its individual members change, but equally, those individuals can be recognized through their 'family resemblance.'" *The English Romance in Time: Transforming Motifs from Geoffrey of Monmouth to the Death of Shakespeare* (Oxford: Oxford University Press, 2004), p. 8 and relevant notes.

[69] "'What's in a Name?'" p. 143.

would be idle to deny that it is primarily a history play and that its effect on audiences differs significantly from that of *Pericles*, for example. *The Two Noble Kinsmen* resists all the familiar Shakespearean categories, although its heroic story, taken from Chaucer and Boccaccio, and its mixed ending give it certain affinities with the romances and with other examples of Jacobean tragicomedy. Stylistically, at the level of sentence and line, these two plays exhibit most of the same properties as do the four romances that precede them. If the thesis of this book is that Shakespeare's distinctive late style came into being as a vehicle appropriate to these romances – that the style and structure are manifestations of the same theatrical impulse – how does one account for the appearance of that style in plays that don't much resemble those for which the style was devised?

The answer to that question, I believe, is that after *The Tempest*, for reasons that we cannot fully know but that have something to do with collaboration and gradual disengagement from the company, Shakespeare began to change again. In other words, the metamorphosis that began as he gave up writing tragedy continued through the period of the romances and led him to move in still different directions. Here it is helpful to remember that no group of plays is absolute and autonomous, and that while "the romances" may constitute a family group, they nevertheless exhibit resemblances to other plays not in the group. Just as *Othello* and *King Lear* have connections with *Measure for Measure*, so the romances may be related to the tragedies that precede them, e.g. *Antony and Cleopatra*, and to the strange hybrids that follow them, i.e. *Henry VIII* and *The Two Noble Kinsmen*. As Mowat and others have amply shown, the "romances" are themselves hybrids. For example, *Cymbeline* was considered a tragedy by the editors of the Folio, and some recent critics have urged that it be regarded as a history play.[70] The surprise ending of *The Winter's Tale* gives it a particular resemblance to the tragicomic style of Beaumont and Fletcher, with its "surprise packet" altering everything that has gone before.[71] The two last plays show a greater degree of hybridity than, and fewer familial links with, the familiar four than

---

[70] See A. Kent Hieatt, "*Cymbeline* and the Intrusion of Lyric into Romance Narrative: *Sonnets*, 'A Lover's Complaint,' Spenser's *Ruins of Rome*," in *Unfolded Tales: Essays on Renaissance Romance*, ed. George M. Logan and Gordon Teskey (Ithaca: Cornell University Press, 1989), pp. 98–118. Also see King, *"Cymbeline": Constructions of Britain*.

[71] I have borrowed the very useful phrase from F. P. Wilson, *Elizabethan and Jacobean* (Oxford: Clarendon Press, 1945), p. 128.

those four do with one another. But, again, the resemblances are sufficient to warrant discussing them in the same terms, and one of the chief resemblances is their distinctive, complex verse style.

STYLISTICS

Fundamentally, then, this is a book about decorum, about the calibration of dramatic speech to the content and shape of the narrative being staged, and reference to such a relation introduces the question of critical principles. Rather than weary the reader with a series of preliminary battles against imaginary adversaries, specifically debates about the value of stylistic criticism, I proceed with my analysis under the narratologist Gérard Genette's "methodological postulate . . . that what is true of individual elements is equally true of larger units."[72] Delineation of such identities assumes that the smallest grammatical and poetic details not only correspond to larger narrative or dramatic preferences but also serve, especially in the aggregate, as reliable indicators of an artist's way of apprehending the world. In other words, parallels between speech and structure are not merely resemblances but manifestations in different registers, such as dialogue and the disposition of events, of the same artistic impulse.

In support of such parallelism I refer occasionally to models that succinctly and persuasively demonstrate the value of detailed stylistic inquiry. The first is that of Tzvetan Todorov, who has written on the identity of narrative and style in the fantastic tales of Henry James. Arguing that "the secret of Jamesian narrative is precisely the existence of an essential secret, of something not named, of an absent and superpowerful force which sets the whole machinery of the narrative in motion," he goes on to show that "the complexity of James's style derives entirely from this principle of construction and not from a referential (for instance, psychological) complexity. 'Style,' 'feelings,' 'form,' and 'content' all say the same thing, all repeat the same figure in the carpet."[73] The second model derives from the reading of Ezra Pound's *Cantos* by Hugh Kenner, who enlists the ideas of the mathematician Benoit B. Mandelbrot: "The phrase 'self-similarity' is promoted . . . to describe

---

[72] Gérard Genette, *Fiction and Diction*, tr. Catherine Porter (Ithaca: Cornell University Press, 1993), p. 113n.

[73] Tzvetan Todorov, "The Secret of Narrative," in *The Poetics of Prose*, tr. Richard Howard (Ithaca: Cornell University Press, 1977), pp. 145, 158.

configurations that, viewed from varying distances, seem imitations (not duplicates) of themselves . . . Mandelbrot makes claims for 'the fractal geometry of nature,' 'fractal' being his term for a look of irregularity that turns out to be self-similar at varying scales . . . Small units, when they have integrity, imply wholes."[74] In Shakespeare's late work, grammatical sentences, poetic lines, and distinctive expressive habits offer access to what Todorov calls "the whole machinery of the narrative," in this case the dramatic narrative. Such minute properties also compare fractally with the recursive complexity and the episodic structures of Shakespeare's romantic stories. Further help with such reflective study is provided by Peter Brooks, who has written helpfully on the "grammar" and "syntax" of narrative, demonstrating the way that narrative structures often behave – work upon a perceiver – in the way sentences do.[75] Brooks is a specialist in prose fiction, but most of his insights are readily adaptable to drama.

The reader will recognize in this brief prospective *apologia* the principles of structuralist poetics, a theoretical framework I find illuminating and productive. Thinking about dramatic verse with the structuralist paradigm in mind helps to distinguish stylistics from the aims and methods of New Criticism, and even at this late hour the assertion of such a distinction is probably in order. Jonathan Culler, in his retrospective Preface to the Routledge Classics edition of *Structuralist Poetics* (2002), shows why structuralist analysis ought not to be identified with New Criticism. "Anglo-American New Criticism had made hermeneutics or interpretation the orthodoxy of literary studies, and I argued that rather than aim at discovering new yet sound interpretations of literary works, literary studies should seek to understand how works produced the effects they have for readers (effects such as meanings)."[76] As Culler goes on to prove, structuralist analysis does not proscribe the insights of deconstruction, historicism, feminism, or any of the major schools of critical practice that have gained prominence in the last three decades; rather, it can accommodate and even employ them as a means of refining its conclusions. In other words, the identification of poetic conventions, formal properties, generic codes and the dynamic relations among them is not invalidated but enriched by the exceptions and asymmetries that

[74] Hugh Kenner, "Self-Similarity, Fractals, Cantos," reprinted in *Historical Fictions* (San Francisco: North Point Press, 1990), pp. 319 and 325.

[75] Peter Brooks, *Reading for the Plot: Design and Intention in Narrative* (New York: Alfred A. Knopf, 1984).

[76] Jonathan Culler, *Structuralist Poetics: Structuralism, Linguistics, and the Study of Literature*, with a new preface by the author (London and New York: Routledge, 2002), pp. vii-viii.

post-structuralism, with its generally skeptical points of view, has succeeded in isolating. As Culler puts it, "One might say that the critique of the goal of a science of literature accompanies the scientific project, dogging its footsteps, and making the scientific impulse, in the most interesting and productive structuralist thinkers, above all a quest to make explicit the conditions of possibility, especially when the objects evade or play against those conditions."[77]

I hope to show that the patterns and fractals apparent in Shakespeare's late plays are significant literally, that they signify or function as carriers of meaning. Style and genre help to clarify – indeed help to create – ideas by supplying them with shape, making them easier to perceive; style and genre also direct the audience's responses, both intellectual and emotional. To notice a similar structure among multiple components of a dramatic work confirms the value of each in promoting meaning and controlling response. However, verbal configurations do more than prop up themes to be admired. Poetry in particular contributes to our experience of a Shakespeare play in a fashion independent of the specific propositional content it helps to display. Sometimes, of course, particularities of rhythm or other sounds will cooperate with the sense by seeming to echo the denotations of the words. Responding to what is probably the most obvious example in the last seven plays, the chaotic metrical scheme in Leontes' ravings about sexual infidelity, critics proudly note the indisputable parallel between the unstable verse and the unstable mind. "The rough and abrupt phrases, which huddle upon one another so as almost to break the texture of the line, represent the mind of Leontes maddened by his distemper of jealousy."[78] The problem with this tidy argument, of course, is that many persons in *The Winter's Tale* – and indeed in all the last plays – speak similarly irregular blank verse.

Such instances of poetic mimesis, satisfying as they may be, are for the most part anomalous, and in this respect I hold with critics such as Stephen Booth and Mark Womack who have sued for a divorce between "acoustic functions" and "semantic ones."[79] They can claim a powerful advocate in Dr. Johnson, who upholds the autonomy of sound and the peril of linking meter to meaning in his reply to Pope's famous "the

---

[77] *Structuralist Poetics*, p. x.
[78] Evans, *The Language of Shakespeare*, p. 206.
[79] Mark Womack, "Shakespearean Prosody Unbound," *Texas Studies in Literature and Language*, 45 (2003), 1–19; and Booth, *An Essay on Shakespeare's Sonnets*.

Sound must seem an Eccho to the Sense": "This notion of representative metre, and the desire of discovering frequent adaptations of the sound to the sense, have produced, in my opinion, many wild conceits and imaginary beauties."[80] The debatable question of mimetic prosody rears its head frequently in the following pages. For now, suffice it to say that the structures of verse and narrative answer to more removed meanings, meanings reflecting not the character's frame of mind but the larger "design" of the play. Such meanings serve as pointers to the playwright's thinking about his material and thus as guides to audience response. As James Sutherland puts it, after quoting the jerky, convoluted, puzzling dialogue that opens *Cymbeline*, "I suspect that the person who is thinking rapidly, breaking off, making fresh starts, and so on, is not the character, but Shakespeare himself."[81]

STYLE

An exceptionally clear statement of the problems presented by the late verse was written almost exactly one hundred years ago:

> After *Hamlet* the style, in the more emotional passages, is heightened. It becomes grander, sometimes wilder, sometimes more swelling, even tumid. It is also more concentrated, rapid, varied, and, in construction, less regular, not seldom twisted or elliptical. It is, therefore, not easy and lucid and in the more ordinary dialogue it is sometimes involved and obscure, and from these and other causes deficient in charm.[82]

This is A. C. Bradley in the third lecture from *Shakespearean Tragedy*, accomplishing in four sentences more than most of us can manage in four chapters. While the first phrase and the context disclose that Bradley is thinking chiefly of the very last tragedies, he also observes the same qualities in the plays composed after *Coriolanus* and *Antony and Cleopatra*. The third sentence identifies with exceptional precision those characteristics that make the language of the late plays so challenging – "concentrated," "varied," "less regular," "twisted," "elliptical" – and from these

---

[80] Samuel Johnson, *Lives of the English Poets, Volume III: Swift – Lyttleton* (Oxford: Clarendon Press, 1925), p. 230. See also the prudent summary by James Wimsatt: "While rhetorical effects are important, especially in the later periods of English poetry, the mystical all-encompassing mimological power, direct and indirect, asserted for them does not exist . . . Even with the most mimetic poetry, we must look beyond the rhetorical for the whole import of poetry's sounds, which reside primarily in the musical force of the phonetic pattern independent of the verbal statement." "Rhyme/Reason, Chaucer/Pope, Icon/Symbol," *Modern Language Quarterly*, 55 (1994), 24.

[81] "The Language of the Last Plays," p. 146.

[82] Bradley, *Shakespearean Tragedy*, p. 68.

adjectives most later treatments of the late style derive. For example, S. L. Bethell in 1956 describes the verse of *The Winter's Tale* as follows:

Rhythms for the most part are not smooth and regular as in the early plays, nor do they directly suggest the rhythms of ordinary speech as do those of Shakespeare's middle period. We are aware of the blank verse pattern and we can hear at the same time the tones of speech, but the total effect is new, a blank verse which is tense, springy, contorted. Among the means employed to achieve this are a daring use of harsh sound to express harsh feelings, the frequent omission of words properly required by the syntax – this is called "ellipsis" – and a sometimes violent distortion of word order.[83]

This is relatively helpful and relatively generous, as stylistic criticism goes, but its debt to Bradley is clear. The analysis that follows also constitutes an elaboration of the Bradleyan categories.

No matter how challenging the syntax or the metrical pattern becomes, *what* the lines mean is considerably easier to discern than *how* they deliver their meanings. Although what Stephen Booth calls the "physics" of many passages remain unexplained after centuries of discussion, usually the listener or reader is able to grasp the main idea. Booth's remarks about certain difficult passages in the sonnets pertain equally, perhaps especially, to the last plays. Sometimes, he says, "a reader will see the speaker's point without understanding (or knowing that he has not understood and cannot in any usual sense understand) the sentence that makes the point," and he goes on to claim that "even where the lines are vaguest and most ambiguous they are usually *also* simple and obvious."[84] We know what's being said, but we can't quite say, or even know, how we know. Stephen Orgel takes a slightly different position in his Introduction to *The Winter's Tale*, arguing that Shakespeare may not have expected the audience to apprehend every line, that what some of the most difficult passages

conveyed to the Renaissance audience was pretty much what they convey to us: intensity, vagueness and obscurity. How we interpret this obscurity – as a function of character, or of the Sicilian court, of the language of kings, of the

---

[83] S. L. Bethell, Introduction to *The Winter's Tale* (Oxford: Oxford University Press, 1956), p. 19.

[84] Stephen Booth, *Shakespeare's Sonnets* (New Haven: Yale University Press, 1977), xii. Frank Kermode makes a similar point, citing Booth, in *Shakespeare's Language*, pp. 153–54. See also J. H. P. Pafford, in his introduction to the Arden2 edition of *The Winter's Tale*, p. lxxxv: "It is worth noting, too, that the incoherence of this language can be exaggerated. There are only one or two passages which are difficult to understand when heard or read quickly. The general sense is clear . . . and since this is so it is as much an error to treat this language as a 'difficulty' as it is to bother about anachronisms and loose ends. On the stage there is no difficulty." This seems to me to overstate the case somewhat.

complexities of public discourse, of the nature of stage plays themselves in the Renaissance – is the real textual question, and it remains an open one.[85]

This book represents an effort to supply a partial answer to that open question.

I propose that we interpret the verbal obscurity and poetic difficulty of the late style as a product of Shakespeare's increasingly sophisticated way of thinking about the world, a stylistic manifestation of his ever developing view of human experience. It seems clear, as Roger Warren puts it, that the poet is "trying to pack in a great deal, to communicate this or that emotion in all its complexity, even at the sacrifice of immediate clarity."[86] The difficulties of the late verse, in other words, attest to a straining after greater subtlety, an effort to represent many complex and at times virtually contradictory ideas. Shakespeare is frequently said to be deliberately seeking to intensify the virtual experience, trying to propel listeners beyond mere verbal denotation, contriving to make them participate in the feeling represented. And if that way of putting it is too abstract or mystical, we might say that years of putting words in the mouths of others had led the playwright to pursue new ways of expressing thought and emotion. Harley Granville-Barker identifies the link between this increasingly sophisticated mode of thought and the poetic style devised to communicate it: "Shakespeare himself, intent more and more upon plucking out the heart of the human mystery, stimulated his actors to a poignancy and intimacy of emotional expression – still can stimulate them to it – as no other playwright has quite learned to do . . . His verse was, of course, his chief means to this emotional expression."[87]

My primary aim is to describe the components of that verse, to attend to the acoustic surface of the late style and thereby to assemble an illustrated taxonomy, a survey more specific and wide-ranging than any attempted so far. While hardly exhaustive, my study catalogues in successive chapters some of the major poetic and grammatical features of this verse, offering a relatively detailed account of their mechanical operations, affective functions, theatrical contributions, and thematic potentialities. Such an account identifies formal particulars (letters, syllables, words, phrases, sentences, and lines), notices the relations among these elements,

[85] Introduction to *The Winter's Tale*, p. 12.
[86] Roger Warren, "Theatrical Virtuosity and Poetic Complexity in *Cymbeline*," 46.
[87] Harley Granville-Barker, "Introduction," *Prefaces to Shakespeare*, 2 vols. (London: Batsford, 1958), I, 11–12.

describes the mechanics of their interaction, and observes some of the aural patterns they compose. In studying textual details I usually employ non-technical vocabulary, avoiding the diction of linguistic scholarship: at least in the study of early modern dramatic verse, such specialized terminology usually impedes rather than fosters clarity and understanding.

The technical features that make Shakespeare's late style demanding can be enumerated in a few sentences. Ellipsis exerts a constant pressure on the sound and sense as the poet concentrates expression, omitting phonemic and verbal units that in an earlier phase of composition he would have retained. Connectives between clauses are sometimes removed, creating the effect of asyndeton: the words and phrases that remain make the verse sound unusually "distilled." Syntax becomes convoluted, often confusingly so, and even though word order in early modern English is much less standardized than it has since become, the number of deformed phrases, directional shifts, and intricately constructed sentences is exceptional for the period and exceptional for Shakespeare. Related to this grammatical complexity is the dependence on parenthesis, what one critic refers to as "parenthomania, the alarming outbreak of brackets."[88] Repetition of various units – letters, words, phrases, rhythms – becomes more prominent and sometimes almost obsessive, patterning heard clearly in the incantatory doublings in *Macbeth* and resounding most audibly in the extraordinary echoing effects of *The Tempest.* Blank verse, usually a guarantor of order and regularity, is now aggressively irregular, encompassing enjambments, light or weak endings, frequent stops or shifts of direction, and other threats to the integrity of the line. Metaphors tend to be introduced and often succeeded rapidly by others, not articulated at length. Finally, governing all these technical features is a pervasive self-consciousness, an artist's playful delight in calling attention to his own virtuosity.

An article of critical agreement is that the mature Shakespeare divides language from speaker, or at least the connection between style and character has been attenuated. On this point, at least, Strachey ("no longer interested . . . in . . . who says what") may claim victory. That Shakespeare learned, as he reached professional maturity in the mid-1590s, to make his speakers sound like themselves is one of the triumphs of his craft, one of the talents for which he is celebrated and by which he is differentiated

---

[88] Keir Elam, "Early Modern Syntax and Late Shakespearean Rhetoric," in *Early Modern English: Trends, Forms and Texts*, ed. C. Nocera Avila, N. Pantaleo, and D. Pizzini (Fasano: Schena Editore, 1992), p. 69.

from lesser dramatists. Prince Hal, Falstaff, King Henry, Hotspur, Owen Glendower – none of these speakers will be confused with the others.[89] Indeed, so confident of their distinctive voices is their creator that he even allows some speakers to parody others with the certainty that the audience will get the joke. Such verbal differentiation obtains throughout the middle plays, allowing the listener to distinguish among the various speakers in *Othello*, for example. However, about 1607 or so Shakespeare begins to weaken the link between speech and speaker.

The most persuasive articulation of this principle is Anne Barton's elegant analysis: "Shakespeare has adjusted his language and dramatic art to the demands of a new mode: one in which plot, on the whole, has become more vivid and emotionally charged than character."[90] Although most of her illustrations come from *The Winter's Tale*, Barton's general argument applies as well to the other late work. She notes, for example, that in *Pericles* "Shakespeare appears to be using Marina less as a character than as a kind of medium, through which the voice of the situation can be made to speak."[91] Many astute readers have noticed that to make sense of certain puzzling passages in the late work we must, in the words of John Porter Houston, "have recourse to the notion of some general design in the language of the play rather than to that of character or scene."[92] I am persuaded that we might move beyond the boundaries of the individual play and locate that "general design" in the last plays as a group, with each text representing different aspects of that design.

To return briefly to Bradley, his summary captures in a single phrase one of the major problems inherent in the poetry of this phase: "it is also." The critic must immediately confront the multiplicity of the late style, or putting it another way, the frankness of its inconsistencies. So varied and unpredictable is the verse that almost any generalization about its

---

[89] Among many writers on this point, see Daniel Seltzer, "Prince Hal and Tragic Style," *Shakespeare Survey 30* (1977), 13–20.

[90] "Leontes and the Spider," pp. 180–81.

[91] *Ibid.*, p. 168. A more recent statement of this view is Simon Palfrey's contention that "unlike the appropriative masteries of a Mercutio, Rosalind, Falstaff, of a Hamlet or Iago, speech is now manipulated in the service of Shakespeare's supra-characterological ambitions" (*Late Shakespeare: A New World of Words*, p. viii).

[92] Houston, *Shakespearean Sentences*, p. 207. S. L. Bethell, in his Introduction to *The Winter's Tale*, makes a similar point: "this same kind of verse is spoken by most of the characters most of the time . . . in *The Winter's Tale* only the old Shepherd is given a characteristic style. The jealous Leontes, the faithful Florizel, the gracious Hermione, even the forthright Perdita, all speak with twisted rhythms, 'realistic' vocabulary, and metaphysical wit. The style represents Shakespeare's mind, not the character's; indeed, it draws our attention *away from* the speaker to what is spoken about" (p. 22).

elements and their uses requires modification and, in some cases, contradiction as well. Everyone recognizes that the late verse is "concentrated" and "elliptical," for example, and yet everyone also admits that the thought can frequently be expansive and the verse sentences digressive. A text like *The Tempest* is both elliptical and unashamedly pleonastic. These contradictory descriptions attest to the countervailing pressures built into the verse: the forces of coherence, such features as repetition and identification, compete with and complement the forces of irregularity, such features as ellipsis and syntactic digression. Conscious of these incongruities, disturbed by the frequent semantic difficulties, and puzzled by the idiosyncratic poetic choices, critics have struggled to provide comprehensive descriptions: the late verse has been called "metaphysical" (S. L. Bethell and Anne Barton), "a strange mixing of artifice and simplicity" representing "a new euphuism of imagination" (Harley Granville-Barker), "the clotted rhetoric that is the poetry of a man who has finished with action . . . the style of old age" (Theodore Spencer), "straining after the maximum of intensity" (James Sutherland). Various explanations for these conditions have been offered: that the poet was bored (Lytton Strachey's famous charge), that he suffered from "imaginative exhaustion" (Ifor Evans), that he "was writing at speed" (Sutherland), that he was striving for "greater intensity," a more sophisticated mode of expression (Roger Warren). The variety of labels and explanations notwithstanding, most commentators would seem to agree with J. M. Nosworthy's conclusion that much of the late verse is "experimental," and that Shakespeare around 1608 is "a man in search of a style."[93]

In 1850 James Spedding, sensing the presence of an alien hand in *Henry VIII*, published an essay on the two distinct kinds of verse he heard, and in so doing contributed an exceptionally helpful piece of analysis. He catches precisely those properties that distinguish Shakespeare's verse from that of Fletcher and also from his own earlier practice. The most valuable paragraph comes as Spedding recounts his experience of reading the first scene:

The opening of the play – the conversation between Buckingham, Norfolk, and Abergavenny, – seemed to have the full stamp of Shakespere, in his latest manner: the same close-packed expression; the same life, and reality, and freshness; the same rapid and abrupt turnings of thought, so quick that language can hardly follow fast enough; the same impatient activity of intellect and fancy,

---

[93] Introduction to *Cymbeline*, p. lxii.

which having once disclosed an idea cannot wait to work it orderly out; the same daring confidence in the resources of language, which plunges headlong into a sentence without knowing how it is to come forth; the same careless metre which disdains to produce its harmonious effects by the ordinary devices, yet is evidently subject to a master of harmony; the same entire freedom from book-language and common-place; all the qualities, in short, which distinguish the magical hand which has never yet been successfully imitated.[94]

Multiplicity, bravado, unusual music, spontaneity – most of the qualities that later listeners have found in the late style are identified here.

Informing Spedding's survey is his awareness of a single quality, an essential property of the late style that has not been accorded adequate notice: pace. This is not pace in the metrical sense – the work of Pope's "swift Camilla" – but rather speed of thought, the celerity with which our minds are expected to process multiple poetic effects and ideas. Metaphor offers perhaps the most revealing insight into this mercurial manner: Gordon McMullan speaks of Shakespeare's "febrile use of metaphor" at this period,[95] thus identifying an effect almost everybody has sensed, that Shakespeare supplies fewer details about the metaphoric likeness he proposes and expects the audience to make the transference more rapidly. Whereas in earlier plays he usually developed, or more precisely, allowed the speaker to develop, the terms of the comparison, here he barely introduces the figure before moving quickly to another and perhaps still another. We ourselves are expected to register the terms of similitude and then pass immediately to another demanding figure.

Speed of thought, elliptical constructions, and syntactical idiosyncrasies produce a sense of spontaneity, an impression of characters in the act of thinking. This poetic style is distinctly Shakespearean. Emerson, in his essay on Shakespeare in *Representative Men*, caught the flavor of this style when he noticed the two distinct poetic voices in *Henry VIII*. Taking up a scene by Fletcher, he misses "the metre of Shakespeare, whose secret is that the thought constructs the tune, so that reading for the sense will best bring out the rhythm; here the lines are constructed on a given tune."[96] In other words, the dramatic moment governs the music of the passage, and Shakespeare has mastered the art of seeming artless – the poetry

---

[94] James Spedding, "Who Wrote Shakespere's *Henry VIII?*," *The Gentleman's Magazine*, August 1850, 115–23, p. 118.

[95] Gordon McMullan, review of Simon Palfrey's *Late Shakespeare, Notes and Queries*, 46 (1999), 120. This description confirms the view of metaphor proposed many years ago by Frank Kermode: see Chapter 1, p. 46.

[96] Quoted in Vickers, *Shakespeare, Co-Author*, p. 364.

convincingly represents people in the act of speaking and talking. Fletcher's lines tend to be much more obviously crafted; he exerts much greater control over the shapely unfolding of his sentences; his patterned language calls attention to its arrangement.[97] Nosworthy's remark that around 1609 Shakespeare was "a man in search of a style" derives probably from the quickness and multiplicity of the verse, its tendency to shift into another key or to move on to contrasting effects before the listener is able to get a purchase on it. *Brevitas* and *amplificatio* work together: Shakespeare removes much of the detail used to elaborate a poetic sign – say, a metaphor – in his earlier work, while at the same time he has increased the number of signs we are expected to absorb. The "tune" that Emerson speaks of is now pared down, fractured into smaller phrases that flicker and are quickly supplanted by another phrase. A provisional way of describing the late verse would be to call it a kind of synecdochic style, a set of codes that the listener must act upon so as to follow the mind of the character and the dramatist. This is what A. C. Partridge means when he says that Shakespeare's "ideas outstrip his syntax," or Bradley when he argues that in many passages "the sense has rather to be discerned beyond the words than found in them."[98]

STYLE AND STORY

In constructing a repertoire of stylistic features on which the late plays depend, I propose to demonstrate the fractal relationship between the late verse and the new kind of story to which Shakespeare was contemporaneously attracted. Nosworthy believes that Shakespeare's turn to a novel theatrical mode would naturally have altered the texture of his poetic style: "romance, which imposes a new species of action and a changed process of character portrayal, would, by implication, call for new forms of expression."[99] Writing in the 1950s, he unhesitatingly speaks of

---

[97] See, among others, Cyrus Hoy, "The Language of Fletcherian Tragicomedy," in *Mirror up to Shakespeare: Essays in Honour of G. R. Hibbard*, ed. Douglas Gray (Toronto: University of Toronto Press, 1984), and Chapter 5, below.

[98] A. C. Partridge, *Orthography in Shakespeare and Elizabethan Drama: A Study of Colloquial Contractions, Elision, Prosody and Punctuation* (Lincoln: University of Nebraska Press, 1964), p. 147, and Bradley, *Shakespearean Tragedy*, p. 69.

[99] Introduction to *Cymbeline*, p. lxii. It is worth reiterating a point made earlier, however, that we must be careful not to read backwards: as Shakespeare worked on the last acts of *Pericles* or prepared to adapt the historical and fictional stories that resulted in *Cymbeline*, the playwright himself may not have known that he was preparing to write his "last plays" or even that his next several productions would all be some form of theatrical romance.

"romance." The debates over nomenclature notwithstanding, most readers will agree that the late plays exhibit many of the defining properties of romance fiction, but "romance fiction" is notoriously difficult to define. In 1909 W. P. Ker concluded his lecture to the English Association with the claim that "Romance means almost everything," a statement with which subsequent authorities, from Eugène Vinaver to Helen Cooper, have concurred.[100]

Romance is so resistant to definition that I intend for the moment to proceed without one, confident that most readers are aware of the problem, acquainted with the general properties of the mode, and willing to entertain various descriptions and emphases during the course of the analysis. Such an evasion receives support from Barbara Fuchs, who begins her study of the form by admitting the indefinite nature of the object she has undertaken to consider: "Romance is a notoriously slippery category. Critics disagree about whether it is a genre or a mode, about its origins and history, even about what it encompasses. Yet, paradoxically, readers are often able to identify romance when they see it."[101] Certainly those familiar with early modern fiction know romance when they see it. A specialist in comparative literature, Fuchs expresses the modern scholar's impatience with the way Shakespeare has tyrannized the category, thus "obscuring the many genres with a claim to being considered English Renaissance romances, all of which are typically neglected for the highly anomalous category of dramatic romance."[102] Nonetheless, she and others who share her reservations admit the shared materials and moods of Shakespearean and other examples of romance fiction: adventures, journeys and wandering, shipwrecks, divided families, desert places, temporal leaps, apparent death, providential intervention, joy after despair. For the study of verse style, however, these narrative topoi are less useful than two identifying organizational features of romance: narrative amplitude and structural looseness. As Shakespeare adapts his source materials to the task of telling stories on a stage, his arrangement of his dramatic materials corresponds, in shape and effect, to his ordering of the poetic constituents. Staging the unstable realm of romance produces narrative equivalents of those convolutions, reversals, ellipses, delayed

---

[100] W. P. Ker, *Romance* (London, 1909), p. 12. A recent authority slyly understates the problem: "The meaning of the term 'romance' is complicated by the fact that both in medieval and modern times it has been used loosely." *New Princeton Encyclopedia of Poetry and Poetics*, ed. Alex Preminger and T. G. V. Brogan (Princeton, 1993), p. 751.

[101] Barbara Fuchs, *Romance* (London: Routledge, 2004), pp. 1–2.

[102] *Ibid.*, p. 94.

grammatical units, repetitions, additives, and other stylistic mannerisms to which the ear must become attuned.

Syntax offers an instructive preliminary example. The two chapters devoted to sentence structure will illustrate the particulars of what is generally called the "loose parenthetical syntax" of Shakespeare's late period,[103] and that same phrase might be profitably applied to his organization of his chosen sources. Verbal syntax is fundamentally a matter of recognized, meaningful relations among words and grammatical units. In Shakespeare's last plays, the difficulties of the loose syntax are attributable to the playwright's having weakened or suppressed certain normal relations among the parts of sentences, or between and among the several sentences in a larger speech or verse paragraph. This technique is a version of what the Renaissance rhetoricians referred to as "asyndeton." A sentence coheres and delivers its meaning by virtue of its adherence to certain agreed upon forms, but the liberty with which the speaker or writer distributes those syntactical units may stretch or even seem to defy the rules of coherence. Shakespeare's late style, comprising as it does hundreds of sentences very casually tied together, is recapitulated structurally in the episodic, disjointed unfolding of dramatic romance.

The unexpected juxtapositions, surprising turns of plot, and temporal shifts characteristic of the action represent a mode of storytelling that might be called narrative asyndeton. Romance fiction is noted – and valued – for its neglect, even its defiance, of the canons of logic; in their place we are given magic, surprise, providential intervention, and other manifestations of an alogical domain. Integuments among plots, relations among characters, motives of action, or links among locations are by no means inevitable and often puzzling, the conditions of the mode having relieved the storyteller of the obligation to clarify such connections and furnish background. Thus, to offer a specific instance, the realm Shakespeare has created in *Cymbeline* is exceedingly disjointed. The characters are loosely related and physically separated: we begin with the parting of Imogen and Posthumus, as he removes to Rome; she has never seen her brothers, stolen from their father's court in infancy; the royal family also includes an adopted son and a stepmother; the relation of the British-Roman tribute plot to the story of Imogen's putative infidelity is, narratively speaking, very tenuous. While various cues imply an eventual reunion and perhaps even a happy ending, how such a reconciliation will

---

[103] Pafford, Introduction to *The Winter's Tale*, p. lxxxv, n.2.

be achieved is by no means obvious. *Cymbeline* is the play in which Shakespeare seems to have set himself the greatest challenge in dispersing and then bringing together the threads of action.[104]

Many of the terms that critics use to describe the late style – "extravagant," "reckless," "loose" – also pertain to the sprawling, episodic, casually organized dramatic structures that Shakespeare favored from *Pericles* forward. In responding to both poetic style and dramatic structure, the audience remains aware of the controlling hand of the dramatist. Chance would seem to govern the unpredictable course of events, but the theophanies or oracular interventions that mark each play suggest providential agency. The spectacular appearance of Jupiter in Act 5 of *Cymbeline* is one such intercession. Through a complicated network of ironies (to be explored in Chapter 6), the effect of such a divine agent is, paradoxically, to highlight the supervisory role of the playwright. Throughout the dazzling last scene of *Cymbeline* the audience remains conscious of and indeed enjoys being conscious of the managerial virtuosity of the dramatist, particularly his skill at concealing, diverting, revealing, and above all controlling the multiple strands of the action. The managed complexity generates a feeling of pleasurable uncertainty. Likewise, the listener often feels the same combination of perceptual anxiety and security about the semantic direction of the verse sentences. It is as if, for the purposes of the theatrical experience, the providential agent is the poet, delaying comprehension and finally delighting the listener with clarification.

This correspondence between smaller and larger units is more than an analogy, however, something greater than a simple parallel between style and structure. Rather, noticing the correspondence between minute grammatical particulars and broad organizational principles helps to show how style makes meaning. As patterned sound passing from actor's throat to listener's ear, verse constitutes one of the primary conduits of transaction between playwright and audience, the actor serving as intermediary. In fact, the early modern terms for actor, *persona*, and for the creation of character, "personation," derive from the Latin for "speaking through." The kind of language spoken determines how the audience experiences the story and thus controls its perception of events and their significance. Metrically, for example, the contest between the order of the blank verse pattern and the threats to that order posed by the energies of the sentence

---

[104] I use the name "Imogen" throughout, following the *Riverside* and Folio texts, rather than the emended "Innogen" of *The Oxford Shakespeare*, on the grounds that the question is not yet settled. Ros King, in *"Cymbeline": Constructions of Britain*, points out that while the princess is called Innogen in Holinshed's text, his index lists "Imogen" (p. 72).

imparts to the listener or reader a physical apprehension of the fictional conflicts that the structure of romance is calculated to emphasize. This stylistic recapitulation is most obvious in a speech like Leontes' "Too hot, too hot" or Imogen's headless man speech, but the same principle obtains throughout each of the late works. And at all times the audience is granted the safety of virtuality.

PROCEDURE

This kind of insistence on the *minutiae* of the theatrical event is as deadening as those accounts of poems in which a critic bothers us with his impressions, word by word, sound by sound.

Michael Hattaway[105]

The degree of detail in a book of this sort, intended to survey the components of a particular style of dramatic poetry, can be deadening. Aware of that peril, I have tried at all times to relate poetic *minutiae* to larger questions of dramatic form and purpose. Chapter 1 locates in three late tragedies, *Macbeth*, *Coriolanus*, and *Antony and Cleopatra*, the origins of the turn to romance. These tragedies display certain poetic properties (especially insistent repetition) and complementary attitudes towards verbal expression (distrust of language on the one hand and delight in it on the other) that help to fix contexts for Shakespeare's embrace of the new form and development of the new style. The central chapters explore and illustrate the major traits that make up the late style, grouped roughly as follows: Chapter 2 is devoted to strategies promoting ellipsis, Chapter 3 syntactical divagation, Chapter 4 syntactical suspension, and Chapter 5 repetition. In the concluding chapter, I suggest how these stylistic properties work together to create meaning, meaning particular to the kind of stories the dramatist has chosen to tell.

In the last quarter of his career something in Shakespeare changed. We cannot know what event or process of thought led to his revaluation of experience, but we discover in the last plays a refreshed view of language, an affirmative attitude towards theatre and representation generally, and a renewed faith in his own profession. At least for a time such renewed confidence becomes apparent. Then it seems to dissipate again. A more nearly complete understanding of those fundamental changes may be found through close study of the late style.

---

[105] Michael Hattaway, Review of *Reinterpretations of Renaissance Drama*, ed. Norman Rabkin and Max Bluestone, *The Yearbook of English Studies* 1 (1971), 236–37.

CHAPTER 1

The idioms of the late tragedies

Women are wordes, Men deedes.

Thomas Howell, 1581[1]

A point of origin for the late Shakespearean style does not immediately present itself. Analysis might reach as far back as *2 Henry VI* or *Love's Labour's Lost*, since even these very early texts contain the roots and forecast the development of the main stylistic features in the late plays. In other words, since Shakespeare's treatment of dramatic poetry developed over the course of his career, and since the late verse represents a metamorphosis or revision of earlier poetic practices, any decision about where to begin is to some degree arbitrary. Practically speaking, however, a later starting point is necessary. One of the ambitions of this book is to show that the distinctive properties discernible in the late verse are intimately related to the shift from tragedy to romance, that the altered style and the new mode express Shakespeare's renewed sense of values and refreshed artistic purpose. A concomitant goal is to demonstrate that this exchange of modes may be ascribed, at least in part, to Shakespeare's evolving and contradictory opinions about language itself, so that his rejection of tragedy derives also from conflicted and developing opinions about the stage and about his own professional status. Therefore I begin with the distinctive idioms of three tragedies written just before, or perhaps just as, Shakespeare took up the form of dramatic romance: *Macbeth*, *Coriolanus*, and *Antony and Cleopatra*.

Collectively, these tragedies constitute a kind of pivot for the shift from one mode to the other. In the present context, their particular utility resides chiefly in their intimation of certain stylistic habits that characterize the late work. *Macbeth* is an unusually indicative stylistic predictor because it is uncommonly poetic or musical, especially compared to some

---

[1] *Howell's Devises 1581, With an Introduction by Walter Raleigh* (Oxford: Clarendon Press, 1906), p. 31.

of the dramas written shortly before it, such as *Measure for Measure* and *King Lear*. Its text abounds in aural pleasures, poetic configurations such as frequent rhyme, the chanting associated with the demonic, and what seems to be an obsessive devotion to repetition, or doubled sounds. It is not too much to say that *Macbeth* exhibits a fascination with and a delight in poetic artifice that seem more akin to the romances than to the tragedies. Paradoxically, it seems that such musical echoing threatens to compromise the terms of representation, hinting at the playwright's eventual move away from mimesis and towards a frank dramatic poesis. The two Roman tragedies are also valuable indicators of stylistic metamorphosis, although their particular poetic qualities may not at first be so perspicuous. These three tragedies are also pivotal because they entertain opposing ideas about the vices and virtues of language, exhibit anxiety about gender and its relation to dramatic and poetic representation, and express concern about the value of the stage, particularly about the role of the playwright.

Timon of Athens might also have been included, of course: it shares stylistic traits with the other three (and with the late plays as well) and evinces profound concerns about words, women, and the world of the theatre. Its desperate negativity has seemed to some critics to denote an authorial blockage relieved by the shift to romance: to Clifford Leech, for example, *Timon* "seems to mark the end of Shakespeare's tragic writing and, because it reached an impasse, to lead into his new development in the last plays."[2] But debates about its date, its collaborative origins, and its uncertain state of completion conveniently justify putting it aside, and readers will recall from it many of the properties and ideas considered here. *Macbeth*, *Coriolanus*, and *Antony and Cleopatra* suffice to demonstrate, in their similarities, that Shakespeare was engaged in a serious revaluation of his professional direction and his poetic medium; in their differences, they disclose profound ambivalence about the theatre and his future in it.

"MACBETH, MACBETH, MACBETH"

The inordinately compressed language of *Macbeth* forecasts precisely Shakespeare's ongoing effort, one which becomes more and more audible,

---

[2] Clifford Leech, "Masking and Unmasking in the Last Plays," in *Shakespeare's Romances Reconsidered*, ed. Carol McGinnis Kay and Henry Jacobs (Lincoln: University of Nebraska Press, 1978), p. 49.

to reduce poetic expression to essentials. Stylistically speaking, it looks to the future: its extravagant verbal music makes it sound more like the last act of *Pericles* than, say, the last act of *Julius Caesar*. This reiterative poetic texture exposes with unusual clarity the playwright's mixed feelings about language, its irresistible attractions and inherent duplicity. What seems especially important, as it will in *Coriolanus* and *Antony and Cleopatra*, is that Shakespeare associates ambiguous speech especially with predatory females, in this case with demonic women. An affiliation between women and wicked words is suggested by the distinctive sound of the "witch language" that opens the play and infects many of its characters. And yet beguiling language is also the instrument of artistic creation, the sine qua non of the tragedy. These conflicted feelings about his own medium are hardly new and certainly not confined to *Macbeth*: they underlie the rhetorical brilliance of Richard of Gloucester, for example, with his ability to "moralize two meanings in one word," and they animate (to a greater or lesser extent) each of the other major tragedies. But such ambivalence seems especially paradoxical for a dramatist and poet. By 1606 or so the feelings of skepticism have tilted dangerously to the negative, and yet shortly thereafter renewed faith in language is one of the prompts for the shift to a new theatrical mode.

Macbeth is among the shortest plays in the canon, and even if the Folio text, the only surviving version, represents an abbreviated script prepared perhaps for court or touring performance, still the play is calculated to seem short, the effects of speed and brevity contributing to its power.[3] Without the subplots of *Hamlet* and *King Lear*, the action is concentrated and propulsive, and the distillation of the story is enhanced by the hitherto unprecedented concentration of verbal means. Bradley's description of Shakespeare's style after *Hamlet* – "concentrated," "elliptical," "involved and obscure" – was probably written with *Macbeth* very much in the critic's ears. Many passages illustrate exactly the phenomenon described by Stephen Booth, that the audience often understands what a passage says without understanding precisely how that understanding comes about, as in "And to be more than what you were you would / Be so much more the man" (1.7.50–51).[4] Rarely has dialogue seemed so

[3] On the status of the text, see A. R. Braunmuller's thorough discussion in the Introduction to his edition (Cambridge: Cambridge University Press, 1997), esp. pp. 95–96.

[4] See Introduction, p. 31. Also see Stephen Booth's "Close Reading without Readings," in *Shakespeare Reread: The Texts in New Contexts*, ed. Russ McDonald (Ithaca: Cornell University Press, 1994), pp. 42–55.

poetically compressed. But the sonic effects of this distillation have been insufficiently noted. A major result of such extreme verbal compression is to magnify the relations between similar words and sounds, making their identities more audible and more potentially, or at least apparently, significant. As I shall argue in more detail in Chapter 5, such echoing is aurally satisfying and intellectually tantalizing: it seems to give "the word of promise to our ear."

Less than five minutes into the first act the Scots Captain recounts for King Duncan the invasion of the Norwegian army:

> As whence the sun gins his reflection,
> Shipwracking storms, and direful thunders
> So from that spring, whence comfort seem'd to come,
> Discomfort swells. Mark King of Scotland, mark. . .
> (1.2.25–28; Folio punctuation)

As the Cambridge editor notes, this is "a complicated and ambiguous passage, but the main meaning is clear: in circumstances that seem positive, a threat unexpectedly appears."[5] The impulse to concentrate meaning into few words accounts for the aphetic "gins," perhaps for the absence of a verb in line 26, and for the conversion of "shipwrack" into a participle, the first known example of that usage. Pope emended line 26 by adding the verb "break" at the end, a suggestion taken up by some modern editors but not others. The critic wants to avoid assigning significance to a feature that turns out to be a compositor's error, but the fact is that such an elliptical line is typical of the verse to come. Here, the conversion of noun into participial adjective creates brief grammatical uncertainty: "shipwracking" might at first seem to be a progressive verb in a clause in which "sun" is the subject, instead of a modifier attached to "storms." Likewise, the two parts of the simile's vehicle, contrasting affirmative and negative effects emanating from the same source, are compressed and elliptical. For all the distillation, however, the passage echoes with reiterated sounds: the incantatory "Mark King of Scotland, mark," the characteristically Shakespearean play on the antithetical "comfort" and "discomfort," the triple repetition of "com" in "come," "comfort," and "discomfort," the sibilants throughout, and the cluster of consonants – *c, m, d* and *s* – in lines 27 and 28. Throughout *Macbeth* this tension between reduction and pleonasm manifests itself in diction, metrics, and syntax. It is also a primary feature of the late style and a major source of its difficulty.

---

[5] Braunmuller, *Macbeth*, p. 105n.

Readers will easily recall speeches, lines, metaphors, and turns of phrase in which evocative or distilled language conveys its meaning in apparent defiance of logical or literal sense. An obvious case in which intuitive understanding precedes grammatical cognition is the passage beginning "pity, like a naked new-born babe . . ." (1.7.21–25), of which Dr. Johnson said "the meaning is not very clear" and over which Cleanth Brooks labored so valiantly. Another is Lady Macbeth's "Was the hope drunk wherein you dressed yourself?" (1.7.35–38), with its succession of apparently illogical images. This darting from one metaphor to another apparently unrelated image, which has frequently puzzled editors and critics, is a practice that Shakespeare will pursue uncompromisingly throughout the last phase, forcing the listener's mind to accelerate at a dizzying rate. Frank Kermode's remark that in *The Tempest* "metaphor gleams momentarily, and is rarely extensive enough to be catalogued and analyzed,"[6] is pertinent to the late style generally; and *Macbeth*, notwithstanding its famous vegetative and sartorial clusters, exhibits the roots of this gestural, condensed use of figurative language.

Syntactical experiments that alter the listener's response to the speaker also become more prominent about this time. The romances are notorious for their intricate syntax, some of it so clotted as to resist comprehension and to defy adequate paraphrase. Much of this complexity is attributable to the elliptical urge, in that the omission of non-essentials, particularly verbs and relative pronouns, markedly reduces the elements of the sentence and sometimes creates unfamiliar, puzzling grammatical relations. Yet a frequent source of syntactical difficulty is the poet's additive impulse, usually his continuation of an apparently completed sentence by appending non-restrictive relative clauses. Macbeth's instructions to the murderers about Banquo's death are articulated in such a manner:

> Now, if you have a station in the file, 101
> Not i' th' worst rank of manhood, say't,
> And I will put that business in your bosoms,
> Whose execution takes your enemy off,
> Grapples you to the heart and love of us, 105
> Who wear our health but sickly in his life,
> Which in his death were perfect.
>
> (3.1.101–7)

---

[6] Introduction to *The Tempest* (London: Methuen, 1954), p. lxxix.

Such an articulated structure might plausibly be linked to character or theme: the sequence of clauses, "Whose . . . Who . . . Which . . ." could be said to capture the hero's nervous efforts at criminal justification, or to replicate stylistically the succession of murders that will make up the second half of the play. Without wanting to disallow such readings, one is compelled to point out that passage after passage in *Cymbeline, The Winter's Tale,* and *Henry VIII* is spun out by just such an aggregation of clauses. Macbeth's few lines reveal other poetic tactics that will become more prominent, particularly the ellipses in line 102, the late line pause also in 102, casual repetitions ("business in your bosoms"; "in his life / . . . in his death"), and flickering metaphor ("wear" in line 106). Furthermore, the separation between speaker and verse begins to emerge noticeably in *Macbeth*. Nicholas Brooke, citing the First Murderer's lyrical evocation of evening, "The west yet glimmers with some streaks of day; / Now spurs the lated traveller apace / To gain the timely inn" (3.3.5–7), points out that the lines "belong absolutely to the play and are alien to the speaker."[7]

The auditory pattern that overrides all others in *Macbeth* is unremitting repetition. This is a striking technique in such an exceedingly short play: echoing sounds register with unusual force because they reverberate in so short a space. Not only are words repeated ("double, double, toil and trouble") but consonants and vowels are doubled and trebled, rhythmic configurations repeated insistently, and phrases and images reiterated, not just immediately but memorably, across several scenes. An efficient way of indicating the scope of this technique is to mention a few gifted readers and the patterns they have helped to identify. L. C. Knights, although more celebrated for the derisive title of his essay ("How Many Children Had Lady Macbeth?") than for the sensitivity of his ear, catches the "sickening see-saw rhythm" characteristic of the witches: their trademark sound pattern is audible in the catalectic line of trochaic tetrameter, "Fair is foul and foul is fair."[8] It is a commonplace that Macbeth echoes their diction in his entrance line, "So foul and fair a day I have not seen" (1.3.38), but it is less frequently noted that he soon begins to reproduce their distinctive rhythms: "This supernatural soliciting cannot be ill, cannot be good" (1.3.130–31). A. R. Braunmuller, responding to the

---

[7] Introduction to *Macbeth* (Oxford: Oxford University Press, 1990), p. 11. For further discussion of the importance of this separation of speaker and style, see my Introduction, pp. 33–34 and notes.

[8] L. C. Knights, *Explorations: Essays in Criticism Mainly on the Literature of the Seventeenth Century* (London: Chatto and Windus, 1946), p. 20.

abundance of rhyme, notes that in *Macbeth* Shakespeare concludes more scenes with couplets than in any other play, both proportionately and absolutely: this is a telling statistic in light of the play's unusual brevity.[9]

Braunmuller also acutely analyzes the unusually dense patterns of alliteration, such as Macbeth's "But now I am cabin'd, cribb'd, confin'd, bound in / To saucy doubts and fears" (3.4.24–25), lines in which, in addition to the repeated initial consonants, the terminal *d* of the participles is recapitulated in "bound" and "doubt," monosyllables which duplicate a vowel sound.[10] Most recently David Kranz, in a detailed account of reiteration in *Macbeth*, associates the "general patterns of linguistic repetition" with the duplicitous influence of the weird sisters. For example, he captures the paradoxical effect of poetic patterning: "the repetitive (possibly numerological) verbal patterns in *Macbeth* represent, in such a manner that divine will always remains a mystery, the existence of a supernatural order in which possible but indeterminate providential designs work through demonic and human actors to bring changes to the history of Scotland and England."[11] Kranz provides one of the few attempts to understand both the local, musical effects of patterning and its larger dramatic significance, and his reading is also a rare acknowledgement of the negative and positive implications of such figuration.

Other manifestations of musical repetition call attention to themselves. Insufficient attention has been paid to the effect of the vowels in *Macbeth*, particularly their contribution to the spooky atmosphere. Although historical phonology is uncertain about many subtleties of early modern pronunciation, most of the time it is possible to sense the tonality supported by the vowels. Vowel combinations (and consonants, too, for that matter) color Macbeth's meditation on the growing darkness as he contemplates the murder of Banquo:

> light thickens, and the crow
> Makes wing to th' rooky wood;
> Good things of day begin to droop and drowse,
> Whiles night's black agents to their preys do rouse.
>
> (3.2.50–53)

[9] Introduction, pp. 51–52.   [10] Introduction, pp. 52–53.

[11] David Kranz, "The Sounds of Supernatural Soliciting in *Macbeth*," *Studies in Philology*, 100 (2003), 346–83; the passage quoted is on page 382. Other modern critics who have written helpfully on these repetitive structures include Maynard Mack, Jr., *Killing the King* (New Haven: Yale University Press, 1973), pp. 160–64; Madeleine Doran, "The *Macbeth* Music," *Shakespeare Studies* 16 (1983), 153–73; Barbara Everett, *Young Hamlet: Essays on Shakespeare's Tragedies* (Oxford: Clarendon Press, 1989), and George Walton Williams, "Time for Such a Word: Verbal Echoing in *Macbeth*," *Shakespeare Survey 47* (1995), 153–59.

Macbeth also contains an exceptionally high quotient of passages in which words are repeated, either identically or polyptotonically, in the same or successive lines.

> If it were done, when 'tis done, then 'twere well
> It were done quickly.   (1.7.1–2)

> Might be the be-all and the end-all – here,
> But here . . .   (1.7.4–5)

MACB.   If we should fail?
LADY M.   We fail?
                    (1.7.59)

> Still it cried "Sleep no more!" to all the house;
> "Glamis hath murdered sleep, and therefore Cawdor
> Shall sleep no more – Macbeth shall sleep no more."
>   (2.1.38–40)

Such echoing – in the last excerpt suggestive of incipient madness – reaches its apogee in Lady Macbeth's desperate monologues in the sleep-walking scene (5.1): "The thane of Fife had a wife . . . To bed, to bed . . . Come, come, come, come . . . To bed, to bed, to bed." The desolate coda to this music sounds in Macbeth's response to her death: "Tomorrow, and tomorrow, and tomorrow . . . "

Perhaps the most aurally exciting effects occur when semantic repetition is joined to sonic echo in a group of crucial, highly charged words, some of which are repeated identically and some of which are varied, thus offering a related repetitive pleasure. "Do" and its multiple sonic and semantic cognates represent perhaps the most insistent example: "do," "deed," "done," "undone," "dunnest," "Duncan," and "Dunsinane." Other less obvious instances enrich the texture of the dialogue, words such as "clear," "present," "success," and "consequence," not to mention "fair" and "foul" again. Occasionally such semantic repetition is less assertive, but still meaningful. The word "trifle," for instance, is heard early, in Banquo's warning that "the instruments of darkness tell us truths, / Win us with honest trifles, to betray's / In deepest consequence" (1.3.124–26). (The sounding of "consequence," soon to resound in Macbeth's soliloquy in 1.7, is also notable.) In the next scene, the executed Thane of Cawdor is said to have thrown away his soul "As 'twere a careless trifle" (1.4.11). After the murder, the Old Man laments that "this sore night / Hath trifled former knowings" (2.4.2–3). This is the night, of course, in which Macbeth has trifled with his own soul, throwing it carelessly away, and former "knowings" are nothing compared to the spiritual knowledge that will come to torture him.

Accompanying such lexical iteration is the frequent return of a striking image, such as "milk." In a play haunted by children and the absence of children, Lady Macbeth in her first appearance speaks of the "milk of human kindness," invokes the "murdering ministers" to "take [her] milk for gall" (i.e. either transform it into gall or consider it as bitter as gall), and in dialogue with Macbeth claims to "know / How tender 'tis to love the babe that milks [her]." The noun is echoed semantically in her drugging of the grooms' "possets," a drink of hot milk and wine, and we recall it much later when Malcolm, forecasting the predations of his rule, threatens to "Pour the sweet milk of concord into hell" (4.3.98). Finally, in this same vein, the famous families of metaphor are among the strategies that make the play seem poetically dense: clothing, seeds and plants, and children, connected both to seeds and to milk. These metaphors, which have attained notoriety as grist for the New Critical mill, are more than just clusters of images that figure the unnatural quality of the Macbeths' crime. They also constitute major groups of identical units in a highly artificial poetic text, a self-conscious construct built on reflections, repetitions, and significant sequences.

Shakespeare's augmentation of the verbal patterns at which I have glanced in *Macbeth* will bring about a stylistic transformation, a metamorphosis that accompanies his exchange of tragedy for romance. But these changes in style are much more than simply the technical experiments of an active artistic intelligence. Rather, they result from and help to reveal the playwright's acute ambivalence towards language at this moment in his career. It might be argued that such a mixed opinion informs virtually every one of his plays, his awareness of the potentialities and the limitations of language being a commonplace. But *Macbeth* (like the tragedies that follow it) exposes with unusual clarity the dramatist's creative struggle with competing ideas about his medium and about the ends to which theatre and poetry are put.

The repetitions that create the music of *Macbeth* are enchanting, dangerously and thrillingly so. Just as Macbeth unconsciously takes over the see-saw rhythms of the weird sisters, so an audience can scarcely resist the incantatory allure of the protagonists' speech. From the beginning Shakespeare secures our emotional collusion with the Macbeths by giving them soliloquies and secret dialogues to which we alone are privy, and in responding to their poetry we place ourselves, unwittingly but certainly, in sympathy with them and their deeds. Shakespeare acknowledges – and fears – the physical effect of beguiling sounds. With these people in this world, any talk can be double talk, and apparently innocent sounds can be pressed into the service of the pretense and lies by which the couple seeks to take advantage. The fatal ambiguities of words inhere in the significant wordplay: "done" is the cardinal example, but there are many other instances of equivocal language. Those dangers also emerge from Lady Macbeth's verbal "spirits," in the "valor of [her] tongue" (1.5.27), and in the bewitching words of "those juggling fiends . . . / That palter with us in a double sense" (5.8.19–20).

And yet, both in its story and in its status as a theatrical event, the play also confirms authorial faith in the affirmative power of words. That the play is still immensely popular with audiences attests implicitly to this positive effect. The fiction of self-disgust which Malcolm spins out in the English scene, testing Macduff's loyalty to Scotland and ultimately persuading him of Malcolm's honesty, illustrates the affirmative potentialities of speech. Or so it seems. But these naive fictions are themselves virtuous permutations of the lies that have brought Macbeth to power. The scene leaves open, if only very slightly, the possibility that the prince's self-condemnation might be part of a larger fiction, one of several turns in a scenario of false humility and concealed ambition. Words are not inevitably false; representation is not necessarily misrepresentation; but language affords us no reliable means of knowing the difference.

The aural and ideational patterns of *Macbeth* attest to Shakespeare's unusually severe anxiety about the magical, sinister powers of words, and seductive sounds are here associated, as they are in the tragedies that follow, both with witchcraft and with women. The weird sisters begin the play with chants, charms, and prophecies, tempting the hero with equivocal words. Their tetrameter couplets, rhymes, and songs link them with music, with poetry, and later with spectacle. They are also identified, of course, with Lady Macbeth, herself the mistress of seductive speech: "Hie thee hither, / That I may pour my spirits in thine ear . . ." (1.5.25–26). This apostrophe figures her words to her husband as a metaphorical version of the wine – literal spirits – with which she has poisoned the grooms' drinks. Witchcraft, treacherous women, spectacle, slippery words, illusion, fiction – all are identified with one another in *Macbeth*, and all are sources of peril. Noting Shakespeare's reticence to identify the witches as fantastic or mortal, Stephen Greenblatt comments:

Macbeth manifests a deep, intuitive recognition that the theater and witchcraft are both constructed on the boundary between fantasy and reality, the border or membrane where the imagination and the corporal world, figure and actuality, psychic disturbance and objective truth meet. The means normally used to secure that border are speech and sight, but it is exactly these that are uncertain; the witches, as Macbeth exclaims, are "imperfect speakers," and at the moment he insists that they account for themselves, they vanish.[12]

All speech is inherently imperfect, theatrical language especially so. As Greenblatt reminds us, "Shakespeare was part of a profession that made its money manipulating images and playing with the double and doubtful senses of words."[13] At this point in his career, Shakespeare is becoming increasingly conscious of and troubled by this aspect of his occupation.

THE VICE OF VOICE, OR CAIUS WITHOUT CONJUNCTION

It is unclear whether *Coriolanus* or *Antony and Cleopatra* immediately succeeded *Macbeth*, or whether *Timon* or perhaps *Pericles* somehow intervened, but for my purposes the sequence is irrelevant. Both Roman tragedies explore the fallibility of language, and both stand as triumphant examples of verbal possibility. Thus they serve as valuable pre-texts for studying the generic reversal to come. *Coriolanus* seems to convey a darker, more nearly satiric tragic vision than does *Antony and Cleopatra*. Chronologically, therefore, one might suppose that the darkness of *Macbeth* carried over into *Coriolanus*, that shortly thereafter the playwright began to think more affirmatively, and that the imaginative freedom apparent in *Antony and Cleopatra* opened the way to the creation of the romances. Unfortunately, we have no external evidence for such a satisfying sequence. For all its darkness, *Coriolanus* may be the last of the tragedies.

Caius Martius professes a distrust of language, but he speaks one quarter of the play's 3200 lines, a part longer than any in the tragedies except for Hamlet, Iago, and Othello. Martius's laconic style of speech represents a skeptical response to the instabilities of all language, and it is fair, if ironic, to say that Shakespeare poured a good deal of himself into the creation of his uncommunicative hero. This play restages his concern, familiar from the earlier tragedies, especially *Macbeth*, with the infidelity

---

[12] Stephen Greenblatt, "Shakespeare Bewitched," in *New Historical Literary Study: Essays on Reproducing Texts, Representing History*, ed. Jeffrey N. Cox and Larry J. Reynolds (Princeton: Princeton University Press, 1993), p. 123.

[13] *Ibid.*, p. 127.

of verbal signs and the limits of representation, but here the skepticism concerns the faulty verbal foundations of politics. Much of the play's political vocabulary derives etymologically from words having to do with speech, and their reiteration asserts the necessity, in the political realm, of dialectic, contingency, and multivocality.

The most striking critique of the verbal foundations of political process appears in the elaboration of the terms "voice" and "voices" in the central movement of the play. Shakespeare borrowed the noun from North, who took it from *voix* in Amyot's translation of Plutarch. As D. J. Gordon pointed out long ago, the appearance of the word owes something not only to the classical source but also to contemporary Jacobean political procedures, specifically the customary method of parliamentary election.[14] In the tribunes' declaration that "the people / Must have their voices" (2.2.139–40), the word is a synonym for "votes," as it is in modern French; and this declaration begins to suggest other possible senses – "opinion," "will" (as in "the voice of God"), "desire," and "choice."

Neither Plutarchan source nor narrative demand, however, can account for Shakespeare's inspired worrying of the word, a preoccupation culminating in the protagonist's bitter reiterations:

> Here come moe Voyces. – 125
> Your Voyces? for your Voices I haue fought;
> Watcht for your Voices: for your Voices, beare
> Of Wounds, two dozen odde: Battailes thrice six
> I have seene, and heard of: for your Voices,
> Have done many things, some less, some more: 130
> Your Voices? Indeed I would be Consull.
>
> (2.3.125–31)

I depart from the modern text to cite the Folio, where the consistent capitalization of "Voices" in this (and only in this) passage would seem to imply authorial intention (or a compositor with an Empsonian critical sensibility).[15] The word "voices" is used fifty-four times in the Shakespeare

---

[14] D. J. Gordon, "Name and Fame: Shakespeare's Coriolanus," in *The Renaissance Imagination*, ed. Stephen Orgel (Berkeley: University of California Press, 1975), pp. 203–19. On the uses and abuses of etymology in literary studies, see Derek Attridge's fascinating essay, "Language as History/ History as Language: Saussure and the Romance of Etymology," in *Poststructuralism and the Question of History*, ed. Derek Attridge, Geoff Bennington, and Robert Young (Cambridge: Cambridge University Press, 1987), pp. 183–211.

[15] *The Norton Facsimile of the First Folio of Shakespeare*, prepared by Charlton Hinman (New York: W. W. Norton, 1968). Elsewhere in the play, "voice" and "voices" are sometimes capitalized, sometimes not. I am grateful to Richard Proudfoot who, commenting on an oral version of this material, alerted me to the Folio's unusual capitalization.

canon, two-thirds of them (thirty-six) in this play, twenty-seven times in this scene alone.[16] Its prominence has to do with its synecdochic function: it stands for the instability and contingency that Coriolanus deplores in human interaction, of which politics is the epitome and language the flawed medium.

It is one of the great ironies of *Coriolanus* that the hero's credo, his intolerance for verbal ambiguity, should be founded upon a pun, the paronomastically unstable "vice" and "voice." Kökeritz demonstrates the frequent leveling of the dipthong OI and the long I, offering an especially pertinent example when he shows that the Folio spelling of *voyce* for *vice* in Cloten's discussion of music in Act 2 of *Cymbeline* is not a misprint but a quibble.[17] *Coriolanus* may be thought of as a study of the vice of voice, or the political complexities deriving from the weaknesses of the word. Several heads, many voices, "the multitudinous tongue" – these are the conditions of politics that Coriolanus wishes to control or escape because they are incompatible with his need for unity and independence. Shared responsibility in political affairs, expressed in Coriolanus's fears about what happens "when two authorities are up," corresponds to shared meaning of words: the protagonist's horror of polysemy is another form of his contempt for political representation. His idealism affords him the illusion of freedom, from the constraints of language or of any other such limits, and that grand illusion is the source of his destruction.[18]

In the clash of the hero with his mother, the tragedy stages a contest between antithetical views of language. Presenting such a conflict, Shakespeare addresses again some of the fears adumbrated in *Macbeth*, this time drawing upon controversies over expressive styles that run deep in the literary and academic cultures of the sixteenth and seventeenth centuries. Caius Martius's passionate solipsism and hubris express themselves in his contempt for flattery, his discomfort with spoken praise, and his unwillingness to state his desire for the consulship, each of these refusals being an expression of what might be called linguistic absolutism.[19] We

---

[16] My source for the statistics of usage is Marvin Spevack, *A Complete and Systematic Concordance to the Works of Shakespeare* (Hildesheim: Olms, 1968), vol. III, *The Tragedies.*

[17] Helge Kökeritz, *Shakespeare's Pronunciation* (New Haven: Yale University Press, 1953), pp. 151–52.

[18] For a thorough analysis of the masculine desire for self-generation, see Janet Adelman, *Suffocating Mothers: Fantasies of Maternal Origin in Shakespeare's Plays, "Hamlet" to "The Tempest"* (London: Methuen, 1991), pp. 147–64.

[19] Since language itself is so important an issue in *Coriolanus*, it is treated in some detail in general studies, especially those by G. Wilson Knight, *The Imperial Theme* (Oxford: Oxford University Press, 1931); Derek Traversi, *An Approach to Shakespeare*, 2nd. edn. (New York: Doubleday, 1966);

recognize his kinship with Cordelia, another verbal purist, when he objects to the public account of his military victory as "acclamations hyperbolical" and "praises sauced with lies." Love of fighting is accompanied by fear of speech: "yet oft, / When blows have made me stay, I fled from words" (2.2.71–72). Another analogue is found closer to Rome: Aufidius, speaking after his defeat at Corioles, declares his contempt for "condition," or the terms of surrender, by mocking and distancing himself from the word (1.10.3–16). As with "voice," the etymological context is also linguistic: "condition" derives from *con* and *dicere*, or "speaking with." Aufidius is the ignoble double of Caius Martius, and it is telling that both of them abhor "terms." This dubious view of speech reflects the discursive constraints of the hero's occupation, the militaristic privileging of action over words, reluctance to reveal too much, and belief in the self-evident rightness of a cause.

In announcing his distaste for the word, Martius echoes Plutarch's frequent emphasis on the reticence or plain speech of the Spartan soldiers, a bias known in Renaissance England as Lacadaemonian or Laconian or Laconick. He thus makes explicit the strain of suspicion about language that the early modern humanists had inherited from the ancients. Erasmus, as Patricia Parker has reminded us, spent considerable energy illustrating the ancients' attitude towards the waywardness and unreliability of the tongue:

After example upon example of the "wanton tongue" ("intemerpantis linguae") of men, Erasmus turns to the styles of oratory, singling out the Spartans as men of deeds ("facti strenui"), sparing of talk ("verbis parcissimi") and contemptuous of empty garrulity ("inanem arrulitatem") . . . The Spartans, he writes,

Maurice Charney, *Shakespeare's Roman Plays* (Cambridge, Mass.: Harvard University Press, 1961); Norman Rabkin, *Shakespeare and the Common Understanding* (New York: The Free Press, 1966); Jonathan Goldberg, *James I and the Politics of Literature* (Baltimore: Johns Hopkins University Press, 1983); and Adelman, *Suffocating Mothers*, pp. 146–64. More specific studies of Coriolanus's problems with words include Lawrence Danson, *Tragic Alphabet: Shakespeare's Drama of Language* (New Haven: Yale University Press, 1974), pp. 142–62; James Calderwood, "*Coriolanus*: Wordless Meanings and Meaningless Words," *SEL*, 6 (1966), 185–202; Carol M. Sicherman, "*Coriolanus*: The Failure of Words," *ELH*, 39 (1972), 189–207; Page du Bois, "A Disturbance of Syntax at the Gates of Rome," *Stanford Literature Review*, 2 (1985), 185–208; Leonard Tennenhouse, "*Coriolanus*: History and the Crisis of the Semantic Order," *Drama in the Renaissance: Comparative and Critical Essays*, ed. Clifford Davidson, C. J. Gianakaris, and John H. Stroupe (New York: AMS Press, 1986), pp. 217–35; and Lisa Lowe, "'Say I Play the Man I Am': Gender and Politics in *Coriolanus*," *Kenyon Review*, n.s. 8 (1986), 86–95. Indispensable are Kenneth Burke, "*Coriolanus* and the Delights of Faction," *Hudson Review*, 19 (1966), 211–24, and Stanley Cavell, "*Coriolanus* and the Interpretation of Politics ('Who does the wolf love?')," rpt. in *Disowning Knowledge in Six Plays of Shakespeare* (Cambridge: Cambridge University Press, 1987), pp. 143–77.

considered it "just a theatrical trick" when orators claimed to be able to "shrink the mightiest topics ["res amplissimas"] into a small compass, and to amplify absolute trivialities into a vast theme" by the power of language. By contrast, they worshipped Hercules because he was successful in action rather than words ("bene gerendae rei, quam bene dicendi").[20]

Shakespeare's Roman warrior exemplifies his Spartan bias and his concomitant devotion to verbal purity on his first entrance: his opening sentence is "Thanks."

The laconic style makes itself felt chiefly by means of syntactic reticence. There are no superfluous words, few smooth transitions, little decoration. Grammatically speaking, even greater specificity is possible: Martius rarely employs conjunctions. His speeches eschew connectives, both within and between sentences, and such withholding creates a disjunctivity that sets every utterance apart from every other.[21] The pertinent rhetorical figure here is *asyndeton*, the omission of conjunctions between words, phrases, or clauses. Puttenham describes asyndeton as "loose language," judging it "defective because it wants good band or coupling"; it violates the rhetorician's sense of communicative decorum because it is discontinuous, neither smooth nor effectively integrated into a natural-sounding whole. Puttenham identifies the military pertinence of such verbal patterns when he illustrates the figure with "I came, I saw, I overcame." In Caesar's famous triplet, the conqueror "wrote home to the Senate in this tenour of speach no lesse swift and speedy then his victorie."[22] Although asyndeton normally describes the relation of clauses within sentences, Shakespeare has effectively magnified the grammatical figure by also suppressing the couplings between sentences so as to create a severely limited economy of verbal means.

Coriolanus affords numerous examples of this laconic technique, beginning with the hero's fierce attack on the multitude in the opening scene. A memorable moment in the action also illuminates the effect of Martius's grammatically sundered style, his request for merciful treatment of the Coriolan citizen who had befriended him: "I sometime lay here in Corioles, / At a poor man's house: he us'd me kindly. / He cried to me; I saw him

---

[20] Patricia Parker, "On the Tongue: Cross Gendering, Effeminacy, and the Art of Words," *Style* (1987), 448. See also Philip Brockbank's Introduction to his Arden edition (London: Methuen, 1976), pp. 68–71.

[21] Throughout this discussion I depend heavily upon the excellent analysis of John Porter Houston, *Shakespearean Sentences: A Study in Style and Syntax* (Baton Rouge: Louisiana State University Press, 1988), especially chapter 7, "Syndeton and Asyndeton in *Coriolanus*," pp. 159–78.

[22] George Puttenham, *The Arte of English Poesie*, a facsimile reproduction ed. Edward Arber, with an Introduction by Baxter Hathaway (Athens, Ohio: Kent State University Press, 1988), pp. 185–86.

prisoner" (1.9.82–84). With characteristic irony, Shakespeare employs the spare style for an expression of generosity, and the ungenerous syntactic patterns register the warrior's impatience with the niceties of rhetorical progression. Rarely in Coriolanus's speeches is the movement from one sentence to the next made explicit; rather, the transition is usually achieved by force. Moreover, the hero's language is not only grammatically asyndetic: in vocabulary and tone it also gives the impression of stinginess. His normal syntax is rather strictly paratactic and simplified, marked especially by "enumeratory patterns," a form of expression implying simplicity, order, and lack of argumentative subtlety.[23]

It is not difficult to see how Shakespeare's most emotionally isolated hero should speak a language in which the interdependence of sentences is suppressed, clauses do not touch, and the prevailing tone is firm and unyielding.[24] His speech constitutes the grammatical equivalent of his famous desire for freedom from familial or other kinds of relation, his desire to "stand / As if a man were author of himself, / And knew no other kin" (5.3.35–37). Such values and patterns are appropriate to tragedy, a mode which moves toward separation and extinction and is usually given over to a solitary male hero. The laconic, separated speech of Coriolanus is not only a military style; what is even more pertinent is that it is coded historically as a masculine style.

Coriolanus's stylistic independence helps to extend the critique of masculine self-sufficiency that Shakespeare inherited from his sources and exploited narratively, grammatically, and prosodically. "Manlines" is a principal topic in Plutarch's introductory sketch of Martius's character, and Shakespeare depicts an early version of the masculine mode of behavior in Volumnia's approving words about her grandson: "He had rather see the swords and hear a drum than look upon his schoolmaster"

---

[23] Houston, *Shakespearean Sentences*, pp. 160, 161–62. This spare grammatical base line causes eccentricity or deviation to stand out. G. Wilson Knight finds a surprisingly large number of bizarre words, many of them polysyllables, that obtrude from a plainer style of diction, words such as "conspectuities," "empiricutic," "directitude," "factionary." "Many of these cause blank amazement among the rabble, or Volscian menials: and are thus related to the main idea of the aristocrat contrasted with commoners. So, in our line units, there is, as it were, an aristocrat among a crowd of plebeian words, and often that protagonist word falls with a hammer-blow that again reminds us of metal" (*The Imperial Theme*, p. 160).

[24] Page du Bois helpfully notices that one figure which gains especial prominence is *anacolouthon*, or the breaking off in the middle of a thought and resuming again in a different form. "Anacolouthon is the appropriate rhetorical figure for this tragedy, which is about breaks in lines – not just breaks in lines of speech or thought, but breaks in descent, in lineage, breaks in city walls, breaks in bodies, wounds, breaks in the continuity of surfaces. *Coriolanus* is about the failure to follow" ("A Disturbance of Syntax," p. 187).

(1.3.55–56). The separation of "words" from "swords" (the first noun contained in the second) plays on a parallel familiar to London audiences at least as early as *Tamburlaine*, and here the quibble helps to clarify what it means to say that boys will be boys: the child, attracted by the eloquence of military action, shuns the schoolmaster who teaches him language arts. The son exhibits "a con*firm*'d countenance"; the father attacks the patriciate for being soft on the populace. Plutarch reports that Martius "dyd so exercise his bodie to hardnes" that he always won at wrestling or games of strength, and those who lost to him "would say when they were overcome: that all was by reason of his naturall strength, and hardnes of warde, that never yelded to any payne or toyle he tooke apon him."[25]

This emphasis on physical "hardnes" manifests itself repeatedly, perhaps most notably when Aufidius speaks of his enemy's body, "where against / My grained ash an hundred times hath broke, / And scarr'd the moon with splinters" (4.5.107–9). Coriolanus's body, in other words, is as hard as his head or his heart, and his stony mien represents one of Shakespeare's most effective subversions of the ideal of manly self-sufficiency and impenetrability. Coriolanus fulminates that the competing claims of plebeians and patricians will allow "confusion" to "enter 'twixt the gap of both" (3.1.110–11) and fears that yielding to popular demands sets a precedent "which will in time / Break ope the locks a' th' Senate" (3.1.137–38). He asks leave to depart during Cominius's praise of him because he cannot stand to hear his "nothings monstered," thus drawing upon the sense of "monster" as a malformation or unnatural creature, part brute and part human. What is aurally striking is that Shakespeare has found a stylistic equivalent for integrity and manly impenetrability. Wilson Knight's impressive list of metallic images – fins of lead, lead roofs, iron walls, metal gates, stone barriers – suggests a harsh visual background sustained by what we might call the syntactic and prosodic angularity of the work.[26] Shakespeare's stark arrangement of the hero's grammatical forms creates an aural impression consistent with his "phallic aggressive pose."[27]

---

[25] Quotations from Plutarch are taken from Geoffrey Bullough's *Narrative and Dramatic Sources of Shakespeare*, 6 vols. (New York: Columbia University Press, 1964), v: 506–7.

[26] *The Imperial Theme*, pp. 155–57.

[27] Janet Adelman, *Suffocating Mothers*, p. 151. The section on *Coriolanus* originally appeared as "'Anger's My Meat': Feeding, Dependency, and Aggression in *Coriolanus*," *Representing Shakespeare: New Psychoanalytic Essays*, ed. Murray M. Schwartz and Coppélia Kahn (Baltimore: Johns Hopkins University Press, 1980). See also Robert J. Stoller, "Shakespearean Tragedy: *Coriolanus*," *Psychoanalytic Quarterly*, 35 (1966), 263–74.

The habit of discursive withholding, of limitation and parsimony, makes Coriolanus particularly uncomfortable in the marketplace, where his most formidable challenges occur and where the discourse of commerce clashes with his reticence and ideal of self-sufficiency. In other words, the military hero can't make it in the business world. The marketplace depends upon the language of exchange, a flexible discursive economy in which the rhetorically rigid soldier will not participate. He "pays himself with being proud" (1.1.33–34), as one of the citizens puts it, and the narrative context of dearth, beggary, and unfair distribution supplies added point to the emphasis on Coriolanus's "sufficiency" and refusal to negotiate, his unwillingness to show his wounds in public or to bargain for the consulship.

> Better it is to die, better to starve,
> Than crave the hire which first we do deserve.
> Why in this woolvish toge should I stand here   115
> To beg of Tom and Dick that does appear,
> Their needless vouches. Custom calls me to't.
> What custom wills, in all things should we do't,
> The dust on antique time would lie unswept,
> And mountainous error be too highly heap'd   120
> For truth to o'erpeer. Rather than fool it so,
> Let the high office and the honor go
> To one that would do thus. I am half through:
> The one part suffered, the other will I do.
>   (2.3.113–24)

The commercial dimension of this desire for independence is captured paronomastically in his attack on tradition as "custom": he will not become the people's customer. Seeking even greater distance from the plebeians, with whom he has been bickering in prose, he shifts into rhyme, thus underscoring his declaration of independence from tradition. But the step into the more formal register may also be said to undo his argument about ceremony, as the couplets ironically connect line to line in poetic interdependence.

Ceremony, ritual, politics, all forms of exchange (except the speechless interchange of physical combat) are repugnant to him. Volumnia seeks to overcome her son's class- and gender-based fear of the marketplace, and she comes close, in Act 3, scene 2, to teaching him the art of "policy" or negotiation. Her urging of compromise and diplomacy is another way of asking her son to lower his moral price, but his absolutism forbids such haggling. He makes an effort to get with the patrician program, resolving to go "to the market-place," "mountebank their loves, / Cog their hearts from them, and come home belov'd / Of all the trades in Rome" (3.2.132–34). Facing the crowd in the political theatre, however, he betrays an unbearable consciousness of being bought. This self-disgust appears in his sardonic promise to respond as calmly "as an hostler, that for th'poorest piece / Will bear the knave by th' volume" (3.3.32–33). The climax of this central public episode, the hero's banishment, occurs after he is taunted with the word "traitor," one who "turns," who reneges on a commitment or cheats his countrymen. In that term of contempt we may also catch the mercantile sense of "trader."[28] Coriolanus can accept neither denotation and so calls off the deal: "I would not buy / Their mercy at the price of one fair word" (3.3.91–92).

In dramatizing such conflicts Shakespeare exploits the connotative interchangeability of economics and sexuality. Coriolanus's contemptuous wish to be possessed by "Some harlot's spirit" in order to sustain the performance in the marketplace partakes of both discourses, since "harlot" comes from the Old French word for vagabond, and his inability to "discharge" the part contains an economic metaphor embedded in his refusal to act. This mixture of the verbal, the economic, and the sexual recalls the connection between discourse and discharge apparent in Volumnia's loquacity, her endless need to relieve herself verbally. We hear it also in the first scene in the political marketplace: "for if he show us his wounds and tell us his deeds, we are to put our tongues into those wounds and speak for them" (2.3.7–9). One need not be adept at psychological criticism to feel the effect of this cluster of images: the political "custom" of showing wounds and asking approval is an act of commercial exchange, the buying of the consulship, and this process becomes a complicated verbal and sexual transaction, the taking of the tongue/phallus into the wound/hole which then becomes a mouth.[29] To Coriolanus, real men do not play the receiver in the sexual act; nor do they sully themselves in business. All intercourse – political, commercial, sexual, theatrical, or verbal – is debased, amounting to a form of prostitution. It becomes increasingly clear that Coriolanus's distrust of language is a fear of dependency and vulnerability, with a particular abhorrence of the feminine.

---

[28] I owe this idea to a conversation with Professor Catherine Loomis.

[29] Adelman is especially illuminating on this passage, since the oral imagery is an essential ingredient in the dependency theme: see *Suffocating Mothers*, pp. 153–55.

MEN AND WOMEN AND STYLE

Shakespeare's self-consciousness about the perils and opportunities of language coincides with the contemporary debate over the available forms of prose style and the philosophical implications of those positions. A brief review of the controversy reminds us that the old-fashioned Ciceronian model, with its elaborate syntactical constructions, symmetrical patterns of words and clauses, and devotion to ornament, came into conflict with the self-consciously modern approach, modeled on Seneca, with its obviously broken periods and asymmetrical grouping of words, a severity of vocabulary and sound, and a Spartan disdain for decoration.[30] In the late Roman world, Ciceronian eloquence was thought of as Asiatic or exotic, Senecan directness as Attic or classical.[31] The foundations of these two opposed attitudes are quickly discernible: the Ciceronians valued language for its own sake and considered stylistic extravagance a just exploitation of its linguistic value and possibility; their opponents, passionate about clarity of expression and dedicated to a utilitarian view of the word, condemned such ornamental arrangement as likely to magnify the potential treachery of language and increase one's vulnerability to it.

Roger Ascham defended his taste for Cicero and the elaborate style by accusing his detractors as follows: "Ye know not what hurt ye do to learning, that care not for words but for matter."[32] In other words, to privilege meaning and to overlook the means by which that meaning is communicated neglects such important factors as persuasion and instruction. At the other pole stood the formidable Francis Bacon, who considered the imitation of Cicero the primary error of modern education, "for men began to hunt more after words than matter." "Then did Car of Cambridge, and Ascham with their lectures and writings almost deify Cicero and Demosthenes, and allure all young men that were studious,

---

[30] The historical background is found in Morris W. Croll, *Style, Rhetoric, and Rhythm*, ed. J. Max Patrick, Robert O. Evans, et. al. (Princeton: Princeton University Press, 1966), and George Williamson, *The Senecan Amble* (Chicago: University of Chicago Press, 1951). Jonas A. Barish's *Ben Jonson and the Language of Prose Comedy* (Cambridge, Mass.: Harvard University Press, 1960) offers a useful development and application of these principles.

[31] See Rosalie Colie, *Shakespeare's Living Art* (Princeton: Princeton University Press, 1974), pp. 168–207, for a brilliant discussion of this stylistic and cultural opposition. A more recent treatment may be found in Madhavi Menon, *Wanton Words: Rhetoric and Sexuality in English Renaissance Drama* (Toronto: University of Toronto Press, 2004), chapter 1.

[32] Roger Ascham, *The Schoolmaster*, ed. Lawrence V. Ryan (Charlottesville: University of Virginia Press for the Folger Shakespeare Library, 1967), p. 114.

unto that delicate and polished kind of learning."[33] Antithetical values are
at issue here: the elaborate versus the plain, the delicate versus the rough,
the roundabout versus the pointed, form versus content. It is an understatement to say that the debate over kinds of writing involved a good deal
more than syntactical preferences. Is language a medium and nothing else?
Or since language is necessary as an expressive tool, oughtn't the writer to
develop and relish its manifold properties?

This debate is self-evidently grounded in conceptions of sexual difference and related to the figuration of language as feminine and action as
masculine in medieval and early modern language theory.[34] This misogynist tradition propagates the identification of language and women as
treacherous and unreliable, subject to extravagance, malleability, and
error. It originates in the classical period and receives virulent expression
in the writings of some of the Church Fathers, particularly Tertullian,
St. John Chrysostom, and St. Augustine. As Howard Bloch has demonstrated in some detail, this gendered conception is responsible for the
series of identifications, still with us, of the masculine with the primary,
with essence, with form, with unity; and of the feminine with the
secondary, the accidental, the material, the duplicitous or ambiguous.[35]
In the most notorious anti-feminine passages in medieval literature, a
familiar and loudly asserted complaint against women is their proclivity
for loud complaint. Garrulousness, nagging, shrewishness, bickering,
demanding – the most common laments from the *molestiae nuptiarum*,
or the tradition of anti-marriage literature, have to do with the verbal
miseries inevitably attendant upon the taking of a wife. In other words,
the attack on women is often a simultaneous attack on language.

Commentators reach as far back as Eden to connect the female with the
decorative, the artificial, the inessential: in the Genesis account, Eve's
verbal seduction of Adam into eating the fruit of the Forbidden Tree led
to the need for covering, and from that time forward there existed a
contest between the natural body and the dressings invented for it. As
Tertullian put it, "with the word the garment entered." In a related

---

[33] Francis Bacon, *The Advancement of Learning*, ed. Arthur Johnston (Oxford: Clarendon Press, 1974), p. 26.
[34] The most thorough discussion of this tradition is found in Howard Bloch, *Medieval Misogyny and the Invention of Western Romantic Love* (Chicago: University of Chicago Press, 1991), pp. 13–35. For background on some of the patristic writers, particularly the Platonic roots of their gynophobic thinking, see also Jonas A. Barish, *The Antitheatrical Prejudice* (Berkeley: University of California Press, 1981), chapters 1 and 2.
[35] *Medieval Misogyny*, pp. 18–30.

treatment of the topic, St. Augustine distinguishes between numerical signs as masculine and verbal signs as feminine: "From that time forth she [Reason] found it hard to believe that the splendor and purity [of numbers] was sullied by the corporeal matter of words. And just as what the spirit sees is always present and is held to be immortal and numbers appear such, while sound, being a sensible thing, is lost into the past."[36] Numerals are identified with the virtues of constancy, order, and clarity, in short, with the spirit. Words connote corruption and impermanence and are linked with the body, specifically with the female body and its traditional adornments – clothing, makeup, hairstyle, jewelry.

We might now return to Bacon's attack on Ciceronian style as "that delicate and polished kind of learning" that "allured" the boys from Cambridge: "delicate and polished" is a gendered phrase, pejorative adjectives denoting a sissified style. Patricia Parker summarizes this debate with a major instance from the early Tudor period:

Erasmus in his *Ciceronianus* (1528) speaks of seeking in vain in Ciceronian eloquence for something "masculine" and of his own desire for a "more masculine" style. Ciceronian copia in these discussions is both effeminate and the style of a more prodigal youth, to be outgrown once one had become a man: "I used to imitate Cicero," writes Lipsius; "but I have become a man, and my tastes have changed. Asiatic feasts have ceased to please me; I prefer the Attic."[37]

And this bias appears also in the Renaissance view of the femininity of verse and the Puritan attack on the effeminacy of the stage: we remember Sidney's *Defence*, written as a rejoinder to the attack on theatrical poetry as immoral, frivolous, and unmanly. The sentence cited at the beginning of this chapter, Thomas Howell's "Women are wordes, Men deedes,"[38] should remind us of Hotspur, that quintessential man of action, who proclaims his contempt for "mincing poetry" and who on the battlefield is infuriated when the King's effeminate ambassador addresses him in "many holiday and lady terms." The still-prevalent view that poetry or dramatics is for girls, while science or mathematics – real learning – is best left to boys, descends from this ancient derisory association of women and words.

It is an easy leap from this traditional identification of the ungoverned female tongue with speech in general to Shakespeare's juxtaposition of the

---

[36] Tertullian's "cum voce vestris intravit" is from *De Pallio*, Augustine's remarks from *De Ordine*: both are quoted in Bloch, *Medieval Misogyny*, pp. 46, 220.

[37] Patricia Parker, *Literary Fat Ladies: Rhetoric, Gender, Property* (London: Methuen, 1987), p. 14.

[38] *Howell's Devises 1581*, p. 31.

loquacious Volumnia and her laconic son. Most pointedly in Act 3, scene 2, the episode in which she coaches him for his appearance in the market-place, she employs her limitless verbal energies to modify his absolutism, urging flexibility, compromise, and interpretation; another way of putting it is to say that she attempts to open his closed text, to puncture his wall of impenetrability, to seduce him into performing a fiction of humility. After asserting the value of "gentle words" in taking in an enemy city and commending the need to "dissemble" in the proper cause, Volumnia lowers her sights somewhat and tells him that if he cannot speak the proper words as he asks the citizens for the consulship, then at least he can appear to be accommodating. She sets forth in one extraordinary sentence the way he ought to look and the way he ought to sound:

> I prithee now, my son,
> Go to them, with this bonnet in thy hand,
> And thus far having stretch'd it (here be with them),
> Thy knee bussing the stones (for in such business   75
> Action is eloquence, and the eyes of th'ignorant
> More learned than the ears), waving thy head,
> Which often thus correcting thy stout heart,
> Now humble as the ripest mulberry
> That will not hold the handling: or say to them,   80
> Thou art their soldier, and, being bred in broils,
> Hast not the soft way which, thou dost confess,
> Were fit for thee to use as they to claim,
> In asking their good loves, but thou wilt frame
> Thyself, forsooth, hereafter theirs, so far   85
> As thou hast power and person.   (3.2.72–86)

The immediate relevance of this passage is found in its grammatical structure, particularly the contrast with Coriolanus's masculine style.

Even if the passage is punctuated so as to divide into two sentences, there is no break in thought. The length and the syntactical involutions suggest the association of women and copia: the paratactic, additive form of the plea, supported and extended as it is by the participles, connotes the endlessness of female speech, the ungoverned tongue familiar from the misogynist tradition; at the same time, the hypotactic intrusions and parentheses attest to the indirections and potential waywardness of women and their words. Metrically, the expectations of regularity established by the pentameter are frustrated by the liberty and variety of the phrasing: the semantic demands and wayward rhythmic drive introduce disruptions that poke holes in the order of the line and threaten a kind of aural chaos.[39] Other kinds of gaps yawn as well – the elision of words, the breaking in of parenthetical phrases, the opening of logical fissures as words and ideas tumble out pell-mell. In this plea for duplicity we hear a forecast of the complicated verbal patterns to be developed in the romances.

Coriolanus, then, presents a contest of styles, with each side sexually marked. The Baconian, phallic position informs the laconic speech of Coriolanus, who flees from words. Volumnia, on the other hand, embodies Ciceronian loquacity and indirection. The "tradition of the copia of discourse" described by Patricia Parker seems particularly relevant to this conflict between mother and son, feminine and masculine: as she puts it, "Augustine in the *Confessions* has a whole chapter devoted to 'increase and multiply,' (XIII.xxiv) in the sense of the interpreter's opening and fruitful extension of a closed or hermetic scriptural text, what the rhetorical tradition would call 'dilating or enlarging of the matter by interpretation.' But this 'matter' and its enlarging also easily joined with *mater*."[40]

The matter on which this mater enlarges in the great oration before the gates of Rome is a feminine plea for language as a sign of connection, and her speech begins with an effort to tempt her son away from his linguistic chastity. She has become, like the plebeians in the first scene, a beggar from whom Coriolanus deliberately withholds his "good word": "Speak to me, son"; "Why dost not speak?"; "Yet give us our dispatch." Begging for mercy, suing for the word of reconciliation instead of the deed of destruction, she saves Rome by an act of oral interpretation. Playing the go-between from which the word *interpreter* etymologically derives, she unfolds the multiple senses of the texts of "loyalty" or "honor" or "nobility." She is supported by two women and a child, and she presses a "suit" or "petition" asking, significantly, that Coriolanus "reconcile" the two sides, that he "show a noble grace to both parts." It is a demand that her monomaniacal son acknowledge duality, and her eloquent and extravagant defense of the city constitutes an appeal, if an unconscious one, for the values of exchange, community, communication, and multivocality. Coriolanus has already declared his refusal to "capitulate / Again with Rome's mechanics" (5.3.82–83), and the word "capitulate," deriving from

---

[39] See the rich discussion of how Shakespeare makes meaning from this pervasive contest between line and sentence in George T. Wright, *Shakespeare's Metrical Art* (Berkeley: University of California Press, 1988), chapters 14 and 15.

[40] *Literary Fat Ladies*, p. 15.

the process of organizing an oration under headings, is essentially another verbal metaphor: he will not come to terms. When he does give in, he surrenders not only to the relentless claims of the female, but also to the inescapability and conditionality of language. Volumnia's victory is limited, however: although she seems to persuade him of the need for human connection, his submissive deed is accomplished ironically without language, as the famous stage direction indicates: "He holds her by the hand, silent." I want to suggest that we read this surrender of son to mother, of masculine verbal purist to feminine verbal seducer, as an allegory of Shakespeare's professional uncertainties around 1607.

CAESAR VERSUS CLEOPATRA

Allegories, as Mrs. Malaprop knew, are found on the banks of the Nile, and the relevance of *Antony and Cleopatra* to the topic of language and gender will be immediately clear.[41] The contest between the masculine and the feminine or the Senecan and Ciceronian is encoded in the several poetic and rhetorical patterns that the sophisticated but fundamentally binary structure of the play serves to promote. Some of these contrasts, most of them obvious on a single reading of the play, include the imagistic tension between a masculine Rome and a feminine Egypt; the contest between the hyperbolic and deflationary and the tendency of the former to tip over into the latter but to recuperate itself nevertheless; the identification of Cleopatra with abundance and Caesar with scarcity; the opposition between the Attic and Asiatic discourses.

Worth articulating here, first, is the way Shakespeare appeals to the misogynist-linguistic tradition in his creation of the Egyptian queen, both invoking and rejecting the censure implicit in it, and second, the way the characters produce and are produced by the stylistic effects of the play. As Rosalie Colie puts it in her brilliant analysis: "'Style' is – especially in the

---

[41] *Antony and Cleopatra* has generated a number of stylistic studies, of which David Bevington's Introduction to the New Cambridge Edition (1990) provides a useful survey. For my purposes, the most helpful discussions include those of G. Wilson Knight, *The Imperial Theme*, pp. 199–262; Colie, *Shakespeare's Living Art*, pp. 168–207; Janet Adelman, *The Common Liar: An Essay on "Antony and Cleopatra"* (New Haven: Yale University Press, 1973); Doran, "The *Macbeth* Music"; G. R. Hibbard, "*Feliciter Audax: Antony and Cleopatra*, I, I, 1–24," in *Shakespeare's Styles: Essays in Honor of Kenneth Muir*, ed. Philip Edwards, Inga-Stina Ewbank, and G. K. Hunter (Cambridge: Cambridge University Press, 1980), pp. 95–109; and Charney, *Shakespeare's Roman Plays*. Also useful, although less specifically concerned with style, is Robert Ornstein's "The Ethic of the Imagination: Love and Art in *Antony and Cleopatra*," in *Later Shakespeare*, ed. John Russell Brown and Bernard Harris (London: Edward Arnold, 1966), pp. 31–46.

Attic–Asiatic polarity – a moral indicator, but here displayed as deeply thrust into the psychological and cultural roots of those ways of life. In this play, a given style is never merely an alternative way of expressing something: rather, styles arise from cultural sources beyond a character's choice or control."[42] In this case, those cultural sources include, among many others, the misogynist disparagement of the female tongue, the Puritan anti-theatrical polemics that had been loudly sounding since the 1570s, the traditional association of Cleopatra with witchcraft and deception, and the incompatibility of words and swords.

The infinitely various Cleopatra is the embodiment of those values for which Volumnia so eloquently and lengthily pleads: multiplicity, equivocation, and – in the political and the sexual senses – compromise. An audience's difficulty in judging Cleopatra derives partly from Shakespeare's clever strategy of giving her no soliloquies. Artfully enshrined on the barge through the medium of Enobarbus's encomium, she is the play's signifier of verbal prowess and ambiguity, the focus of its concern with the transgression of limits, whether of nations or genders. The detailed attention to her clothing, most notably her appearing "in the habiliments of the goddess Isis," associates her with the moon-deity, a figure of pagan mystery and mutability.[43] Moreover, that get-up locates her in the region of theatre and language, of coverings and tissues and mysterious femininity, and such associations give greater point to her unmanning Antony by dressing him in her tires and mantles.

Her changeability makes her poetic voice exceptionally difficult to classify, as she mimics Roman seriousness, plays with words for the material pleasure they offer ("music – music, moody food / Of us that trade in love"), and assumes the language of tragic heroine in the final scene. One of her familiar gambits is her penchant for *ecphonesis*, and in prominent places:

THID. He knows that you embraced not Antony
       As you did love, but as you fear'd him.
CLEO.   O!

(3.13.56–57)

The "infinitely meaningful phoneme" creates the sense of flexibility and openness that is coded as female and represents speech – the word – at its

[42] *Shakespeare's Living Art*, p. 179.
[43] See Adelman, *Suffocating Mothers*, pp. 183–84, and Colie, *Shakespeare's Living Art*, p. 195.

most fundamental.[44] The frequency of "O" is matched in this play by a host of pleonasms, as in the repetitions of "Come" (and "welcome") during the monument scene and succeeding episodes: "Where art thou, death? / Come hither, come! Come, come, and take a queen / Worth many babes and beggars!" (5.2.45–47). As this excerpt indicates, Cleopatra's language at the last becomes not only more elevated but more "poetically" marked, with a noticeable increase in alliteration, internal rhyme, and other reverberating effects. The final speeches also employ a remarkable range of syntactical structures. The reverie addressed to her maids immediately after Antony's death ("No more but e'en a woman") is full of exclamations, questions, sentences of varying length, and stops and starts, not to mention the prominent images and their poetic presentation ("Our lamp is spent, it's out"). It is unnecessary to elaborate on such poetic properties: what is important is that they sustain the association of Cleopatra with language and its creative powers.

This female realm of discourse is disturbing to Caesar because it is inimical to Roman values. Indeed, "the scarce-bearded Caesar" shares with the "boy of tears," Coriolanus, a preference for deeds to words. Well aware of the Roman bias, Antony offers a conciliatory promise to Octavia before the wedding: "Read not my blemishes in the world's report. / I have not kept my square, but that to come / Shall all be done by th' rule" (2.3.6–8). But like the marriage itself, the words are mainly for Caesar's benefit, expressing succinctly the regularity of the Octavian code. "Report" is fallible and untrustworthy, for words are roundabout and irregular. Caesar declares himself in the negotiations with Pompey: "There's the point" (2.6.31). This masculine commitment to the point, the purpose, the job to be done, reinforced by his impatience at circumlocution and inefficiency, stands in contrast to Antony's dalliance with Cleopatra, a geographical and emotional digression that not only effeminizes him but makes him the subject of talk. Caesar's view of amorous passion is figured in terms that carry a discursive charge, images explicitly linked with the Asiatic style: slack, effeminate, inflated, voluptuous.[45] Sharing Coriolanus's professedly Spartan view, he distrusts words as uncertain, dislikes conversation, and associates language with liquor and

---

[44] The phrase is David Willbern's, from his suggestive essay "Shakespeare's Nothing," in Schwartz and Kahn, *Representing Shakespeare*, pp. 244–63; the quotation appears on p. 249. On this point I have also profited from an unpublished paper by Edward Snow, "Cleopatra's O," delivered in the plenary session at the 1989 meeting of the Shakespeare Association of America.

[45] See Colie, *Shakespeare's Living Art*, pp. 199–200.

other threats to manhood and duty. These fears emerge as he departs from Pompey's galley after the bacchanal:

> Strong Enobarb
> Is weaker than the wine, and mine own tongue
> Spleets what it speaks; the wild disguise hath almost
> Antick'd us all. What needs more words? Good night.
> (2.7.122–25)

Earlier Caesar has lamented Antony's metamorphosis into "an ebb'd man," and the diction of this passage brings together the causes of such degeneration: the splitting tongue, "disguise" as a term for revelry, unruly behavior, pointless talk.

If we are to read Shakespeare's development allegorically, as I have proposed, then Antony stands in for the dramatist poised stylistically between the masculine and the feminine, the Attic and the Asiatic, tragedy and romance. The hero's conversion to Egyptian pleasure is censured by Octavius in language of dissolution (the "ebb'd man"), and Antony himself adopts such locutions in the celebrated passage from his suicide scene (4.14.1–14). It begins with the image of the shifting cloud, continues with the liquid metaphor of lost difference ("as indistinct / As water is in water"), and ends with deliquescence, "Here I am Antony, / Yet cannot hold this visible shape." Stylistically, the distinction between masculine and feminine loses its outline in the union of Antony and Cleopatra, and the verbal subtleties make the play even more clearly indicative than *Coriolanus* of the direction Shakespeare will soon take.

Our familiarity with the visual, imagistic stress on permeability, dissolution, and the losing of recognizable shape should be supplemented with an awareness of the aural equivalent. As the rhythms and the syntax of *Antony and Cleopatra* indicate, the contours of Shakespeare's verse tend to melt in the heat of the Egyptian sun. Metrically the play is uncommonly subtle, even for Shakespeare, even for this phase, and both the untutored and the experienced ear will find it more aurally various and appealing than *Coriolanus*. One of its determining properties is the frequency of the short sentence, the brief outburst that acts to challenge the sovereignty of the pentameter line. Very frequently "the sense runs over into the next line, a tendency facilitated by Shakespeare's radically increased usage of weak and light line-endings," or what are sometimes called feminine endings.[46] If *Coriolanus* exhibits its hero's dedication to a disconnected,

---

[46] See Wright, *Shakespeare's Metrical Art*, p. 222.

masculine verse, much of *Antony and Cleopatra* displays the complementary form, a style that is irregular, digressive, and, according to the conceptions of the period, feminine. Rhythmically, the sense "o'erflows the measure" of the line.

In its syntax, *Antony and Cleopatra* depends heavily on the figure known as *hyperbaton*, or, as Puttenham Englishes it, "the trespasser." Its description is found in Book III of the *Arte*, "Of Ornament," the section prefaced by his elaborate comparison of writing with the sartorial splendor of "Madames of Honour." The most notable of these figures "of tollerable disorder" is the parenthesis, or in its English equivalent, "the inserter." After providing an unusually extended example, Puttenham comments that "This insertion is very long and utterly impertinent to the principall matter, and makes a great gappe in the tale," and he cautions that "you must not use such insertions often nor too thick, nor those that bee very long as this of ours, for it will breed great confusion to have the tale so much interrupted."[47] Such an account of discontinuity pertains to both the grammatical and the scenic syntax of *Antony and Cleopatra*: not only is the incidence of inverted word orders and disrupted sentences uncommonly high, but the interpolated episodes, digressive scenes, and disordered geography make for a notoriously choppy theatrical narrative, a feature that contributed to neo-classical discomfort with the work. The increasing metrical irregularity and syntactic disorder combine with other grammatical and rhetorical propensities, such as frequent ellipsis and a reliance on verbless constructions, to create a verse-style that is closer to prose than in almost any of the earlier works. Formally speaking, the dramatic verse of the tragedy is copious, unruly, showy, and demanding. It is also a preview of coming attractions.

The final movement, from Antony's suicide to Caesar's eulogy, may be considered a bridge between the tragedies and the romances because it attests to Shakespeare's developing attitude toward fictional language. Cleopatra seems to have occupied Shakespeare's imagination, making a great gap in Plutarch's tale by inserting herself into, and thereby transforming, what might have been simply the tragedy of Antony. She not only memorializes Antony in a virtuosic act of poetic construction but also stages her own spectacular end by the creative manipulation of costume, setting, and words. The represented death of the historical female is for Shakespeare the birth of the fictional Cleopatra, or, in

[47] *The Arte of English Poesie*, pp. 180–81.

Sidneyan terms, the exchange of history for imagination. But this final movement depends upon a theatrical scrambling of gender, a recombination of the masculine and feminine. Cleopatra, a boy actor neither man nor woman, talks her way into the male role of tragic hero, using women's weapons and speaking much of the time about a man. Janet Adelman contextualizes this imaginative compounding of gender:

> In the tragedies that follow from *Hamlet*, heroic masculinity has been constructed defensively, by a rigid separation from the dangerous female within and without; founded in the region of scarcity, the self-protective and niggardly manliness of Macbeth or Coriolanus illustrates the impasse at the end of this defensive construction . . . By locating Antony's heroic manhood within Cleopatra's vision of him, Shakespeare attempts in effect to imagine his way beyond this impasse.[48]

This imaginative union of the masculine and the feminine helps to account for Shakespeare's re-conceived attitude towards words, dramatic mode, and the theatrical enterprise itself.

FROM TRAGEDY TO ROMANCE

Shakespeare's exchange of tragedy for romance is a fascinating and, perhaps from this distance, inexplicable move. It would be tendentious to deny that a variety of influences, many of them practical, had an effect on his alteration of his professional course around 1607. Beaumont and Fletcher were making themselves known at just this moment, exhibiting in their collaborative and individual efforts familiarity with the theatrical scene, a keen interest in the popular dramatic modes, and a desire to experiment with new ones. Queen Anne's promotion of the masque was changing the shape of theatrical spectacle at court and thus influencing the professional companies. The King's Men were about to expand in new directions, having taken possession of the performing space at Blackfriars and preparing to attract new audiences.[49] The company may have needed someone to assist George Wilkins in the completion of *Pericles*, or may have needed to finish it for him.[50] The London playhouses were shut for

---

[48] *Suffocating Mothers*, p. 177.

[49] See especially Gerald Eades Bentley, "Shakespeare and the Blackfriars Theatre," *Shakespeare Survey 1* (1948), 1–15.

[50] See MacDonald Jackson, *Defining Shakespeare: "Pericles" as Test Case* (Oxford: Oxford University Press, 2004), Brian Vickers's *Shakespeare: Co-Author* (Oxford: Oxford University Press, 2002), and Suzanne Gossett's Arden3 edition of *Pericles* (London: Thomson Learning, 2004).

most of 1607, presumably giving a dislocated Shakespeare more time than usual to read and write and perhaps think about the future.[51] But all the external causes notwithstanding, Shakespeare's turn to romance and the concomitant changes in poetic style are to a large extent attributable to a change within him, a revised conception of language, of the theatre, and of human experience generally. Bound up with these changes are his altered views of masculinity and femininity.

Theatre, language, and gender seem to have been intimately associated in Shakespeare's mind, a matrix of connections consistent with the prevalent views of early modern English culture generally. The negative identification of women and words took its most extreme form in anti-feminine tracts such as Joseph Swetnam's *Arraignment of Lewd, Idle, Froward, and Unconstant Women* (1615), but the linking of chastity and female silence was a fundamental tenet of the Pauline strain of Christian doctrine (and the source of the name of the loquacious Paulina in *The Winter's Tale*). Shakespeare's earlier plays are replete with passages that exploit the link, either seriously or ironically: Richard of Gloucester's question when he is prevented from killing Queen Margaret, "Why should she live, to fill the world with words?" (*3 Henry VI* 5.5.44); the men's discussion of Kate in *The Taming of the Shrew* and Beatrice in *Much Ado about Nothing*; Hamlet's "like a whore unpack my heart with words." This cultural stereotype accounts for the religious attack on the stage as unmanly and a threat to sexual boundaries. As I shall document more fully in Chapter 6, the anti-theatrical polemicists expressed their opposition to the stage in terms of gender. In the most extreme statements of this view, such as Prynne's *Histrio-mastix,* seductive women, clothing, ornament, words, lies, and fictions are all identified, and Shakespeare's representation of predatory females in the tragedies partakes of these cultural fears.

For whatever reason Shakespeare's thinking about the feminine and his representation of women begin to change markedly at about this time, thus reversing a similar turn that had occurred when he gave up romantic comedy around 1600.[52] *Hamlet* and *King Lear* especially depend upon

---

[51] A detailed consideration of the theatrical scene and Shakespeare's place in it is found in Leeds Barroll's *Politics, Plague, and Shakespeare's Theatre: The Stuart Years* (Ithaca: Cornell University Press, 1991).

[52] A survey of Shakespeare's depiction of female sexuality in this late phase is found in Cyrus Hoy, "Fathers and Daughters in Shakespeare's Romances," *Shakespeare's Romances Reconsidered*, pp. 77–90. Illuminating work in this line has been done more recently by C. L. Barber and Richard Wheeler, *The Whole Journey: Shakespeare's Power of Development* (Berkeley: University of California

Shakespeare's portrayal of female sexuality as degenerate and predatory, and in *Macbeth* that portrayal has become even darker, tainted with witchcraft and possible demonic possession. But the conception of both the feminine and the masculine in *Macbeth* is complicated by Shakespeare's critique of the violence of masculinity, Lady Macbeth's attempt to "unsex" herself, and the ambiguous gender of the witches. Then, in *Coriolanus* and *Antony and Cleopatra*, Shakespeare renegotiates the relations between masculine and feminine, thinking about gender and genre in ways that make possible a rehabilitated understanding of women. In the romances the malignant female is not imaginatively banished, surviving in Dionyza, the Queen in *Cymbeline*, and Sycorax, with perhaps a tinge, for ironic purposes, in Paulina. But such iniquity is complemented and finally overwhelmed by the power of the creative and nurturant woman. This recuperation of the feminine accounts also for Shakespeare's revised, affirmative view of language and of the theatre.

Genre, we should remember, was typed according to gender. For the early modern spectator and reader, tragedy, with its historical authority, was evidently masculine, a prejudice that survives in the long-standing privileging of tragedy over comedy: love stories are merely pleasurable tales, useless fictions for and about women; men prefer tragedies. A vivid embodiment of these divisions is found in the Induction to *Mucedorus*: "*Enter Comedy ioyfully, with a Garland of Bayes on her head.*" This feminine, accommodating figure is immediately menaced by the blustering figure of Envy, whom Comedy ultimately, although with difficulty, subdues:

> Vaunt bloody cur, nursed up with tigers' sap,
> That so dost seek to quail a woman's mind;
> *Comedy* is mild, gentle, willing for to please,
> And seeks to gain the love of all estates:
> Delighting in mirth, mixed all with lovely tales;
> And bringeth things with treble ioy to pass.[53]

These commonplaces form the backdrop against which, around 1607, Shakespeare exchanges the masculine for the feminine mode, relinquishing

Press, 1986), and Coppélia Kahn, *Man's Estate: Masculine Identity in Shakespeare* (Berkeley: University of California Press, 1981). The most persuasive treatment of gender in this phase is Adelman's *Suffocating Mothers*. See also Alison Thorne, *Shakespeare's Romances* (New York: Palgrave Macmillan, 2003).

[53] *A Most Pleasant Comedy of Mucedorus* (London, 1598). I have modernized the spelling.

what has been called the "end-stopped form" of tragedy in favor of the more "open" form of romance.[54]

The end of the tragic sequence implies, in the rejection of Coriolanus's view of words, in the failure of aggressive masculinity, and in renewed faith in values considered feminine, a new commitment to theatre and language. In other words, Shakespeare embraces a style of poetry implicitly marked by his culture as female, returning to Ciceronian principles of ornament and verbal pleasure. The masculine, separated, univocal style associated with Coriolanus yields to a verse given to extravagance and multiplicity. The last two tragedies are exceptional in that individual speakers of the appropriate gender express themselves in language coded as masculine and feminine, but even here, with these relatively schematic divisions, the subtlety of Shakespeare's conception proscribes crude distinctions. The "femininity" of Volumnia and Cleopatra is complicated by the masculine associations with which they are tinged, such as Sicinius's contemptuous question to Volumnia after the banishment, "Are you mankind?", and Cleopatra's remembrance of wearing Antony's "sword Phillipan." To assert Shakespeare's turn to feminine values with respect to language and genre, however, is not to suggest anything so bald as that all the major dramatic voices, from Pericles' to Prospero's to Henry VIII's, be considered "female." Rather, it is to say that the palpable difficulties of the late verse are illuminated by the historical affiliations of style and gender, and that the dramatist's voice, devoted as it is to pleasure, artifice, and circumlocution, reflects a creative attitude associated by his culture with the feminine.

The romances give us a reconstituted conception of the theatre, an admission that while theatrical illusion and the words that compose it may not adequately represent reality, they can provide an alternative version. Suspicion of the word continues to haunt plays like *The Winter's Tale* and *Henry VIII*, with its ironic alternative title, *All is True*, but distrust is accompanied by a resignation to or acceptance of such limitations and a simultaneous pleasure in the possibilities of fictional language.[55] The destructive verbal illusions of the tragedies – Iago's lies, the equivocal prophecies in *Macbeth*, the flattery of Timon's friends – are not eliminated, but they are now complemented by theatrical fictions that delight and console.

---

[54] See Adelman, *Suffocating Mothers*, pp. 73–4, 190.
[55] Anne Barton, "Shakespeare and the Limits of Language," in *Essays, Mainly Shakespearean* (Cambridge: Cambridge University Press, 1994), pp. 51–69.

The verse in which these fictions are delivered, however, is unusually challenging. Exploitation of the mid-line caesura, the juxtaposition of short and long sentences, the piling of clause upon clause, the frequency of ellipsis, the inversion of subject, verb, and object, the extremes of hyperbatonic syntax, the high incidence, almost one in three, of extra-metrical lines and light endings – all these features constitute a poetic reconfiguration that audibly sets the romances apart from the tragedies. The verse embodies grammatically and metrically the conflicts of sexual difference exhibited in the dramatic narratives.[56] Aurally demanding and self-consciously artificial, the romantic style involves a contest between sense and form, between the semantic energies of the sentence and the restrictions of the pentameter. These stylistic tensions and resolutions grow directly from the sexual conflicts that Shakespeare explores in the late tragedies and develops, with new resolutions, in the romances. If there is a single property of the late style that distinguishes it from the earlier verse, it is the unusual freedom with which its various components, from clauses to words to lines, are joined together in an uneasy but finally successful equipoise. We might say the same for the various forms of sexual relations, healthy and unhealthy, in the romances.

The difficulties of the late style amount to a form of play, a sporting with poetic effects that reflects Shakespeare's newly developed recreative view of language and that suits the thematic emphasis on recreation permeating the late work. His reevaluation of the feminine has ramifications that go beyond language to the kind of stories such language presents and the way those stories are told. The discursive extravagance of Volumnia and Cleopatra is helpful in thinking about this formal shift, since the word "extravagant" derives from the Latin for straying or errancy, and one of the principal characteristics of romance is its dependence upon wandering, doubling, and excess.[57] After the Roman spareness of *Coriolanus* and the Caesarean sections of *Antony and Cleopatra*, Shakespeare offers his audience – with a vengeance – the staples of romantic

---

[56] All these features have been given some attention by the few commentators who have remarked on the later style. See especially J. M. Nosworthy's Introduction to the New Arden edition of *Cymbeline* (London: Methuen, 1955), F. E. Halliday, *The Poetry of Shakespeare's Plays* (London: Gerald Duckworth & Co., 1954); James Sutherland, "The Language of the Last Plays," in *More Talking of Shakespeare*, ed. John Garrett (London: Longmans, 1959), pp. 144–48; N. F. Blake, *Shakespeare's Language: An Introduction* (London: Methuen, 1983); and Wright's *Shakespeare's Metrical Art*.

[57] See Harold Bloom, *A Map of Misreading* (New York: Oxford, 1971), p. 103, as well as Patricia Parker, *Inescapable Romance: Studies in the Poetics of a Mode* (Princeton: Princeton University Press, 1979).

fiction: stolen infants, wicked stepmothers, wronged wives, Italian villains, shipwrecks, tearful reunions, oracles, witches, magic potions, airy spirits, and, everybody's favorite, a voracious bear. Moreover, the presentational style confirms the triumph of artifice: Gower in *Pericles*, the intruding Time in *The Winter's Tale*, the ironic prologue in *Henry VIII*, and many other such instances of self-consciousness – of winking at the audience – differentiate these plays similarly from the tragedies that precede them. In poetic and theatrical styles, limitation is replaced with amplification, simplicity with extravagance, mimesis with poesis.

CREATURES SITTING AT A PLAY

It is difficult to imagine Caius Martius Coriolanus attending a theatrical performance. His distaste for pretense and verbal prolixity would make the pleasures of the stage unavailable to him, and for all his complaints about excessive speech, one suspects that he couldn't sit still without talking back to the actors. Macbeth, on the other hand, possessing an imagination active enough to hallucinate a dagger, willingly attends the demonic theatre of the witches in Act 4. Antony discovers the attractions of performance late in life, a turn for which Caesar despises him; Cleopatra enters the theatre only as the star performer, and only in carefully chosen parts. All these refractions of the stage in the late tragedies point to Shakespeare's reconsideration of his own profession. We might conceive of the playwright as an Antony giving up the serious work of history and tragedy for the Cleopatra of imagination and romance. Having moved back and forth from Scotland to Rome to Alexandria, Shakespeare gazes beyond these historical locales to undocumented realms, the seacoast of Bohemia and a mythical island somewhere between the Mediterranean and the still-vexed Bermoothes. For a time, at least, he does so: even now we may need to be reminded that *The Tempest* is not the end of the story.

CHAPTER 2

Elision

Writing is not like painting where you add. It is not what you put on
the canvas that the reader sees. Writing is more like a sculpture
where you remove, you eliminate in order to make the work visible.
Even those pages you remove somehow remain.

Elie Wiesel[1]

Less is more.

Ludwig Mies van der Rohe[2]

The most distinctive feature of Shakespeare's late style, the property that
contributes more than any other to the acoustic imprint of the dramas, is
its radical compression. Complex ideas are packed into few words, often
at the expense of the dominant metrical pattern and the expected syntactical forms, sometimes in defiance of ready intelligibility. It is a characteristic that readers have recognized and puzzled over since the earliest days
of academic Shakespeare criticism. The terms of the Bradleyan description, quoted in the Introduction –"more concentrated . . . not seldom
twisted or elliptical . . . sometimes involved and obscure"– have been
endorsed by later critics, although few proceed beyond these abstractions
to specific illustration.[3] Gladys Willcock, for example, suggested in 1934
that the late style exhibits a "compressed, often cloudy, pregnancy."[4]
J. H. P. Pafford, reviewing critical responses to the late style for his 1963
Arden edition of *The Winter's Tale*, records general "agreement that the
plays have a certain elusive quality which is peculiar to them."[5] These
accounts capture the widely shared sense that the language of the last plays

---

[1] Interview in *Writers at Work*, 8th series, ed. George Plimpton (New York: Penguin Books, 1988).
[2] *New York Herald Tribune*, 28 June 1959.
[3] A. C. Bradley, *Shakespearean Tragedy: Lectures on "Hamlet," "Othello," "King Lear" and "Macbeth,"
With a New Introduction by John Russell Brown* (London: Macmillan, 1972), p. 68.
[4] Gladys Willcock, *Shakespeare as Critic of Language* (London, 1934), p. 3.
[5] J. H. P. Pafford, Introduction to Arden2 edition of *The Winter's Tale* (London: Methuen, 1963), p. xliii.

is veiled and ineffable, that it points to something beyond itself but frustrates any effort to apprehend that something directly.

The favored adjective for identifying this elusive quality, a term especially useful to editors or annotators faced with an intractable passage, is "elliptical." J. M. Nosworthy, for example, remarks that in *Cymbeline* (and the late style generally) "ellipsis and elision contribute greatly to stylistic economy, and short speeches in particular are sometimes so concentrated as to be perplexing."[6] A. C. Partridge, in the midst of describing Shakespeare's style generally, includes some relatively specific observations: "On the track of the telling and indelible image, he may leave behind anacolouthons and hanging relative clauses in the most inconsequent fashion; he compresses his meaning and tortures his syntax, so that while the effect of the passage may be poetically grand, the meaning is wrung from it with extreme difficulty."[7] Some of these effects will be treated in this chapter and some in the next two: as Partridge indicates, it is difficult to separate ellipsis and syntax.

The general rule is that, as his poetic career proceeds, Shakespeare gives the audience less and less help – literally so, in his removal of articles, auxiliaries, and other such units. By 1607 or so the effects of elimination have become extreme. D. A. Traversi explains this process of reduction, showing how ellipsis accelerates the pace in Menenius's lines from *Coriolanus*, "For the dearth, / The gods, not the patricians, make it, and / Your knees to them (not arms) must help" (1.1.72–74):

It is impossible not to feel that this is an example of the unique free mastery of Shakespeare's later verse. We should be aware of the conciseness of the last sentence, of the way in which the "not arms" parenthesis enables us to grasp the essential contrast without the distraction that would result from a full statement of the alternatives; it is a telescoping of language that follows the movement of living thought.[8]

The example is helpful, but this is about as concrete as anybody gets. Those who speak of an elliptical style almost invariably intend the word figuratively, as a synonym for "puzzling."

I propose to take the word "elliptical" literally and seriously. If we are to do more than rehearse impressionistic reactions to the poetry, most of them derivative and comfortably vague, then we should specify the nature

---

[6] J. M. Nosworthy, Introduction to the Arden2 edition of *Cymbeline* (London: Methuen, 1955), p. lxii.

[7] A. C. Partridge, *Orthography in Shakespeare and Elizabethan Drama: A Study of Colloquial Contractions, Elision, Prosody, and Punctuation* (Lincoln: University of Nebraska Press, 1964), p. 147.

[8] D. A. Traversi, "*Coriolanus*," *Scrutiny*, 6 (1937), 44.

of Shakespeare's verbal omissions, the effect of such ellipsis on the listener, and the semantic and theatrical ramifications of such a stylistic habit. In seeking intensity, the mature Shakespeare experiments with a poetic method based on distillation and reduction, on the suppression of certain grammatical elements (and the corresponding promotion of others), on subordination and casting away. He vigorously omits syllables from words, discards verbs from sentences, eliminates conjunctions between clauses, dispenses with relative pronouns wherever possible, and collapses potentially lengthy clauses into participial or infinitive phrases. The removal of disposable syllabic and lexical signs consequently places intense pressure on those sounds and signs that remain and often transforms the poetic surface, playing havoc especially with metrical regularity.

The effect of poetic ellipsis is magnified because the late verse is also extravagantly pleonastic. As he abbreviates, Shakespeare also supplements, adding semantically unnecessary words, repeating syntactic structures, and reduplicating sounds, words, and phrases to create a poetic texture that seems reiterative and incantatory. As Roger Warren suggests about *Cymbeline* in a passage cited earlier, such "inclusiveness" represents an effort "to pack in a great deal,"[9] and, as he implies, any discussion of stylistic distillation must also include an awareness of stylistic surplus. This reciprocal effect of elimination and supplementation gives the late verse its peculiar dynamic, a simultaneous impression of sketchiness and amplitude. This dual impulse may perhaps be traced back to Shakespeare's primary education. According to Norman Blake,

There are two features of the teaching of Latin grammar which had an impact on Shakespeare and his composition in English. They were the development of compound sentences and extensive noun groups, on the one hand, and the imitation of the compression of Latin expression through ellipsis in English, on the other hand. Latin being a synthetic language it appeared that one could say much more in fewer words. Shakespeare and his fellow pupils learned many Latin proverbial utterances by heart and these were echoed and imitated in his own writings.[10]

More than thirty years later, Shakespeare has had considerable practice at the expansion and contraction of English speech. The impulse both to omit and to include elements in the production of this compressed,

---

[9] Roger Warren, "Theatrical Virtuosity and Poetic Complexity in *Cymbeline,*" *Shakespeare Survey* 29 (1976), 46.
[10] N. F. Blake, *A Grammar of Shakespeare's Language* (Houndsmills: Palgrave, 2002), p. 17.

gestural poetic style attests to a confidence and security that we might expect from Shakespeare at this stage in his career.

But his distillation of the verse also has significant implications for the direction and emphasis of his late work. Susan Wolfson has suggested that we come to know works of art more thoroughly when we are able to see "the local form invested with macroformations,"[11] and in the case of Shakespeare's late plays the vital relation is between the poetic line and the chosen dramatic mode. The dynamic of distillation and supplementation may be seen as deriving from the same motives that impelled the playwright to experiment with dramatic romance, that famously episodic form that skips over great gaps of time, neglects logical connections in favor of less predictable sorts of juxtaposition and sequence, and regularly withholds satisfactory accounts of human motive or supernatural influence. The theatrical spectator is required to fill in gaps, to ignore or forgive unclear sequences and logical faults in the structure of romance fiction. Likewise, the concentrated and intense poetic style demands of the auditor heightened concentration and imaginative participation. It is further appropriate, of course, that such an elliptical poetic form should be developed for a kind of play that often takes its dramatic motive from the experience of loss. Characters are repeatedly made to look beneath surfaces, often to find, by virtue of a double irony, that the truth they sought is clearly visible on the surface. The operation of the verse engages the audience physically and mentally in this complex interplay of surfaces and depths.

The challenge of relating particular formal elements to larger expressive aims and methods is compounded in the case of ellipsis because here the critical effort involves the analysis of poetic elements that don't exist. While the dropping of letters and syllables in the service of meter or rhythm is familiar from Shakespeare's earliest work – indeed such prosodic fidgeting is often a sign of the poetic tyro – his last plays exhibit a far greater devotion to the practice than might normally be expected of such an experienced poet. In the illustrative analysis that follows I shall attempt to develop specifically Frank Kermode's recent claim that Shakespeare's

---

[11] Susan Wolfson, "Introduction" to *Reading for Form*, a special issue of *Modern Language Quarterly*, 61.1 (2000), 14. Many of the essays in this collection pursue the correspondence between particular formal traits and their macroscopic significance. On this point see also Peter Brooks, *Reading for the Plot: Design and Intention in Narrative* (New York: Alfred A. Knopf, 1984); Tzvetan Todorov, *The Poetics of Prose*, tr. Richard Howard (Ithaca: Cornell University Press, 1977), esp. pp. 143–77; and Patricia Parker, *Shakespeare from the Margins: Language, Culture, Context* (Chicago: University of Chicago Press, 1996), *passim*.

"later language, and so his theatre, does not lose all contact with the eloquence of his early work, but moves deliberately in the direction of a kind of reticence that might . . . be thought close to silence."[12] This chapter, then, is devoted to what Shakespeare leaves out.

POETIC THEORY AND COMPRESSION OF THE LINE

Latin rhetoricians and Elizabethan schoolmasters predictably have much more to say about ornament and amplification than they do about elimination. (The decorator's job is to sell and arrange furniture, not pitch it out.) Still, the major commentators do offer formulae and strategies for poetic economy, specifically for reducing words with too many syllables and clauses with too many words. Such prescriptions as Quintilian's notes on *detractio* (9.3.58) are designed to assist the versifier in meeting simultaneously the demands of semantics and metrics and thus tend to fall under the category of "poetic license."[13] The generic term for such aural adjustment is *metaplasm* (Gr.: "to mold into new form"): it refers to the shifts by which the poet may drop letters, elide vowels into a single syllable, eliminate opening or terminal syllables, and perform other such aurally reductive maneuvers, usually for the sake of protecting the integrity of the metrical frame. George Gascoigne's *Certayne Notes of Instruction* (1575) acknowledges the value of such metaplasmic tactics and demonstrates both the principles of addition and subtraction: "This poetical licence is a shrewd fellow, and covereth many faults in a verse. It maketh words longer, shorter, of more syllables, of fewer, newer, older, truer, falser; and, to conclude, it turkeneth [twists] all things at pleasure, for example, *ydone* for *done, adown* for *down, o'ercome* for *overcome, tane* for *taken, power* for *powre, heaven* for *heav'n* . . . and a number of other[s]."[14] The "faults" to be covered are metrical; syllabic elision ensures regularity; one kind of fault prevents another.

George Puttenham, in his introductory discussion of poetic ornament, displays his awareness that minute changes can affect the larger poetic system and reveals in the ordering of his own sentence a highly structured

---

[12] Frank Kermode, *Shakespeare's Language* (London: Penguin, 2000), p. 13.

[13] References to Quintilian are found in the Loeb Classical Library edition of *The Orator's Education*, edited and translated by Donald A. Russell (Cambridge, Mass.: Harvard University Press, 2001), 5 vols. Parenthetical numbers in my text refer to Quintilian's book numbers and subsections, e.g. (9.3.58).

[14] Quoted in Brian Vickers, *English Renaissance Literary Criticism* (Oxford: Clarendon Press, 1999), p. 168.

conception of language: "Therefore as the members of language at large are whole sentences, and sentences are compact of clauses, and clauses of words, and every word of letters and sillables, so is the alteration (be it but of a sillable or letter) much materiall to the sound and sweetnesse of utterance."[15] Puttenham then proceeds to exemplify the transformation of words by a letter or syllable, demonstrating the flexibility available to the poet who wishes to adjust the medium for metrical or perhaps homophonic purposes without altering meaning. Usefully reminding the modern reader of the extraordinary flexibility of Elizabethan English, he argues that, within limits, the poet is free to shift the accent of words [*éndure* for *endúre*], engage in the "displacing of a sillable" [*de-si-er* for *desire*], or substitute one letter for another in the interest of rhyme [*wrang* for *wrong*]. This last maneuver, the rhetorician cautions, is subject to abuse and ought to be performed sparingly.[16]

The strategies on which Puttenham lavishes the most attention in this context are "your figures of *rabbate.*" The etymology of "rabbate," from the French *rabbatre*, to beat down, suggests violence, the exertion of control, the forcible suppression or omission of dispensable phonetic, lexical, or grammatical elements. Puttenham includes among his recommended adjustments "Your swallowing or eating up one letter by another . . . when two vowels meete, wherof th'ones sound goeth into other, as to say for *to attaine t'attaine.*"[17] The word "rabbate" thus reflects on the authority of the poet, his power to govern the poetic line, to tolerate a certain degree of disorder and even to encourage such license in the name of aural diversity, all the while ensuring the smooth operation of the verse. One of its cognates is "rebate," to deduct, or diminish; another is "rabbit," the noun that survives in modern carpentry for a surface that has been planed down to remove irregularities. In the same section of his treatise, Puttenham includes *eclipsis,* "the figure of default,"[18] and the OED associates "eclipsis" or "eclipse," to cover or obscure, with "ellipsis" or "elision." Thus omission creates in the listener a sense of mystery or lack; something meaningful seems to stand behind or beneath the surface of the line; one is led to look beyond the difficult, crowded signifiers towards an elusive, hidden significance.

Graduating from letters and syllables to more substantial forms of omission, the cataloguers offer the aspiring writer schemes for condensing

---

[15] *The Arte of English Poesie,* a facsimile reproduction, ed. Edward Arber, with an Introduction by Baxter Hathaway (Athens, Ohio: Kent State University Press, 1988), pp. 172–73.
[16] *Ibid.,* p. 174.   [17] *Ibid.,* p. 162.   [18] *Ibid.,* p. 175.

the verse line, most of their suggestions falling under the rubric of concision. Quintilian's advice on the forms of omission offer appropriate solutions to a variety of oratorical requirements and problems. For example, *aposiopesis*, or a breaking off and allowing the listener to fill in the remainder, helps the speaker to preserve modesty or decorum. Asyndeton "is useful when we are speaking with special vigour: for it at once impresses the details on the mind and makes them seem more numerous than they really are" (9.3.50). (Puttenham's helpful remarks on asyndeton are considered below.) Quintilian's definition of omission is fairly broad, including, for example, many tropes we would consider remote from deletion, such as synecdoche and metonymy (8.6.21–23). It is worth noting, moreover, that over several centuries and in different cultures the prescriptive vocabulary can shift significantly: for example, Quintilian reserves the word *ellipsis* for an error or blemish (*vitia*).

Most of the classical commentators and their early modern disciples confess, either openly or implicitly, that economy is not the only goal. Authorial play is a legitimate motive as well, as shown in Quintilian's concluding remarks about aposiopesis: "Neither do I personally call it Aposiopesis in all cases in which something is left to be understood; for example, the thing left to be understood in Cicero's letter: 'Written on the Lupercalia, the day when *Antonius Caesari*,' where Cicero has not suppressed anything, but made a joke, because the only words that could be understood are 'put the diadem on his head'" (9.3.61). This passage implies a vital principle about the value of omission, namely a consciousness of the way that audiences (whether of orations or plays) and readers (whatever the kind of writing) cooperate in the creation of meaning.

Collaboration between speaker and listener is a principle taken up specifically by the Renaissance cataloguers as they adapt the rules of oratory to the making of English verse. Puttenham, after listing the ways in which letters or syllables may be altered or eliminated, mentions the importance of participation when he moves to "Auricular figures pertaining to clauses of speech." These figures delete words or phrases that can be understood from the pattern of words already established, or intuited from the semantic and dramatic context, or, as he puts it, "supplied by common understanding" (175). He declares that "your whole and entire clauses [may] be in such sort contrived by the order of their construction as the eare may receive a certain recreation" (174). Puttenham's description of the pleasing effect of arrangement based on ellipsis is instructive because it implies the means by which that pleasure is created: the ear "receives a certain recreation," enjoys the refreshment that attends the act of exercise. In other words, the listener delights generally in the patterning of words, phrases, and clauses, and, in the case of omitted elements, the recreation arises from the "re-creation" of an implied pattern.[19]

In dramatic verse generally, and especially in the difficult, elliptical style of Shakespeare's late work, the listener must complete the puzzle by filling in the gaps or connecting the dots, and audition becomes a game in which the members of the theater audience are challenged by aural complexity and rewarded with hard-won cognition. Bradley's description of the late verse as "concentrated" and "less regular" is followed by his noticing that in many cases "the sense has rather to be discerned beyond the words than found in them"; as a result, he says, "readers . . . will admit that in traversing the impatient throng of thoughts not always completely embodied, their minds move through an astonishing variety of ideas and experiences."[20] Although Bradley reveals his literary bias – "readers" rather than theatergoers will feel themselves mentally exercised – his comments describe a process that informs all theatrical speech: the listener is forced to draw conclusions and make connections rapidly and partially. Towards the end of his career Shakespeare assists less and less in this process of comprehension so that the auditor's mind must move ever more rapidly, working with even less information and nimbly making connections. In the theater this movement is rapid and exhilarating, giving the listener the sensation of mastery and suggesting the presence, to return to Bradley, of "something beyond the words."

Puttenham's leading example of significant omission is "*eclipsis*, or the figure of default," which he classes with the "defective figures." The OED, citing this passage and an earlier instance from Coverdale's *Prolegomena to the New Testament*, suggests that the word "eclipsis" may have arisen from a confusion with "ellipsis"; the second sense of "eclipsis," the suppression of certain consonants in Gaelic, is related possibly to the word "eclipse," in the sense of "to obscure." The relation between the two words helps to expand our sense of rhetorical possibility in poetic treatment of the verse line. This reference to eclipsing or covering offers a historical source for the critical impression about Shakespeare's later practice captured in

---

[19] This is a familiar Shakespearean pun, of course, used memorably by Leontes after his anagnorisis in the third act of *The Winter's Tale*; he proposes a daily visit to the chapel containing the tombs of his wife and son: "and tears shed there / Shall be my recreation" (3.2.239–40). Penance becomes both pleasure (a daily exercise) and the means to spiritual restoration.

[20] *Shakespearean Tragedy*, p. 69.

Willcock's "compressed, often cloudy, pregnancy." Something meaningful seems to stand behind or beneath the surface of the line. Mostly the
classical orators and Renaissance commentators believed that the reader or
listener knows what is assumed: their examples indicate that the terms to
be supplied are self-evident. Shakespeare, however, often makes the task
of filling in much more challenging. The suppressed words or ideas are
nebulous but apparently meaningful. Quintilian's name for the pleasure
of filling in the blanks is *gratiam*: "At quae per detractionem fiunt figurae,
brevitatis novitatisque maxime gratiam petunt" ("As regards Figures generated by Subtraction, they aim principally at the charm of brevity and
novelty" (9.3.58)). Shakespeare has intensified the gratification by exaggerating the number and the difficulty of his omissions. Listeners find
themselves pleasantly tantalized, suspended between obscurity and revelation. Quintilian's definition of the figure of synecdoche might be helpful
in this context: "it is found when some omitted word is understood well
enough from the others" (9.3.1). Thus we might say that Shakespeare is
attempting something like a synecdochic style, one in which the whole
meaning is taken from the part. I shall return to this suggestion.

Abundant elision has an audible effect on the metrics of the late verse,
and the frustrations attendant upon hearing and comprehending it are
hardly surprising considering the violent diction with which the theorists
describe these acts of poetic adjustment. The forcible "suppression" of
weak and unnecessary letters, the "displacing of a sillable," "your figures
of *rabbate*," cannibalization among consonants and vowels ("your swallowing or eating up one letter by another") – such instructions imply a
connection between poetic composition and social organization. Awareness of such relations of subjection and promotion should also lead us to
wonder about the differences among the practices of poetic dramatists, as
well as about changes in the style of a single practitioner.[21] It is not merely
that Puttenham is conservative and authoritarian when it comes to verse
and to politics, although he famously is so.[22] The point is that the
ordering of the verse line implies selection, the exertion of control, and
the willingness to indulge a certain degree of disorder. As Constance
Jordan reminds us in her study of the romances and the Jacobean

---

[21] James Sutherland describes Shakespeare as a writer "swept along by some inner compulsion, and
whose mind seems at times to be generating an immense energy which he is applying, as a man
might apply a pneumatic drill, to the immediate problems of composition." "The Language of the
Last Plays," in *More Talking of Shakespeare*, ed. John Garrett (London: Longmans, 1959), p. 151.

[22] See Jonathan Crewe, "The Hegemonic Theater of George Puttenham," *ELR*, 16 (1986), 71–85.

discourses of tyranny, the late plays are concerned more directly than we have recognized with the effects of monarchical neglect and misrule.[23] The contest between authority and its opponents that animates plays such as *The Tempest* or *Henry VIII* is also played out in the organization of the verse line. Shakespeare's tolerance for prosodic irregularity has audibly increased in his movement from tragedy to romance: as far as the metrical frame is concerned, there is subversion, no end of subversion, and yet the dominance of the pentameter is never finally overthrown. It would be a blunder to make too much of the political implications of blank verse, but Shakespeare's stylistic recklessness certainly bespeaks a relaxed, playful attitude towards authority and control of the poetic medium. That insouciant attitude seems increasingly pertinent to his philosophical and professional views as well.

DROPPING OUT

In cataloging the mature Shakespeare's propensity to elide, it makes sense to start where Puttenham does, with the eclipsing or beating down of individual letters and syllables. Obviously too much should not be made of those cases in which simple suffixes such as "ed" are reduced to "d," since this is a conventional feature of normal English speech. Nor are contractions necessarily meaningful, although it is hard not to be impressed by Willard Farnham's demonstration of Shakespeare's increasing freedom with such abbreviation. Compared to the six contractions in *The Merchant of Venice*, the Folio text of *The Winter's Tale* contains 154.[24] But any kind of omission, even the simplest and most conventional, assumes greater significance in the midst of other forms of elision. Opening consonants increasingly tend to be dropped, as in "'em" for "them." Frequently phrases and words such as "of the" and "in the" and "it" are stripped of their vowels or consonants and thus deprived of some syllabic weight so that, in metrical terms, a complete iamb or trochee is reduced to half its rhythmic status. Occasionally words may be deprived of their auditory value altogether: in Prospero's "he did believe / He was indeed the Duke, out o'th' substitution" (1.2.102–3), the prepositional "o'th" attaches to "out," so that three potential syllables are collapsed into the

---

[23] Constance Jordan, *Shakespeare's Monarchies: Ruler and Subject in the Romances* (Ithaca: Cornell University Press, 1997).

[24] Willard Farnham, "Colloquial Contractions in Beaumont, Fletcher, Massinger, and Shakespeare as a Test of Authorship," *PMLA*, 31 (1916), 342–44. A taste for contractions seems to have been a characteristic of the scrivener Ralph Crane, who prepared a copy of *The Winter's Tale*, but even so the comparative figures seem significant.

single unstressed syllable between "Duke" and "sub." Shakespeare seems bent on removing inessential syllables so as to pack the line with weightier words, especially to include parts of speech more potent than articles and prepositions. In Prospero's line just cited, the elimination of the "f" in "of" and the "e" in "the" affords room for "substitution." But only barely room: even with the omission of these two sounds, the line remains extrametrical and still sounds crowded.

Prospero's autobiographical narrative (the source of these examples) moves forward with an abundance of such elision. "My brother Antonio," Prospero informs Miranda,

> . . . new created
> The creatures that were mine, I say, or chang'd 'em,
> Or else new form'd 'em; having both the key
> Of officer and office, set all hearts i' th' state
> To what tune pleas'd his ear; that now he was   85
> The ivy which had hid my princely trunk,
> And suck'd my verdure out on't. Thou attend'st not!
>   (1.2.81–87)

Such extreme omission far surpasses Puttenham's limited tips for tidying up the poetic line. In fact, the cluster of examples visible (but not audible) here has rather the opposite effect, disturbing the order of the pentameter and stuffing as many ideas as possible into lines that can barely contain them. The notorious compression of this passage is also apparent in the mercurial quality of its figurative language. A metaphor often lasts only as long as it takes a practiced mind to perceive it, whereupon it is immediately dropped or succeeded by yet another: the "key" in line 83 appears to be a tool for opening locks, but by line 85 it has become a musical image, the key signature of the "tune" dictated by the usurper. Such compression of poetic figures is one of the most striking differences between Shakespeare's late and earlier practice. The last plays contain very few extended metaphors, almost nothing like the memorable conceits from the earlier plays and poems. Compare the passage from *2 Henry VI* in which the Archbishop of York condemns the unreliability of the people:

> Thou, beastly feeder, art so full of him,   95
> That thou provok'st thyself to cast him up.
> So, so, thou common dog, didst thou disgorge
> Thy glutton bosom of the royal Richard,
> And now thou wouldst eat thy dead vomit up,
> And howl'st to find it.   100
>   (1.3.95–100)

The speaker proceeds leisurely and thoroughly, drawing attention to the details of similitude and luxuriating in his specificity. In the romances, the opposite kind of extravagance obtains: the metaphoric vehicle would be reduced to a half-line image.

The compression evident in Prospero's complaint exposes a fundamental opposition between Elizabethan rhetorical theory and Shakespeare's practice in his Jacobean phase. Puttenham's stipulations and instances are calculated to help the poet achieve regularity or smoothness, "to make the metre or verse more tunable and melodious." Shakespeare, with some two decades of experience at composing various kinds of verse for all classes of speakers, now aims at something beyond a regular, unbroken line. In effect, he vastly expands the affective range of the rhetoricians' elliptical goals and formulae. His strategies for condensation tend to make the aural surface of the line even rougher and more irregular, unruliness being the price of extreme reduction and semantic bounty. The omission of dispensable vowels and consonants, not to mention words and larger units, implies the desire to reduce the poetic statement to its essential terms and qualities and to make room for sounds of greater resonance and complexity.

Prospero's opening speeches represent an obviously condensed narration consistent with the intensely elliptical language of the rest of the play. As Anne Barton has pointed out, the play is spiked with unusual compound words – "cloud-capped," "pole-clipt," "hag-seed," "man-monster," "sea-sorrow."[25] So powerful is this elliptical motive that it pervades not only the sentence and the line but the distribution of action as well: in a play that might be seen as a variant of tragicomedy, what would have been the tragic half (such as Acts 1, 2 and 3 of *The Winter's Tale*), is condensed into Prospero's extended narration in the long second scene. Although *The Tempest* is probably the most extreme case, all the late plays offer versions of such disorienting language. And while this rough music is sometimes made to be locally functional, it so thoroughly pervades the last sequence of plays as to defeat most attempts at assigning specific meaning.

The impulse to abbreviate and distill fosters grammatical patterns that make the late verse uncommonly difficult. Many of these patterns involve removing those parts of speech that normally tighten relations between

---

[25] "In compounds like these – and the play is filled with them – nouns strike against nouns or other parts of speech with an immediacy and force which jars both components out of their accustomed meaning." Introduction to her edition of *The Tempest* (Harmondsworth: Penguin, 1968), p. 13.

parts of a sentence, particularly pronouns.[26] Specifically, the relative pronouns "that," "which," and "who" are often discarded, as in Imogen's

> There's other work in hand: I see a thing
> [that is as] Bitter to me as death
>
> (5.5.103–4)

A trickier, more challenging instance introduces Norfolk's condemnation of Wolsey's rise in *Henry VIII*:

> And with what zeal! for now he has crack'd the league
> Between us and the emperor (the Queen's great nephew),
> He dives into the King's soul . . .   (2.2.23–25)

The omission of the conventional connective ("now [that] he has crack'd the league") accelerates the sentence but momentarily obscures the conditional status of the introductory clause, a conditionality that the actor, to ensure comprehension, must be careful to supply vocally. The Old Shepherd in *The Winter's Tale*, humiliated at Polixenes' intervention during the festival, fears that he will not be permitted "To die upon the bed [on which] my father died" (4.4.456). In Hermione's plea for female companionship in prison, "Beseech your highness / My women may be with me" (2.1.116–17), the pronominal subject ("I") is elided in the first clause, perhaps to make space for the unexpected "Beseech"; also elided is the relative "that" which would normally introduce the second clause. Again in *Henry VIII*, Buckingham affirms that he does not exaggerate Wolsey's crimes: "I do pronounce him in that very shape / [In which] He shall appear in proof" (1.1.196–97). In *Cymbeline*, Imogen is described as "one persuaded well of," a phrase complicated by the uncommon use of "persuaded" as a synonym for "thought"; as it stands, it seems to belong to a relative clause lacking the connective pronoun ("one of whom people are persuaded well"). The omission of relative units, words that usually relate one part of the sentence to another, helps to create the generally loose syntax of the late plays and thus accounts for some of their semantic difficulty.

Shakespeare also develops the asyndetic method exploited so effectively in *Coriolanus*, the omission of conjunctive units between clauses.

> My surveyor is false; the o'ergreat Cardinal
> Hath show'd him gold; my life is spann'd already.
> I am the shadow of poor Buckingham . . .
>
> (1.1.222–24)

---

[26] See Blake, *A Grammar of Shakespeare's Language*, pp. 218–19.

This passage from the first climax of *Henry VIII*, the earl of Buckingham's discovery of his entrapment, gains its power from the terse and abbreviated form. The absence of conjunctions gives the speech a sense of finality, a businesslike gravity: the impression is that there is no more to say. In *Pericles*, the wonder and scarcely expressible joy of the hero's awakening arise partly from a similar kind of omission in his epiphanic lines to Helicanus: "strike me, honored sir, / Give me a gash, put me to present pain." Pericles until this point has refused to speak at all: here, rather like Coriolanus (if for different reasons), he confines himself to as few words as possible. When such tactics become habitual they can have a powerful impact on the sound of an entire play. As John Porter Houston has convincingly shown, the syntax of *Cymbeline* is significantly looser than that of plays preceding it, partly because it contains seventy-eight instances of asyndetic construction, nearly twice as many as *King Lear* and *Antony and Cleopatra*, which themselves have more than the earlier tragedies.[27] Asyndeton works by means of juxtaposition rather than coupling, thereby depriving the auditor of the security of clear logical relations. As a result, many passages in a play like *Cymbeline* can give the impression that the inattentive poet is merely piecing phrases together without regard for sequence or interrelation.

The narrative syntax of the late plays also works asyndetically. *Pericles* is the most obvious instance of what might be called serial construction, although the explanatory interventions of Gower serve to lessen the shock of the juxtaposed events. Here, as in romance fiction generally, the narrative sequence eschews logic. Connectives are suppressed, leaving the plot full of temporal and geographical gaps, and these lapses are challenging and exhilarating. Many of the stories, like the verse sentence, engage the audience in a process of mystery and solution, offering riddles and secrets and concluding with the restoration of losses. And even though *Henry VIII* is less a romance than a history, it also strikingly displays a version of such serial construction: major episodes from different times in the Henrician age have been strung together with little transition or attempt to cover the anachronisms or impossibilities. The force of the narrative and grammatical movement seems to validate the authenticity of the historical pageant: *All is True*.

Linkage of two clauses by a conjunction or another relational term often permits a part of the second clause to be eliminated with scant loss

---

[27] John Porter Houston, *Shakespearean Sentences: A Study in Style and Syntax* (Baton Rouge: Louisiana State University Press, 1988), p. 198.

of clarity. In his first appearance in *Coriolanus*, Martius declares that "The rabble should have first unroof'd the city / Ere [*they should have*] so prevail'd with me" (1.1.222–23). Such ellipsis often entails the omission of verbs, as in the following compressed passages from *The Tempest*:

> On their sustaining garments not a blemish,
> But fresher than before.   (1.2.218–19)

In this instance, the first clause lacks a verbal phrase (*there is*), as does the second (*the garments are*). Similarly, in the introductory conditional clauses that Ferdinand blurts out to Miranda,

> O, if a virgin,
> And your affection not gone forth, I'll make you
> The Queen of Naples.   (1.2.448–50)

the first verb and the auxiliary of the second are both deleted.

A characteristic Shakespearean form of compression substitutes a present participle for a longer, more explicit clause or phrase. *The Winter's Tale* is full of such cases, as when Leontes shamefully confesses his attempt to make Camillo kill Polixenes:

> I with death and with
> Reward did threaten and encourage him,
> Not doing it and being done. (3.2.160–62)

To paraphrase: "I threatened him with death if he refused to do it, and I encouraged him with the prospect of reward if he agreed to do it." The logical integument between "not doing" and the "him" on which it depends is initially vague, and the prepositional phrase that would explain "being done" (i.e., "by him") is dropped. Moreover, the shift of voice (from "doing" to "being done") is also perplexing, since it violates the parallelism established in the previous lines. A similar shift marks Florizel's profession to Camillo of his love for Perdita, despite the opposition of his father:

> Why look you so upon me?
> I am but sorry, not afeard; delay'd,
> But nothing alt'red: what I was, I am:
> More straining on for plucking back, not following
> My leash unwillingly.   (4.4.463–67)

Here the effect of manipulated participles is especially telling. In line 466, "straining" modifies "I am" in the previous line, but "plucking," which seems grammatically parallel, is actually inconsistent: Florizel is *being* plucked back, not plucking back himself. The elimination of the noun gives such participles "an absolute status," according to Norman Blake, who thinks it possible that the convenience of the ablative absolute in Latin may have prompted the development of this form.[28] Whether or not this is the origin, Shakespeare's structure in such cases almost certainly derives from the same impulse toward economy that made the absolute construction a staple of Latin verse and prose.

Participles and infinitives deserve particular attention. Their function in the late style is often to stand in for more ample clauses:

> the party tried
> The daughter of a king (*The Winter's Tale* 3.2.2–3)

> If't please the queen to send the babe,
> I know not what I shall incur to pass it,
> Having no warrant. (*The Winter's Tale* 2.2.56–58)

In the first example, the defendant has not yet been brought to trial: "to be" is implied between "party" and "tried." In the second, the omission is more extensive: the infinitive phrase "to pass it" stands in for something like "by permitting it to pass, if I should do so." As a reductive instrument, the participle frequently creates semantic difficulty: in the words of Manfred Görlach, the distinguished historian of the language, "The increase in concision is often achieved at the price of greater obscurity because some syntactical relations tend to become opaque in non-finite forms."[29] The example Görlach offers is "the shooting of the hunters," which conveys any number of different meanings depending on context. In other words, when normal relational pointers are eliminated the listener must work hard to avoid becoming confused.

A more complicated form combines participles, a practice that increases as Shakespeare gains experience. According to the linguist Y. M. Biese:

The average number of compound participles (having gone) in plays of the second period thus works out at about three times higher than in the earlier group. Here *Coriolanus* with six, *Cymbeline* with five, and *Pericles*, *Winter's Tale*, and *Tempest* with four examples each may be said to be typical of the later group of plays . . . compound participles seem to be more frequent in Shakespeare's later works than they are in his early writings.

---

[28] N. F. Blake, *Shakespeare's Language: An Introduction* (London: Macmillan, 1983), p. 102.

[29] Manfred Görlach, *Introduction to Early Modern English* (Cambridge: Cambridge University Press, 1991), p. 127.

This observation is well in accord with the fact that the compound participle with *having* was a construction which established itself in the English language during Shakespeare's lifetime.[30]

A clear example of this compound participle characterizes Miranda's sympathetic lines to Ferdinand about the log he has been made to carry, "when this burns, / 'Twill weep for having wearied you" (*The Tempest* 3.1.18–19). Having threatened the reader's patience in isolating these means of concentration and intensification, I turn to a passage combining several of these tactics, hoping that a more extended sampling will help convey the flavor of the late style.

Various elliptical tactics frequently join to yield a passage of extreme concentration. Among the exaggerated sequence of recognitions in the last scene of *Cymbeline*, one of the most entertaining occurs when the banished Belarius and his two charges, the king's stolen sons, think they recognize the youth ("Fidele") whom they have adopted, found dead, and then buried in the wilds of Wales.

BEL.	Is not this boy reviv'd from death?	120
ARV.	One sand another	
	Not more resembles that sweet rosy lad	
	Who died, and was Fidele. What think you?	
GUI.	The same dead thing alive.	
BEL.	Peace, peace, see further. He eyes us not, forbear.	
	Creatures may be alike; were't he, I am sure	125
	He would have spoke to us.	
GUI.	But we see him dead.	
BEL.	Be silent; let's see further.	

(5.5.120–27)

As the Arden2 editor remarks in his note on this passage, "the ellipsis accords with Shakespeare's later style."[31] Many of the usual devices for achieving compression appear here. Arviragus's terse "What think you?" (122) provokes his brother's verbless "The same dead thing alive" (123), simple expressions that may make their speakers seem rustic. Belarius's admonitions of patience (124–26) are expressed in a paratactic series of imperatives and cautious observations, and the editorial differences on how to punctuate these lines, whether to separate clauses by colons (Folio)

---

[30] Y. M. Biese, "Notes on the Compound Participle in the Works of Shakespeare and his Contemporaries," *Academia Scientiarum Fennica*, 63, no. 1 (1949), 7.

[31] J. M. Nosworthy, *Cymbeline*, p. 178n.

or periods or commas or semicolons, arise from Shakespeare's asyndetic suppression of conjunctive aids. The comparison identifying the youth before them with the "dead" Fidele radically condenses the grammar of the first term, "one sand another"; does the same with the comparative verb, "not more resembles"; and then elides the "two" youths into one, leaving implicit the third of the four terms – the boy walking aside with the King. The degree to which this comparison depends upon intense concentration of means becomes apparent when we recall the similar phrase from the recognition scene in *Twelfth Night*, "An apple, cleft in two, is not more twin / Than these two creatures" (5.1.223–24).[32] Olivia's lines contain all four terms, the two halves of the apple and Cesario and Sebastian, and her grammatical structure is clearly more normative and ample than in the later, distilled version. Arviragus's collapsing of the two boys into "that sweet rosy lad" is apt given that, unlike the situation in *Twelfth Night*, the two are the same. The audience watching *Cymbeline*, in this as in other cases, especially in the last scene, is given greater cognitive responsibility.

The concentrated metaphor of the grains of sand at the center of the passage discloses the paradox of Shakespeare's poetic economy, its typical admixture of omission and supplementation. The radical brevity of "one sand another" is accompanied by "that sweet rosy lad / Who died, and was Fidele," making a sentence that is both unaccountably redundant and poetically spare. For all his efforts to reduce and distill, Shakespeare still permits himself the supererogatory verbal phrase that completes the sentence. This combination of superfluity and omission produces one of the characteristic turns of the late verse: amid the stripped-down, highly-charged construction, the audience confronts an almost entirely gratuitous word or phrase, and such abundant verbiage creates an impression of generosity, a sense of grace. This feeling of the unearned recalls Quintilian's identification of the effect of *gratiam*.

The suggestiveness of the diction employed is significant as well, especially because the remaining words transport the listener, by means of allusion, back through the play to other significant moments and phrases. The sand image recalls Iachimo's "twinn'd stones / Upon the number'd beach" (1.6.35–36), a phrase occurring in a speech praising Imogen; alternatively, it evokes the hourglass on which the providential scheme of the play depends. "Sweet rosy lad" suggests the flowers on the

---

[32] Nosworthy calls attention to the relevance of this earlier passage in his notes to *Cymbeline*, p. 178.

grave of the "dead" Fidele. Guiderius's "the same dead thing alive" is uncommonly pregnant in its overtones: at the opening of the play Cymbeline has condemned his daughter as a "disloyal *thing*," Cloten has been derided in the first scene as "a *thing* / Too bad for bad report," and the oxymoronic modifiers surrounding the noun in the phrase "dead *thing* alive" apply generally to Posthumus, Imogen/Fidele, and Cymbeline's Britain. Finally, the polysemic opportunities of the repeated "peace" resound beyond the immediate conversation to encompass both the international and the sexual politics of the play. Such attention to connotation seems easily warranted here: given Shakespeare's determination to omit, the language that remains becomes uncommonly resonant. The mystifying tendencies of a pared-down verbal style are intensified by the complementary effects of density and allusiveness in the words on which the poet puts the weight. In this passage especially, the ellipticality of the lines is notable because they are dialogic: the abbreviated style has become part of the fabric of the whole.

Typically, the most elliptical and therefore demanding language sounds in longer speeches by single characters, but these need not necessarily be the operatic outbursts. Florizel's entrance lines in *The Winter's Tale* are fundamentally expository, and yet he introduces himself in highly concentrated sentences. Shakespeare repeats his by-now familiar practice of beginning scenes and even whole plays in the middle of a conversation already in progress: one recalls Iago and Roderigo, or the dispute between Philo and Demetrius that opens *Antony and Cleopatra* ("Nay, but this dotage of our general's"). At the beginning of the sheep-shearing the disorienting start is reinforced by the intense concentration of the verse. In other words, the audience is not slowly and comfortably oriented to the narrative facts of the scene:

> These your unusual weeds to each part of you
> Does give a life; no shepherdess, but Flora
> Peering in April's front. This your sheep-shearing
> Is as a meeting of the petty gods,
> And you the queen on't.   (4.4.1–5)

Notable omissions include the verbless construction of lines 2 and 3, "no shepherdess, but Flora / Peering in April's front," the elimination of the verb in the last line, and the elision of "on it." The substitution of phrases for clauses, or the dependence upon verbless constructions, introduces both velocity and weight, a mixture that requires attention on the part of the listener and enhances the impression of sincerity. This is a telling passage because the elliptical verse does not represent an exceptional dramatic moment, neither a mind in crisis nor a sudden outburst nor a heart at odds with itself. On the contrary, the omissions characterize a speech that is conversational, affectionate, unremarkable.

METRICS: SURFEIT AND SCARCITY

For all its fierce abridgements, the late line is also heavy with surplus. In Florizel's speech just cited, ellipsis is matched with supplementation: grammatical gaps go hand in hand with metrical surplus and poetic patterning. Of the four complete lines, three are hypermetrical. The first is egregiously so in that even with "unusual" elided to three syllables, the line scarcely manages to contain its eleven syllables. It may be paradoxical that such a complex line as the first tends to accelerate rather than retard the speaker's progress. In other words, the speaker and auditor are confronted with so many syllables that the line requires a kind of auditory ellipsis in which unstressed syllables, "your un," "ual," "to each," huddle together in subjection to the stressed. This is what Frank Kermode means when he refers to the "ghostly" quality of the iambic pentameter.[33] The speed and propulsion of the lines are aided by familiar tactics of repetition, especially assonance and consonance. The two sentences begin more or less anaphorically ("These your," "This your"). An extraordinary degree of internal rhyme sounds in this brief declaration, especially on *e*: "these," "weeds," "each," "Peering," "sheep-shearing," "meeting," "queen"; "your unusual," "to . . . you," "Is as a."[34] The speech also benefits from consonantal energy, referred to by Stephen Booth as "pulsating alliteration," in which consonants split apart and join together, as in the workings of *p* and *r* and *l* and *f* in the phrase "Flora / Peering in April's front."[35] Such unifying sounds help to bridge the gaps that result from ellipsis, compensating for what has been discarded and enhancing the impression of concentration and contained power.

[33] Introduction to *The Tempest* (London: Methuen, 1954), p. lxxix.

[34] Aware of the uncertainties about early modern pronunciation, I would suggest that there are enough instances of aural resemblance in this and many other passages to make the possible exceptions relatively unimportant.

[35] Stephen Booth, *An Essay on Shakespeare's Sonnets* (New Haven: Yale University Press, 1968), p. 89. In identifying and assessing the contribution of this technique, Booth develops a stylistic insight described earlier by, among others, Kenneth Burke. See "On Musicality in Verse," *The Philosophy of Literary Form* (New York: Random House, 1941), pp. 296–304.

Metrically, phonetically, syntactically, semantically, the mature verse is overloaded and repetitious as Shakespeare insists on crowding the condensed line with additional syllables. The metrical irregularity is generated not only by elimination but also by the high proportion of extrametrical lines. In the early plays, not surprisingly, the average line is far more regular: only one in every ten has an extra syllable. The late plays, however, are exorbitantly hypermetrical: one in every three lines contains at least eleven syllables, and some include as many as thirteen.[36] We can return momentarily to an instance cited earlier, Leontes' "Not doing it, and being done. He, most humane"; in this case, participial abbreviation concentrates a line that also enlarges to the length of an alexandrine. George T. Wright comments on the effect of such excess, looking back to an earlier Tudor model: "Like Wyatt, [Shakespeare] may have realized that a line could gain in richness of sound and sense if its meter trips hurriedly over some syllables, as if the thought or feeling of the speaking character were fuller than its words could quite articulate. To write ten-syllable lines that have, in a sense, eleven or twelve syllables (or eleven and a half) is to crowd the air with meanings only half-spoken, partly concealed. The hypermetrical half-syllables imply that, just as the line contains more in the way of syllables than the meter promises, so too in the meanings conveyed by the words there is more than meets the ear."[37] Wright's reference to the great Henrician innovator is significant in light of Shakespeare's reading at this late stage of his career.[38]

Often repeated consonants and vowels contribute a definite sense of poetic surfeit. Exaggerated assonance and consonance are acoustic hallmarks of the late plays, a topic to be taken up in Chapter 5. For now, one example will suffice, Prospero's reference to Ariel's tree-trap:

> within which rift
> Imprison'd thou didst painfully remain
> A dozen years, within which space she died,
> And left thee there, where thou didst vent thy groans
> As fast as mill-wheels strike. (1.2.277–81)

My fonts only gesture at the extraordinarily poetic sound of the excerpt. In passage after passage, not only letters but also words and even whole

---

[36] For detailed treatment of this increase and its effect on auditory reception, see George T. Wright, *Shakespeare's Metrical Art* (Berkeley: University of California Press, 1988), especially chapters 9 and 11.

[37] *Ibid.*, p. 158.

[38] See Chapter 6, below.

phrases are repeated, and the resounding of these verbal units creates a musical design connoting extravagance and even luxury. Lines are too long, patterns of sound seem prodigal, there seems to be too much to say. It is not merely that the techniques of *brevitas* are accompanied by those of *amplificatio*: the more salient point is that they are functions of the same impulse, the urge to include as much as possible.

The mutual effects of spareness and superfluity create a contradictory dynamic that gives the late line its peculiar acoustic and intellectual energies. This contest between the subtraction and addition of poetic elements is part of a larger rhythmic competition between, on the one hand, the forces of regularity, conformity, and pattern, and, on the other, the forces of chaos, deviance, and individuality.[39] The conflict between the authority of the pattern and the rebellion implied in aberration gives iambic pentameter its dynamic utility. In the rhythm of stressed and unstressed sounds, in the struggle between the semantic claims of the English sentence and the formal demands of the pentameter line we find inscribed an aural version of those power relations represented in the personal and political conflicts of the narrative. Moreover, the diminution of one rhythmic pattern is accompanied by the augmentation of others.

From about 1607 Shakespeare appears to increase various formal co-agulants partly as a check on his urge towards metrical and grammatical audacity. As the iambic repetitions become less audible, as the holes in the line threaten its integrity and regularity, the poet magnifies other forms of identity and coherence, particularly the repetition of vowels, consonants, words, syntactic shapes, narrative patterns. The poetry calls attention to itself, reminding us of its status as verse and asserting its power to maintain order and sense while permitting extravagant deviation. The reverberation of the doubled sounds is thus comparable in effect to ordering efforts in the plot: the matching of narrative episodes and characters in *The Winter's Tale*, for instance, or the parallel usurpation plots in *The Tempest*. Helen Cooper, looking at the romances in the context of medieval tradition, describes the function of narrative symmetry:

The dramatization of longer romances made it especially important to solve the management of episodic structure, and it was often done through . . . processes of parallelisms and symmetry rather than through the kind of organic unity

---

[39] As Wright puts it, "Meter stands (but not simply) for some such principle as order, truth, certainty, completeness – doom; deviation is energy, mischief, trouble – and beauty" (*Shakespeare's Metrical Art*, p. 261).

privileged by nineteenth-century critics. Attention to plot structure in such plays can often therefore be more revealing than characterization or plausibility of action.[40]

She goes on to add, speaking of *Pericles*, that the "sprawl of place and time and the irrelevance of human intention is offset by the precision of its symmetries of structure."[41] Poetically, we hear in the line the same tension between threatened disorder and insistent patterning, and this conflict, whether poetic or structural, hints at one of the fundamental features of the romances, Shakespeare's late preference for the presentational over the representational, for the artificial over the "natural."

RABBATE AND ROMANCE

To scrutinize this inventory of elliptical tactics and to consider the meanings and effects of compression is to be reminded that Shakespeare in the last plays is seldom concerned with consistency of character or with verisimilar speech appropriate to particular persons. Rather, he devotes his attention to the dramatic fable and the meanings precipitated from those conflicts.[42] Recognition of this practice offers a way around the greatest obstacle to understanding the style of the late plays, the desire to explain its irregularities and turbulence in terms of character: when the verse gets rocky, then Prospero or Posthumus or Leontes is said to be under stress, probably raving, and thus difficult to follow. This mimetic account of auditory effects is ultimately an extension of the old-fashioned argument about character, and will be taken up in more detail in Chapter 3. Local interpretation of particularly complex passages is hardly inadmissible, but we must be aware that Shakespeare uses similar effects for different reasons depending upon the dramatic circumstances. We will do better to examine the late style, particularly its irregularity and obliquity, in light of the kinds of stories to which he was attracted and for which he developed such a medium.

---

[40] Helen Cooper, *The English Romance in Time: Transforming Motifs from Geoffrey of Monmouth to the Death of Shakespeare* (Oxford: Oxford University Press, 2004), p. 64.

[41] *Ibid.*, p. 65.

[42] See Introduction, pp. 33–34, and Anne Barton, *Essays, Mostly Shakespearean* (Cambridge: Cambridge University Press, 1994), p. 180. Martin Butler accepts this feature as a given of the late style in his Introduction to the New Cambridge *Cymbeline* (Cambridge University Press, 2005): "Frequently its speakers seem divorced from their own verse, striving after notions that they can barely find words to articulate" (p. 19).

If a highly compressed poetic idiom at first seems incompatible with the expansive narrative form of the last plays, reflection suggests that the abbreviated style is probably a function of some of the same motives – the desire to include more, and still more – that impelled Shakespeare towards the extravagant pleasures of theatrical romance in the first place.[43] Like most of the works in the traditions from which he developed them, his romances exhibit a striking architectural looseness: the multiple episodes that make up the long and complicated stories are very casually linked. *Pericles, Cymbeline,* and *The Winter's Tale,* for example, are notorious for their narrative, spatial, and temporal disjunctions. Near the middle of each play the plot changes direction abruptly and thus, in Puttenham's words, "makes a great gappe in the tale."[44] Even *The Tempest* manages to evoke narrative and spatial amplitude through a series of conventional romantic devices, including shipwreck, its fabulous creatures, and the theophany implied in Prospero's masque. All these plays bear traces of two kinds of structure common to the several European traditions of romance: the linear, iterative form, deriving from stories founded on the quest and described by Northrop Frye as the "and then" type; and the circular, returning form, in which characters and events owe much less to sequence and more to chance, although chance regularly sees to it that ends become beginnings and that which is lost is found.[45] Shakespeare has assimilated and recombined both forms.

The correspondence between the formal difficulties of the late style and the larger units of narrative arrangement is illuminated if we think of the distribution of episodes as a kind of architectural grammar. The elliptical approach to poetic utterance finds its structural counterpart in the spatial and temporal faults for which romance is notorious. The fissures in the grammatical and syntactical structures, the elliptical phrases that require an audience to fill in the blanks and thus complete the sense, represent the stylistic equivalent of narrative discontinuity, "this wide gap of time" in *The Winter's Tale* being the most explicit (5.3.154). In the episodic *Pericles,* with its single wide gap and multiple small ones, the serial construction

---

[43] See Patrica A. Parker, *Inescapable Romance: Studies in the Poetics of a Mode* (Princeton: Princeton University Press, 1979), p. 63.

[44] *The Arte of English Poesie,* pp. 180–81.

[45] Frye's linear model is found in both *The Anatomy of Criticism* (Princeton: Princeton University Press, 1957), and in *A Natural Perspective: The Development of Shakespearean Comedy and Romance* (New York: Columbia University Press, 1965). Suzanne Gossett also comments helpfully on the question of structure in her Introduction to the Arden edition of *Pericles* (London: Thomson Learning, 2004). For further reflections on these two modes of organization, see Cooper, *The English Romance in Time,* Barbara Fuchs, *Romance* (London: Routledge, 2004), and Parker, *Inescapable Romance.*

transgresses both chronological and logical sequence. The dramatist posits no *necessary* connection between the sinister events at Antioch and the hero's rescue of the starving Tharsans. The pirates who burst into theatrical being to abduct Marina from her would-be killer represent an especially outlandish instance of chance's intervention in scene after scene. The plot is full of logical holes: why doesn't Thaisa go in search of Pericles after Cerimon has revived her? Why does Pericles not return to collect Marina before she has become a young woman? There may be hidden motives, as Barber and Wheeler propose: "Pericles does not go to see his daughter for fourteen years, an avoidance unexplained and unremarked, though consistent with fear of repeating Antiochus's sin."[46] In any case, the effect of these narrative suspensions is similar to that of the gaps in the verse. Even as we participate emotionally in the wanderings of the characters, we also stand apart from their trials while attempting to make sense of the larger picture we are permitted to survey. We respond similarly to the omissions and displacements that threaten semantic clarity and metrical regularity. In processing the story and the poetic sentences through which it emerges, the audience learns to exercise what students of romance refer to as "radical perspectivism."[47]

Shakespeare's romances owe much to narrative devices that share a common form, that of the mystery or riddle. The typically gnomic quality of the riddle that initiates the action in *Pericles* establishes a narrative pattern that Shakespeare will develop in the ensuing plays: something is missing; the audience, thanks to the intervention of Gower, has been provided with the missing element; the protagonist must "resolve" the riddle. In fact this problem is especially fascinating because the lack, the missing answer, derives from a surplus: "He's father, son, and husband mild; / I mother, wife – and yet his child" (1.1.68–69). The essence of the riddle is that father and daughter are more to each other than they should be. This formal conundrum is echoed, of course, in the famous language of the recognition scene, as both Pericles and Marina seek to repair the familial losses they have suffered. Marina, for example, defines her orphaned state as something of a mathematical problem: "she speaks, / My lord, that, may be, hath endur'd a grief / Might equal yours, if both were justly weigh'd" (5.1.86–88); her forebears "stood equivalent with mighty kings"; alone and without title, she is at a loss. As Pericles seeks

---

[46] C. L. Barber and Richard Wheeler, *The Whole Journey: Shakespeare's Power of Development* (Berkeley: University of California Press, 1986), p. 310.
[47] See Parker, *Inescapable Romance*, p. 90.

to learn her history, his interrogation of her reverses the questions put to him in the opening episode. Moreover, the need for clarifying the obscure, for understanding the elliptical, is a driving force behind Pericles' attempt to discover his destiny. Throughout the action the emphasis is on the interrogative or the mysterious, from Thaisa's explication of the foreign knights' emblems to Cerimon's mastery of "secret art" (3.2.32) to Diana's deliberately veiled promises in the dream vision.

The solution to virtually all the riddles and prophecies entails restoration of something lost. The oracle in *The Winter's Tale* restores Hermione's good name in apodictic language, its plain prose in contrast to the elliptical, tortured verse that has preceded it. But it riddlingly leaves open the possible return of Perdita, the finding of "that which is lost," the hole in the family and gap in the royal sequence ("the king shall live without an heir"). The book that Jupiter leaves behind after the vision in the last act of *Cymbeline* obliquely promises Posthumus joy and Britain prosperity, and the Soothsayer's "reading" of that prophecy is amusingly juxtaposed to his erroneous interpretation of a dream of Roman victory described in 4.2. The god's appearance to the grieving Leonati fills a teleological gap and corresponds to the similar vision of Queen Katherine in *Henry VIII*. Cranmer's prophetic blessing of Elizabeth at the end of that play carefully praises her for continuing the royal line and passing on to James in an unbroken chain the blessings of her reign, the grammatically linked but problematic "Peace, plenty, love, truth, terror."[48]

Structurally speaking, the looseness of a play like *Cymbeline* is attributable to various locations and temporal settings that are, in Puttenham's phrase, without "good band or coupling." The leaps forward of sixteen years in *The Winter's Tale* and an equivalent period in *Pericles*, facetiously referred to by Gower the presenter as "our fast-growing scene," function in the narrative as grammatical lacunae do in the sentence.[49] The several rhetorical terms for omission or ellipsis belong to a linguistic network that clarifies the relation between narrative and syntactical grammar. These

---

[48] It should be noted, although it scarcely alters the argument here, that this line comes from a segment of the play probably written by Fletcher.

[49] The abutting of any two scenes might be considered to some extent disjunctive: when one group of characters leaves the stage and is succeeded by another, the maneuvers that our brains perform in relating those two groups and their respective concerns are equivalent to the mental work required to connect the matter of successive sentences. Some of the relations are easily achieved: at the beginning of any speech, as at the opening of any play, we grant the speaker or dramatist a degree of latitude, assuming that the connections will come more easily as the passage proceeds. Just as the elliptical quality of the late style may be seen as an exaggerated version of all dramatic speech, so the disjunctions of romance stretch the narrative integuments characteristic of all theatrical representation.

"figures of defect," of which "eclipsis" is Puttenham's first example, produce a sentence in which something is to be understood, a term is suppressed or hidden, something is left out.[50] Further describing the asyndetic effect as that of "loose language" because its connectors are missing, the cataloguer links this device with *brachiologa*, the figure required when we "proceede by all single words, without any close or coupling, saving that a little pause or comma is given to every word."[51] An alternative term for asyndeton, especially helpful in this context, is *dissolutio*, from the Latin *solvere*, "to loosen," "to untie," "to remove." This definition suggests an uncoupling of grammatical and syntactical links, a stylistic loosening that makes greater demands on the attention and patience of the auditor, who must labor to connect the parts and "resolve" the problematic sense of the verse.

So it is with structure and story in the late plays. These fragmented romantic tales, with their divided families, perilous journeys, temporal leaps, and long-delayed recognitions, engage the audience in a tortuous pattern of separation and reunion. They take their extraordinary emotional power from the disappearance and restoration of spouses or offspring, from the tension, in other words, between loss and restitution. In dramatizing these disappearances and returns, Shakespeare plays it different ways, exploiting this anxiety sometimes for irony and sometimes for surprise. On the one hand, the audience witnesses Thaisa's recovery and is privy to the identity of the Bohemian shepherdess, but, on the other, remains ignorant of Hermione's return. In each case a major figure drops out of the text, and what is required is faith in the possibility of restoration. A child is lost (Marina, Perdita, Guiderius and Arviragus, Ferdinand); a spouse is banished or put away (Posthumus, Thaisa, Hermione, Queen Katherine); fraternal relations are threatened (Polixenes and Leontes, Antonio and Prospero, Sebastian and Alonso). In all these instances the family is "dissevered," to use Leontes' participle, and often some mystery or secret cause is responsible for the split. The teleology of the plays asks us to believe that explanation will be forthcoming, that the missing pieces will be supplied. This combination of being in the know

---

[50] Often the omitted term is conjunctive, as in Puttenham's illustration of asyndeton with Caesar's famous triplet, *veni, vidi, vici*, in which he points out the mimetic implications of clausal arrangement: "*Cesar* the Dictator upon the victorie hee obtained against Pharnax king of *Bithinia* showing the celeritie of his conquest, wrote home to the Senate in this tenour of speach no less swift and speedy then his victorie" (185).

[51] He then glosses brachiologa as Greek for "short language" and prescribes its use "when either we be earnest, or would seeme to make hast" (222). Both functions, a rapid pace and the impression of sincerity or solemnity, are vital to Shakespeare in the romantic mode.

and being in the dark, a function of the dramatist's manipulation of both irony and surprise, corresponds to the complementary effects I have described in the verse line – too much and too little.[52]

Gaps demand bridges, and bridges imply faith. The characters' attempts to repair broken bonds often require that they "solve" the mystery, piece together the logical fragments that will reveal the truth, or correct the misunderstanding that initially dissolved the union. Familial or marital reunion ties up the loose ends of the play, bestowing on the audience an emotional resolution all the more powerful for the difficulty of bringing it about.[53] Those moments of gratification are the narrative equivalent of the small cognitive victories that result from close attention to the loose syntactical style. Throughout the late plays, Shakespeare appears to take some pleasure in testing his audience's patience by suppressing those features that would assist comprehension and guarantee progress through both verse sentences and narrative obstacles. Remembering Puttenham's contention that "the eare may receive a certaine recreation" from perceiving the omission and then supplying the missing term, we may apply that principle to Shakespeare's disposition of his scenes. In *Cymbeline*, for example, the entrance of Belarius and his two "sons" in 3.3 offers the audience a form of "recreation" – a pleasure trip to Wales. There the introduction of an unknown set of characters offers a playful challenge to an audience's sense of coherence. Clues have been laid, of course, as to the identity of the boys, and indeed some members of the audience would have been aware already that historically King Kymbeline was succeeded by his own son, but Shakespeare briefly withholds confirmation, just as he sometimes teases the audience grammatically by delaying a needed predicate or refusing to complete a syntactical connection. Stylistically and theatrically, the mood of these fictions is both mysterious and gamesome.

TESTING

Insouciance about the difficulties of the elliptical style is characteristic of Shakespeare's cavalier attitude towards the inconsistencies and disjunctions that mark his last plots and persons, and he exploits thematically the tendency of the style to mystify the audience or test its acuity. The

---

[52] For the classic statement about the complementary effects of suspense and irony in fiction generally, see Wayne Booth, *The Rhetoric of Fiction* (Chicago: University of Chicago Press, 1961), p. 255. Also see Philip Edwards, "The Danger not the Death: The Art of John Fletcher," in *Jacobean Theatre*, ed. John Russell Brown and Bernard Harris (London: Edward Arnold, 1960), p. 164.

[53] On this point see Terence Cave, *Recognitions: A Study in Poetics* (Oxford: Clarendon Press, 1988), p. 286.

listener's capacity for filling up holes and constructing bridges over elliptical passages depends upon faith in the value of doing so. The terse complexity of the late style demands of the auditor the same kind of patience and faith required by the deviations and syntactical disruptions discussed above. As logical connectives are removed and passages from clause to clause made more difficult, the listener must work harder, concentrate more intently on a more concentrated form of verse.

The omissions and abridgments in the late style are valuable indicators of a mode of thought, an authorial attitude towards fiction that accounts for the much-discussed "sophistication" of Shakespearean romance. Instead of the escapist art in which the reader is comfortably led through the contortions and complexities of the narrative, Shakespeare creates a more knowing and mature kind of fiction and fosters a more acute kind of spectator. This self-conscious romance implicates the audience in the process of testing often associated with the hero of romance narrative, as in the trials of Pericles, for instance. Narrative satisfaction, the fate of missing characters, philosophical perspective – all are provided by the authorial figure, agent of irony and closure who may or may not have an obvious surrogate or mediator, such as Gower or Prospero, but who can be counted on as guide and interpreter. Confidence in such a Providential figure supports the audience stylistically, carrying listeners through the ellipses and permitting them to confront and master the strangeness and difficulties of the style. In other words, when the semantic bottom drops out of a speech or sentence, we retain our hope for eventual clarification, just as, when Dionyza unaccountably turns murderous, we still believe in Marina's eventual rescue and reunion with father and mother. As Paulina puts it before the revival of Hermione, "You must awake your faith." The action of moving through the syntactic tangle requires the same patience and belief that govern our response to the dramatic narrative. The need to wait for the fullness of time is as important grammatically as it is theatrically. And the loss of syllables and semantic pointers creates a dynamic struggle within the sentence, a linguistic conflict that mimics the larger contest for narrative and hermeneutic satisfaction. Ellipsis at the very least speeds us along, forcing us to become more attentive and percipient lest we miss something important; and usually it does more than that, threatening us with the loss of coherence or understanding, the restoration of which creates added and apparently unwarranted pleasure.[54]

---

[54] Paul Fussell makes a related point about the workings of poetic contraction in Augustan poetry. "There is evidence, in fact, that the contemporary reader of 18th-c. poetry derived much of his

The mature Shakespeare intensifies the *gratiam*, heightening the impact of our cognitive successes and thus generating a sense of unlooked for satisfaction, a feeling of grace. Although he makes the act of comprehension more taxing by exaggerating the number and the difficulty of omissions, he also generously exceeds the terms of the contract by increasing the aural and theatrical rewards. In each line the audience is deprived of essentials, and yet rescued from incomprehension and showered with poetic pleasures. So in the stories the characters and the audience get more than they expect and usually more than they deserve – the unlooked-for reunion of father, daughter, and wife in *Pericles*, the similar rejoicing at the end of *The Winter's Tale*, Alonso's recovery of Ferdinand and an unexpected daughter in the last act of *The Tempest*, the birth of the infant Elizabeth in *Henry VIII*.

ELISION AND ILLUSION

Grace, belief, recreation – the nouns I have applied to the style and the dramatic structure serve as markers for Shakespeare's refreshed approach, after about 1607, to both the process and the objects of representation. The contests between narrative omission and dilation and between poetic ellipsis and pleonasm may be seen as manifestations of the mature poet's profound ambivalence towards his own medium: that is, the tension between addition and omission corresponds to the mature Shakespeare's simultaneous devotion to language and desire to do without it. The verbal treachery that grounds such tragedies as *Lear* and *Macbeth* is balanced by an acknowledgement of the affirmative possibilities of language, so that doubts are assimilated into a more capacious view of human expression, one that recognizes the duplicity of words while insisting on their compensatory power. *Antony and Cleopatra* is the pivotal text in this respect, the work that appears to have liberated Shakespeare's imagination and moved him beyond the professional impasse that seems to be implicit in *King Lear* or *Timon*.[55] Such a new assessment of the medium entails both fear and pleasure: doubts about the unreliability of verbal signs and

---

aesthetic delight from his deliberate and conscious 'regularizing,' through contraction, of normally irregular phonetic materials." "Poetic Contraction," in *The Princeton Encyclopedia of Poetry and Poetics*, ed. Alex Preminger et al. (Princeton: Princeton University Press, 1993), p. 628.

[55] See Janet Adelman, *Suffocating Mothers* (London: Methuen, 1991), pp. 191–92: "In thus realigning masculinity with the maternal, Shakespeare is able to see his way beyond the either/or of *Macbeth* and *Coriolanus*, and beyond the end-stopped genre of tragedy. The whole of *Antony and Cleopatra* overflows the measure; in its interpretative openness, its expansive playfulness, its imaginative

fascination with their constructive capacity. This conflict is a Shakespearean version of the great conflict between Baconian skepticism and Elizabethan enthusiasm, disputes over linguistic purity, verbal ornament, "natural" expression, the masculine strength of the plain style, the harlotry of theatrical words. The complementarity of ellipsis and surplus would seem to combine the linguistic biases of Bacon and Ascham, of Coriolanus and Cleopatra: on the one hand, the wish to fly from words, to do without language altogether, and on the other the corresponding desire to luxuriate in its material and imaginative pleasures.

Stylistic virtuosity is a sign not only of Shakespeare's reconceived ideas about language but also of his new and sophisticated commitment to virtuality. Although we cannot know for certain, we may guess at some of the sources of this professional reorientation: Shakespeare's creation of Cleopatra, and her creative dream of Antony; his imaginative realignment of the masculine and the feminine; a new theatrical space in which to work; the revival of romance on the London stage around 1607; the tragicomic novelties of Beaumont and Fletcher; old age; the desire of a poet who, in Stephen Booth's analogy, having mastered and grown bored with juggling balls, wants to try hatchets.[56] What is indisputable is Shakespeare's renewed appreciation for the beneficent power of illusion. The lies and shams and cosmetics of the tragedies become, in the last phase, pleasing fictions and spectacles and ornaments. But we must remember, so as not to resurrect the rosy-tinted, Victorian view of Edward Dowden, that this altered conception is not uniformly affirmative. Shakespeare retains a double vision about what he does and how he does it. In other words, he embraces the mode of romance and yet emphasizes its unreality, laments the danger of words and yet celebrates their constructive capacities, imagines an alternative world but mocks it at the same time and then whisks it away. The poet who makes the extravagant line is also the fabulist who invents the theatrical world of romance and the playwright who distributes its narrative events. And the symbiosis of contraction and surplus in the verse provides the audience's initial physical contact with this making and unmaking of the world.

abundance, it seems to me to lead directly to *The Winter's Tale*, where trust in female process similarly bursts the boundaries of the tragic form."

[56] Discussion with secondary teachers, Folger Shakespeare Library, July 1993.

CHAPTER 3

Syntax (I): divagation

Not that *Cymbeline* is a lucid play; its language prevents it being that.

Frank Kermode[1]

"I have observed," wrote the linguist H. C. Wyld in 1919, that syntax is one of those "branches of English studies which many people consider important for somebody else to tackle."[2] Reluctance to generalize about verbal arrangement, even the fundamental conventions of word ordering, has persisted in the community of linguistic scholars and grammarians, and literary critics have partaken of their colleagues' diffidence, thanks in part to the additional complications deriving from the conditions of poetry and drama. If experts hesitate to address the topic of word order in basic speech, expository writing, or prose narrative, then the dearth of commentary about the syntactical properties of Shakespearean blank verse is easily pardoned.

The challenge is especially formidable in confronting the late plays, experts and beginners alike having concurred that the highly complicated syntax of the poetry constitutes one of its most perplexing features, perhaps the major obstacle to comprehension and appreciation. Meaning often seems hampered by circumlocution, capricious placement of words and larger verbal units, starts and stops, and consequent semantic obscurity. The syntax of this phase resists precise description because it encompasses so many different forms: short sentences and long sentences; hypotaxis and parataxis; ordinary conversation and emotional outbursts; inversions and inverted inversions; omission and pleonasm; simplicity and artifice. Moreover, the potential difficulties of the syntax are magnified

---

[1] Frank Kermode, *Shakespeare: The Final Plays*, British Writers and their Work (London: Longmans, Green, 1963), p. 22.
[2] From the Preface to his *A History of Modern Colloquial English*, cited in Bengt Jacobssen, *Inversion in English, With Special Reference to the Early Modern Period* (Uppsala: Almqvist & Wiksells, 1951), p. 7.

by the effects of ellipsis described in the preceding chapter. Such inclusiveness and contradiction have defeated most efforts to label the late style, a challenge that corresponds to the problem of what the late plays ought to be called. So nobody has said much about Shakespearean syntax.

PRELIMINARIES

Commentary on syntactical forms is impeded by a number of particular challenges, beginning with the printing history of the late plays. For each title, the existence of only one authoritative text has reduced editorial possibilities: without a choice among versions and therefore without contemporaneous alternative readings, editors and annotators have been especially bold in their willingness to tamper with what they do not comprehend or approve of. Keir Elam laments such editorial tinkering, illustrating with the first sentence of the "If it were done" soliloquy from *Macbeth*, another single-text play:

the main contributions from the typographical school of thought or exegesis have been in the direction of syntactic and lexical normalizations, and range from Travers's suggesting that we are missing a full stop which would split the opening into two sentences (*then 'twere well. It were done quickly*), to Johnson's inversion of the inversion (*catch with his success, surcease*); to Theobald's correction of the printer's error *shoal* or Pope's correction of singular abstract *ingredience* into plural concrete "ingredients" (presumably an auditory error).[3]

The editorial impatience with syntactical irregularity indicated in Elam's catalogue has made appraisal of the late style all the more taxing. With *The Winter's Tale*, for example, the efforts of editors for more than two centuries to tidy up Leontes' "Affection" speech attest to the widespread wish that Shakespeare had been a little less casual in arranging his speakers' poetic sentences.[4]

Early modern punctuation introduces another layer of uncertainty. The differences between our own and our ancestors' views on pointing – one is

---

[3] Keir Elam, "Early Modern Syntax and Late Shakespearean Rhetoric," in *Early Modern English: Trends, Forms and Texts*, ed. C. Nocera Avila, N. Pantaleo, and D. Pezzini (Fasano: Schena Editore, 1992), p. 65.

[4] For a detailed treatment of this passage, see the Introduction to Stephen Orgel's edition of *The Winter's Tale* (Oxford: Oxford University Press, 1996), pp. 8–9. Orgel proposes that our difficulties with such passages may have been shared by the early modern audience, even its most literate members, and that semantic comprehension, at least in the specific sense of following and processing each clause and phrase, was not necessarily something Shakespeare expected of his auditors (pp. 6–12).

speaking very broadly here – make it exceedingly difficult to know how a verse paragraph printed in 1623 ought to be punctuated in a modern edition, how a sentence should be divided, or when the modern actor should be instructed to pause. In practice, early modern punctuation was consistently inconsistent. It appears to have been rhetorical rather than grammatical, driven usually by a desired theatrical or emotional effect, often momentary. In other words, the use of pauses, periods, and other such conventions was dictated mostly by a sense of dramatic context, not by an agreed-upon set of authorial or publishing conventions.[5] But whose sense of context? It is difficult to assign responsibility for the signals that do appear in the early texts. Do the colons, semi-colons, commas, and periods in a given quarto or in the Folio reflect the tastes of the author? Were they reproduced faithfully, often through several iterations, from the foul papers? Might a professional scribe be responsible, and if so did he have discernible preferences? Did some of the accidentals originate in the printing house, reflecting the habits of the compositor who set that part of the text? Ralph Crane, the scrivener whose fair copies of *Cymbeline*, *The Winter's Tale*, and *The Tempest* were used in the preparation of the Folio, is known to have indulged a "passion for parentheses, apostrophes and hyphens."[6] How are such variables of text production to be factored into a study of prosody, sentence length, and other such properties of style? Recognizing these limitations and admitting that no existing text is ideal for syntactical analysis, I have in this and the next chapter departed more frequently than usual from the *Riverside* text to note a feature of the earliest printed text. My doing so should not be interpreted as assigning greater authority to the punctuation in the Folio, the *Pericles* quarto (notoriously bad in many respects), or the quarto of *The Two Noble Kinsmen*. The strangeness of the original punctuation may provide

---

[5] For helpful discussion of such problems, see A. C. Partridge, *Orthography in Shakespeare and Elizabethan Drama: A Study of Colloquial Contractions, Elisions, Prosody, and Punctuation* (Lincoln: University of Nebraska Press, 1964); Jonathan Crewe, "Punctuating Shakespeare," *Shakespeare Studies* 28 (2000), 23–31; N. F. Blake, *A Grammar of Shakespeare's Language* (Houndmills: Palgrave, 2002), pp. 22–23; and Michael Warren, "Repunctuation as Interpretation in Editions of Shakespeare," *English Literary Renaissance*, 7 (1977), 155–69. A fascinating treatment of the medieval origins of early modern and modern punctuation is M. B. Parkes, "Punctuation, or Pause and Effect," in *Medieval Eloquence: Studies in the Theory and Practice of Medieval Rhetoric*, ed. James J. Murphy (Berkeley: University of California Press, 1978), pp. 127–42.

[6] MacDonald Jackson, "The Transmission of Shakespeare's Text," in *The Cambridge Companion to Shakespeare Studies*, ed. Stanley Wells (Cambridge: Cambridge University Press, 1986), p. 17. See also Stanley Wells and Gary Taylor, with John Jowett and William Montgomery, *William Shakespeare: A Textual Companion* (Oxford: Clarendon Press, 1987).

a slight advantage in making us consider the lines afresh. But to a large extent the choice is arbitrary.[7]

Most of Shakespeare's late speakers deliver themselves of sentences that seem exceptionally complex, but when it comes to the topic of syntax, it is difficult to know what is exceptional or aberrant. Historical changes in the conventions of speech and writing require us to be cautious in generalizing about "normal" grammar and thus about Shakespeare's or anyone else's variations on it. Word order in early modern English was considerably more fluid than it has become.[8] Moreover, so unfixed were many of the conventions of grammar and syntax that some practices seem to have changed markedly even during the twenty years that separate Shakespeare's first plays from his last. This historical shift introduces yet another obstacle to analysis, the difficulty of comparing his late syntax with that of his earlier styles. As a result, not only is the subject inherently difficult to discuss, but the need to identify and discriminate between two or more different syntactical modes multiplies the problems of stylistic analysis.

Certain features permit us to make fairly clear distinctions: for example, the practice of inverting the position of subject and verb – what linguists would call a VS sentence – actually decreases over the course of Shakespeare's career, as it did in English writing generally from the Tudor through the Jacobean period.[9] But often what seems distinctive about the late style is subjective, a matter of impression. I am confident, however, that the impressions generating the analysis undertaken here are reasonably faithful to the stylistic differences between the early and late plays. In other words, while I have not counted the number of sentences in *Cymbeline* that depend on aposiopesis (the breaking off of speech) and then compared that total with the number of similar occurrences in, say, *The Comedy of Errors*, there is no doubt that aposiopesis is an essential feature of Shakespeare's style in 1610 as it is not in 1592. The general rule is enunciated by Keir Elam: "the dramatist's syntax tends to get trickier as he gets older."[10] This understatement covers a broad range of complex forms.

---

[7] See Blake, *A Grammar of Shakespeare's Language*, pp. 2–7.

[8] Vivian Salmon, "Sentence Structures in Colloquial Shakespearian English," in Vivian Salmon and Edwina Burness, eds., *A Reader in the Language of Shakespearean Drama* (Amsterdam: John Benjamins, 1987), p. 268. Also see Charles Barber, *Early Modern English* (Edinburgh: Edinburgh University Press, 1997), *passim.*

[9] See John Porter Houston, *Shakespearean Sentences: A Study in Style and Syntax* (Baton Rouge: Louisiana State University Press, 1988), p. 18.

[10] "Early Modern Syntax and Late Shakespearean Rhetoric," p. 64.

All of these difficulties notwithstanding, it is possible to establish –
cautiously – a profile of the late style, and the way to begin is to say that
the plays exhibit what modern critics and editors have agreed to call "loose
syntax." The relatively unregulated word order of early modern English is
frequently exploited to the extreme: at one time or another most of the
mobile components of the sentence, especially prepositional phrases,
direct objects, and modifying phrases, are eccentrically placed. Multiple
elliptical structures of the kind discussed in Chapter 2 seem to produce
obscurity rather than clarity: these include not only minor omissions
(*o' th'*) but more potentially confusing kinds, particularly the elision of
relative pronouns, the elimination of verbs, and the creation of an
asyndetic mood – the suppression of logical process – by the deletion of
conjunctions. Interpolations, short and long, disrupt the process by which
meaning is perceived. Some utterances break off and resume in another
direction, while other sentences that would seem to have reached completion are extended, often to remarkable length, by the accretion of participial phrases and other modifiers. In many such sentences clause is piled
upon clause, with new ones correcting or reversing semantically those
which have gone before, and such revision produces a sense of nearly
constant digression. Often the listener seems barely able to hang on to the
sense.

If anyone diagrammed sentences anymore, the following passage might
be offered as a challenge.

> Could I finde out
> The womans part in me, for there's no motion
> That tends to vice in man, but I affirm
> It is the womans part: be it lying, note it,
> The woman's: flattering, hers; deceiving, hers: 175
> Lust, and rank thoughts, hers, hers: revenges hers:
> Ambitions, covetings, change of prides, disdain,
> Nice-longing, slanders, mutability;
> All faults that name, nay, that Hell knows,
> Why, hers, in part, or all: but rather all.   180
>   (*Cymbeline* 2.4.171–80; Folio punctuation)

Notorious for both its misogynistic content and its scattered, apparently
incoherent form, this excerpt exhibits many of the properties just enumerated. And in passage after passage, the strategies of compression,
amplification, and circumlocution are so abundant and so extravagant
that critical commentary has not definitely established the mechanics of
meaning. For example, in the second line quoted, readers disagree

over whether we should observe the Folio punctuation reproduced here ("The woman's part in me, for there's no motion"), or adopt Pope's substitution of a dash for F's comma ("The woman's part in me – for there's no motion"), the solution that most modern editors have chosen. It makes a slight difference. When the line is broken with a dash, the speaker's lack of control becomes immediately clear; when it is punctuated with a comma, the shift of direction seems perhaps more composed, as if something logical is to follow. At least this is one reading of the differences in punctuation.

In many of the most tangled passages, the question of responsibility becomes paramount: shouldn't the confused verbal structures be attributed not to the author but to the speaker's disordered state of mind? In speeches such as this one – the same is true of Leontes' tirades – the messy sentence structure indisputably functions to represent the tortured mind of the speaker, as critics have been quick to point out. About the jerky, difficult syntax of the *Cymbeline* excerpt, for example, the Arden editor declares simply that "Posthumus is far too angry to be coherent."[11] Similarly, critics have normally attributed the stops and starts in the extraordinary passage beginning "Ha' not you seen, Camillo / (But that's past doubt: you have, or your eye-glass / Is thicker than a cuckold's horn) or heard?" (*The Winter's Tale* 1.2.267–69) to Leontes' unstable state of mind. The grammarian Norman Blake provides a more generalized statement of this practice, arguing that the poet's resorting to parenthetical phrases "disrupts the normal order of an utterance, and this occurs frequently in the later plays for they are more adventurous in their use of structure to represent emotional turmoil."[12] Without disputing Blake's legitimate perception about Shakespeare's expanded means of representing psychological pressure, I would point out (and the examples given below will indicate) that throughout the last plays various speakers modify or supplement their utterances in the middle, regardless of context.

While Leontes' speech is an especially knotty example, syntactically speaking, the configurations that account for its intricacy are heard throughout the late style from a variety of mouths, so that reading the syntax as an index of passion or mental confusion quickly becomes untenable. As Stephen Orgel puts it, surveying the responses to an even more resistant passage, Leontes' "Affection! thy intention stabs the centre" speech (1.2.138–46),

---

[11] J. M. Nosworthy, ed., *Cymbeline* (London: Methuen, 1955), p. 72, note to l. 172.
[12] *A Grammar of Shakespeare's Language*, p. 267.

few commentators get beyond Pafford's observation that "the speech is meant to be incoherent": Leontes is crazy, and his language is an index to his character. The problem with this is not merely that it commits the play to the imitative fallacy, but that this sort of linguistic opacity is not at all limited to Leontes. Hermione, Camillo, Antigonus and Polixenes all exhibit it on occasion as well.[13]

Although obviously unbalanced characters frequently deliver themselves of incoherent, syntactically puzzling speeches, the properties that make it confusing are essentially the same as those in speeches by every character, the difference being in degree, not in kind. Over the course of the next two chapters, this principle governs the analysis.

The first half of this chapter identifies and describes some causes of the contorted, divagatory style. An illustrated catalogue, moderate in length, leads then to the second part of the analysis, which proposes a correspondence between these several syntactical forms and the larger dramatic structures of the last phase. Again, the notoriously challenging syntax of the romances is a stylistic cognate of the convoluted narrative syntax. And yet the homology between the difficult, circuitous style and the sprawling, roundabout shape of the romance plot represents more than a convenient structural parallel. Almost every dramatic plot, whether composed by Shakespeare or Sophocles or Shaw or Stoppard, consists of a sequence of advances and deferrals, the result of a storyteller's manipulation of the audience's expectations. The same may be said about the organization of the sentences that serve to articulate this network of actions. Both story and syntax are instruments employed by the playwright to manage the transaction between actors and spectators. Geographically, narratively, theatrically, prosodically, especially syntactically – in every sense these plays are all over the map.

Narrative theory can perhaps be helpful here. In *Reading for the Plot*, Peter Brooks summarizes "the linguistic model, applied to narrative analysis" employed by earlier narratologists such as Vladimir Propp, Tzvetan Todorov, and Gérard Genette, concluding that their method can serve "as a suggestive metaphor, alerting us to the important analogies between parts of speech and parts of narrative, encouraging us to think about narrative as system, with something that approximates a grammar and rules of ordering that approximate a syntax."[14] Primarily interested in the "grammar" of prose fiction, Brooks speaks, for example, about the

[13] Introduction to his Oxford edition, p. 9.
[14] Peter Brooks, *Reading for the Plot: Design and Intention in Narrative* (New York: Alfred A. Knopf, 1984), p. 17.

"conjunction" of narrative strands in Dickens's novels. My approach constitutes a modified version of Brooks's: instead of mainly using the conventions of the sentence to analyze the structuring of the fable, I would propose looking in both directions, also using what we know about the shape of the late plays to illuminate the operation of smaller syntactical units. This "janissary" method is especially productive in the case of the romances because critics have historically devoted more attention to the conventions of the mode than to the verbal and poetic structures.[15] Moreover, romance seems especially hospitable to such a method, since plot seems to dominate character and other dramatic features and the audience is led through a series of related actions over a prolonged period of time. In a play like *Cymbeline*, both the shape of the story and the structure of the verse sentences arise from the same artistic impulse, the wish to entertain the audience with a set of self-consciously theatrical means: old-fashioned stories, exaggerated characters, contorted verbal constructs, frank manipulation of dramatic machinery. The syntactical innovations and poetic gamesmanship offer a linguistic version of the audacious, sprawling actions represented on the stage. Our understanding of loosely organized stories can teach us something about the disconnected syntax that seems to give us so much trouble.

The adjective most frequently applied to the syntax of the late plays, as I have indicated, is "loose." Another term occasionally employed by modern scholars derives from the Renaissance rhetorical tradition. "Hyperbatonic" (from Gr: *hyperbaton*), which has come to describe syntactical disruption generally, is translated by George Puttenham as "the trespasser" and treated in his chapter devoted to "your figures Auricular working by disorder." Technically, the term refers to inverted word order, usually for the purpose of emphasis, but as Puttenham suggests, "such disorder may be committed many ways," and the following pages will identify and illustrate some of the specific means by which Shakespeare's syntactical complexity is "committed."[16]

INVERSION

In the repertory of means by which the syntax of the late style is disturbed, the first is the reversal of subject and verb order.

[15] I have borrowed the term from William Poole, "'Unpointed Words': Shakespearean Syntax in Action," *Cambridge Quarterly*, 32 (2003), 27–42.
[16] *The Arte of English Poesie*, a facsimile reproduction ed. Edward Arber, with an Introduction by Baxter Hathaway (Athens, Ohio: Kent State University Press, 1988), p. 180.

> Fight I will no more (*Cymbeline* 5.3.77)

> meets he on the way
> The father of this seeming lady (*The Winter's Tale* 5.1.190–91)

> This avouches the shepherd's son (*The Winter's Tale* 5.2.64–65)

> For a more blusterous birth had never babe (*Pericles* 3.1.28)

As indicated earlier, however, this formation is rather less prominent in Shakespeare's last plays than in his first, and by gradually relinquishing this pattern the playwright seems to have conformed to the stylistic developments of the age: sentences exhibiting such constructions "gradually decreased in number in English prose from the early Tudor period on," and what had been a common syntactic feature became relatively uncommon by the first decade of the seventeenth century.[17] Nevertheless, this minor, comparatively rare type of inversion still appears occasionally and warrants attention in combination with other anomalous forms.

Unusually placed modifiers make a similarly minor but perceptible contribution.

> The silence *often* of pure innocence
> Persuades, when speaking fails (*The Winter's Tale* 2.2.39–40)

> Ne'er mother
> Rejoic'd deliverance more: (*Cymbeline* 5.6.370–71)

> the office did
> Distinctly his full function (*Henry VIII* 1.1.44–45)

> This King of Naples, being an enemy
> To me inveterate (*The Tempest* 1.2.121–22)

A related tactic is the inversion of the complement, placed to precede the nominative and the verbal phrase:

> Troubled I am (*The Two Noble Kinsmen* 1.1.77)

> This satisfaction
> The by-gone day proclaim'd (*The Winter's Tale* 1.2.31–32)

> Great the slaughter is
> Here made by th' Roman (*Cymbeline* 5.3.78–79)

[17] Houston, *Shakespearean Sentences*, pp. 18–19. Also see Matti Rissanen, "Syntax," in *The Cambridge History of the English Language, vol. III, 1476–1776*, ed. Roger Lass (Cambridge: Cambridge University Press, 1999), pp. 264–67.

THAI.   O, my lord,
    Are you not Pericles? *Like him you spake,*
    Like him you are.
PER.   The voice of dead Thaisa!
THAI.   *That Thaisa am I,* supposed dead
    And drowned.
                        (*Pericles* 5.3.31–35)

Several of these instances are instructive because they occur in comparatively unheightened passages, speeches not calculated to increase the emotional temperature or to imitate madness. Sometimes the slight distortion produced by a "postpositive adjective" will be magnified by its alteration of an established pattern. As Jonathan Hope points out, in Pericles' "Celestial Dian, goddess Argentine," the "attributive 'Celestial' is hardly a surprising attribute of the goddess Diana, but postpositional 'argentine' (referring to her associations with the moon, and her silver bow) needs to be worked at."[18] That last phrase, "needs to be worked at," will prove useful in the effort to comprehend the affective and semantic contribution of such syntactical forms.

    Some of the reversals just cited appear in Antigonus's lament on the Bohemian shore about the penalties of sworn duty; also audible therein is another common figure of disorder, the striking placement of a prepositional phrase:

                    Weep I cannot,
    But my heart bleeds; and most accurs'd am I
    To be *by oath* enjoin'd to this.
             (*The Winter's Tale* 3.3.51–53)

Such freedom with mobile grammatical components is a primary source of structural eccentricity in the late verse. Frequently a prepositional phrase will be inserted into a clause before, rather than after, the verb it modifies:

POST.   This is a thing
    Which you might *from relation* likewise reap,
    Being, as it is, much spoke of.
JACH.   The roof of the chamber
    With golden cherubins is fretted. Her andirons
    (I had forgot them) were two winking Cupids
    Of silver, each *on one foot* standing . . .
             (*Cymbeline* 2.4.85–90)

---

[18] Jonathan Hope, *Shakespeare's Grammar* (London: Thompson, 2003), p. 115.

I,

> *Beyond all limit of what else 'i th' world*
> Do love, prize, honor you.
>> (*The Tempest* 3.1.71–73)

> And ye that *on the sands | with printless foot*
> Do chase the ebbing Neptune
>> (*The Tempest* 5.1.34–35)

Such a simple re-ordering of parts is not uncommon in the verse and prose of the period, especially given the general flexibility of early modern syntax; like the other forms of inversion, it appears regularly in the earlier plays. But when heard along with other hyperbatonic transpositions, its contribution becomes more prominent and, in the strict sense, significant: the sensitive listener begins to notice such a habit and to wonder what it signifies.

One effect of such grammatical arrangement is to disrupt, if only momentarily, the expected syntactical order and thus to challenge the listener, to make the transaction between stage and audience slightly more demanding. Again, "expected syntactical order" is a potentially problematic phrase in that adverbial modifiers, as linguists point out, are "highly mobile" and can be situated variously within the clause.[19] Despite such potential flexibility, however, even in early modern English the preposition tends usually to follow the verb, and thus the unexpected placement of such a modifier creates a perceptual effect, and perhaps makes a semantic contribution as well. Grammarians have confirmed the not surprising conclusion that the dislocation of a modifier will tend to add a sense of weight to that modifier.[20] In Posthumus's "Me *of my lawful pleasure* she restrain'd" (*Cymbeline* 2.4.161), with its direct object at the head of the sentence and the prepositional phrase before the pronominal subject and verb, such a small inversion creates a slight logical detour, calling attention to the intruding unit, delaying the arrival of the all-important verb, and thus making the syntactical configuration marginally more theatrical. Puttenham's topographical metaphor is pertinent in thinking about the contribution of such rearrangement: the figure of disorder is known as "the trespasser" because a group of words steps out of place, intruding into territory where it does not belong. These frequent and prominently situated modifiers represent minor diversions along the syntactical road. Those described thus far require only a glance, but others can cause listeners to lose their way.

---

[19] Hope, *Shakespeare's Grammar*, p. 176

[20] As Hope puts it, "The placing of an adverbial in an unexpected position will tend to stress the modifying element," p. 176.

If the formations cited thus far are hardly striking owing to their appearance everywhere in early modern writing, the unexpectedly interpolated
phrase becomes more prominent in Shakespeare's late work. Sometimes
this is a short modifying unit, a stray participle or dependent clause, for
example, one that momentarily alters or colors the sense of the passage in
which it appears.

POST.   I do believe
          (Statist though I am none, nor like to be)
          That this will prove a war
                         (*Cymbeline* 2.4.15–17)

PIS.   nay, you must
          Forget that rarest treasure of your cheek,
          Exposing it (but, O, the harder heart!
          Alack, no remedy) to the greedy touch
          Of common-kissing Titan.
                         (*Cymbeline* 3.4.159–63)

Pisanio's lines are doubly illustrative because the first interruption (line
161) is interrupted ("O") and then succeeded by another intrusive phrase
("Alack . . ."). In addition, the entire parenthetical digression is noticeably
elliptical. The romances contain many of these brief exclamations and
asides within speeches. Sometimes, however, the intruding element will
run for several lines, requiring obvious labor by the speaker to regain the
initial semantic direction.

PAUL.   Good my liege, I come –
          And I beseech you hear me, who professes
          Myself your loyal servant, your physician,
          Your most obedient counselor; yet that dares   55
          Less appear so, in comforting your evils,
          Than such as most seem yours – I say, I come
          From your good queen.

                   (*The Winter's Tale* 2.3.52–58)

Such elaborate interpolations are heard most frequently in *The Winter's
Tale* and, perhaps to a slightly lesser degree, *Cymbeline*, but all the late
plays exhibit them in abundance.

    Help is occasionally available: sometimes a parenthesis will guide the
reader who attempts to follow a semantic path through the thicket of a
difficult passage. *Lunulae*, to use Erasmus's coinage, or "round brackets,"

to use the modern printer's term,[21] are especially plentiful in the printed texts of the late plays: *The Winter's Tale* contains 369 pairs, *Cymbeline* 158, *Henry VIII* 117, and *The Tempest* 97.[22] Again, a percentage of these relatively high numbers may be ascribed to the habits of Ralph Crane, the copyist known to have prepared at least three of the late plays for publication in the Folio. Concerning texts that Crane did not copy, Gary Taylor interprets the existing data to suggest that Shakespeare himself did not frequently use round brackets, but that Compositor B, like Crane, was inclined to add them to the portions of text he set.[23]

Whoever included them, the seventeenth-century conventions for employing parentheses differ from our own. As John Lennard has taught us, early modern writers and editors often enclosed a vocative within brackets, in a way that we would not: "But are they (Ariel) safe?" (*The Tempest* 1.2.217; Folio).[24] However heavy the hands of scribe and compositor at introducing parentheses, the overriding fact is that Shakespeare gave them a great deal of material to enclose: the digressive tendencies of the late style tend to invite bracketing, whether or not printed enclosures appear in the text. Characters stop and start, change direction, amplify or alter an observation just made, interrupt themselves, and treat the integrity of the sentence very loosely indeed. Listeners, lacking the reader's access to the parenthetical signs sprinkled through the text, have no trouble registering the frequency of interpolated statements: they may have trouble, however, maintaining the semantic sense in the face of such constant and distracting interpolations.

---

[21] See John Lennard, *But I Digress: The Exploitation of Parentheses in English Printed Verse* (Oxford: Oxford University Press, 1991), p. 1.

[22] These figures derive from Ashley Thorndike, "Parentheses in Shakespeare," *Shakespeare Association Bulletin*, 9 (1934), p. 33. Thorndike counts those plays "not printed from quartos," and it is worth noting that among all Shakespeare's plays the four for which I have specified numbers occupy the following positions in frequency of parenthesis: *The Winter's Tale* first, *Cymbeline* fourth, *Henry VIII* seventh, and *The Tempest* eighth.

[23] Gary Taylor, "Shakespeare and Others: The Authorship of *Henry the Sixth, Part One*," *Medieval and Renaissance Drama in England* 7 (1995), 145– 205; see also William Montgomery on Crane's habits in Wells and Taylor, with Jowett and Montgomery, *William Shakespeare: A Textual Companion*, p. 619.

[24] *But I Digress*, pp. 1–15. As Lennard points out, parenthetical marks could serve a variety of functions: "where punctuation, conventional or not, is editorial, it is impossible to draw any clear distinction between the extents to which it is supplying for the reader an articulation without which the primary meaning would be lost; or to which it is rhetorical, for example, to indicate the periodic structure of the discourse; or to which it is gnomic, for example to emphasize particular words or phrases. (In the case of rhetorical punctuation it should also be noted that the blocking may be intended to guide or control either written tone or spoken pitch, or both.)" (p. 8).

The contribution of parenthetical elements is exhibited clearly in the Duke of Buckingham's recital of court intrigue at the end of the first scene of *Henry VIII*:

> But our count-cardinal
> Has done this, and 'tis well: for worthy Wolsey
> (Who cannot err), he did it. Now this follows,
> (Which, as I take it, is a kind of puppy
> To th'old dam, treason), Charles the Emperor,
> Under pretence to see the Queen his aunt,
> (For 'twas indeed his color, but he came
> To whisper Wolsey), here makes visitation . . .
> (1.1.172–79).

175

The first parenthetical element ("Who cannot err") is a mordant characterization of the powerful Wolsey, an unnecessary but bitterly amusing relative clause. The second parenthesis introduces the ironic metaphor of treason as dog, in this case a small, young one. The third amplifies the discrepancy between the apparent and actual causes of the Emperor's "visitation." None of these intromissions advances the story Buckingham tells, and yet each adds a splash of color, a memorable detail, an exemplum in the ways of the court. The speaker might have established his argument without digression, might have made his way from point A to point B without detour. But by inviting us to linger briefly, to enjoy a brief, instructive side-trip, Buckingham (and the playwright) teases us with his inside experience, enriches our understanding of the early Tudor political world, and, perhaps above all, diverts us with significant scenic detail as we make our way through the narrative.

Of Puttenham's "figures Auricular working by disorder," the first specific instance is "*Parenthesis* or the Insertour."[25] Such a figure is especially useful, he declares, "when ye will seeme for larger information or some other purpose, to peece or graffe in the middest of your tale an vnnecessary parcell of speach, which neuerthelesse may be thence without any detriment to the rest." Puttenham acknowledges the appeal and temptations of intromission but warns against its excessive use, "for it will breede great confusion to have the tale so much interrupted."[26] The test case for excessive digression is the language proceeding from the ingenious "Italian brain" of Jachimo in *Cymbeline*. His speeches exhibit

---

[25] *Arte of English Poesie*, pp. 180–81.   [26] *Ibid.*, p. 181.

such a high frequency of interruptions because he himself is a figure of disorder, a trespasser who travels from Britain to Rome to Britain, inserts himself into Imogen's bedchamber, disrupts the marriage of Posthumus and Imogen, and "breed[s] great confusion." The flagrantly erratic and parenthetical sentences he speaks, put down in ways that stretch even the elastic conventions of syntax and grammar, typify a heightened form of the divagatory and almost chaotic medium that Shakespeare devised for these romantic tales.

Jachimo's report to Posthumus on returning from his sojourn in Britain is not, syntactically speaking, the most outlandish of his performances, but it offers many characteristic turns:

> JACH. First, her bedchamber
> (Where I confess I slept not, but profess
> Had that was well worth watching) it was hang'd
> With tapestry of silk, and silver, the story
> Proud Cleopatra, when she met her Roman, 70
> And Cydnus swell'd above the banks, or for
> The press of boats, or pride. A piece of work
> So bravely done, so rich, that it did strive
> In workmanship, and value, which I wonder'd
> Could be so rarely, and exactly wrought 75
> Since the true life on't was –
>
> POST. This is true:
>
> (2.4.66–76)

Grammatically speaking, the passage is ambiguous, difficult to classify. The first seven lines constitute a single sentence, more or less, its structure troubled by the substitution of "it" in the third line for "bedchamber" in the first. The second independent unit, beginning "A piece of work . . ." (72), is not a formal sentence at all, lacking as it does a predicate. But the most noticeable stylistic trait is obsessive digression. Jachimo begins as if to offer a logical inventory but instantly veers off into his salacious little throwaway, the joke about what happened there. His tendency to digress grammatically is exceeded perhaps only by that of Leontes.

Detailed scrutiny of this set of Jachimo's interpolations will establish some general principles about the divagatory style. The apparently efficient beginning, with an ordinal adverb and then a modified nominal phrase ("First, her bedchamber"), is immediately compromised by a series of non-restrictive relative clauses. The first, "where . . . I slept not," is itself interrupted with another clause, its relative pronoun omitted, "I confess [that]"; this construction is known to grammarians as an "embedded" clause.[27] This first interruptor is soon followed by a second, the similarly embedded "but [I] profess [that]." The initial interrupting clause ("slept") then re-establishes itself with a conjunction and verb, creating a compound predicate ("slept not but . . . had . . .") and adding another relative clause, this time omitting two relative pronouns and the subject pronoun ("[that] [I] Had that [which] was well worth watching"). The convolutions of my own descriptive sentence might be straightened out slightly by a simple diagram illustrating the fundamental shape of the excerpt:

where	I slept not but		Had that	was well worth watching
I confess [that]	[I] profess [that I]		[which]	

All the bracketed elements demonstrate the elliptical inclinations analyzed in Chapter 2. Here the tactic functions to accelerate the interpolation, tacitly implying that the speaker will quickly return to the main clause.

This digressive string of clauses also glitters with semantic and poetic amusement. The most obvious wink emerges from the play on "slept not": (1) he did not sleep because (2) he was making love to her, all of which is a lie that is ironically true ("slept not") because (3) he neither slept with her nor slept in the room at all. The double irony apparent in (3) is one of Shakespeare's favorite tactics in the late plays: a statement presented as true is in fact false, and yet is true in a sense unintended by the character.[28] Such wordplay itself should be seen as digressive, in that the audience's attention is fleetingly diverted by perception of the double meaning.[29] Aurally the passage is also playful: the chiming *e* vowels (67), the spray of *w* sounds (68), the numerous internal doublings ("not, but," "Had that"), and the shifted prefixes ("con- and pro-fess"). Everywhere in this line-and-a-half the flurry of repeated vowels, consonants, and syllables distracts and pleases the audience while disclosing the speaker's self-conscious pleasure in his performance.

Such repetitions are not only ornamental but also functional, helping to shape a digressive, potentially confusing speech. This particular interpolation, while it interrupts, grammatically speaking, the main business of

---

[27] For clear explanation of this grammatical feature, see Rissanen, "Syntax," p. 297, and Sylvia Adamson, "Literary Language," p. 586, in Lass, ed., *Cambridge History of the English Language.*

[28] See Anne Barton, "Leontes and the Spider: Language and Speaker in Shakespeare's Last Plays," in *Essays, Mainly Shakespearean* (Cambridge: Cambridge University Press, 1994), pp. 165–73.

[29] For more discussion of the diversionary function of puns, see Catherine Bates, "The Point of Puns," *Modern Philology,* 96 (1999), 421–38, and several of the essays in Jonathan Culler's *On Puns: The Foundation of Letters* (Oxford: Blackwell, 1988).

the sentence, relies on certain structuring devices for semantic and poetic integrity, unifying tactics that guide and reassure the audience on their detour from the main point. In this case the most notable such devices are (1) the paired verbs ("confess . . . profess"), matched not only aurally but placed in parallel positions (the assonantal words both stand in identical relation to the clauses they precede, and both could be left out without damage to the meaning); and (2) the exaggeratedly alliterative "[which] was well worth watching." Such reiteration binds together the verbal components of the phrase, thus creating a sense of balance and clarity, preventing the audience from losing the semantic path, despite the convoluted syntax.

But back to the point – always a problem in listening to or describing these passages – the *description* of the bedchamber. After the digression the speaker regains his grammatical balance by supplying the predicate ("– it was hanged") and signaling the resumption of the primary clause by referring pronominally ("it") to the nominal phrase ("her bedchamber"). Having done so, he simultaneously omits and supplements, a dynamic evident in the elision of the verb and pronominal complement ("the story / [was that of] Proud Cleopatra") in combination with the accretion of superfluous visual details in elaborate verbal patterns ("silk, and silver"). This tension between excess and abbreviation emerges again in the next lines, consisting of a verbless construction ("A piece of work / So bravely done, so rich") further concentrated ("it did strive in workmanship and value") and yet freighted with an abundance of modifiers ("so rarely and exactly wrought"). Amid numerous elliptical phrases we hear skeins of repeated sounds, as in:

> With tapestry of s*i*lk, and s*i*lver, the story

Or:

> An*d* Cy*d*nus **s**well'*d* above the banks, **or for**
> The **press** of boats, **or** **pr**ide . . .[30]

Ellipsis is counterbalanced by a sense of poetic richness and even excess.

It is worth stepping back momentarily from poetic and grammatical particulars to point out that the entire description, with the others that sustain this tale, is digressive. Although Jachimo has presented it as proof

---

[30] This is a case in which our uncertainty about early modern pronunciation is relevant but not terribly important: the *C* in "Cydnus" pairs with the *s* sounds if pronounced as a soft consonant, with the *k* in "banks" if pronounced hard.

of his having seduced Imogen, he offers far more information than necessary, so much so that the aim of supplying persuasive evidence almost becomes swamped in visual detail. For example, the continuation of this passage, in which we hear of the chimney-piece depicting the bathing Diana and praise for the natural art of the carver, is similarly excessive. To some degree this superfluity of detail is attributable to character, particularly the performative bent of this fairy-tale Iago. The tale-teller mocks his victim with the sexual undertones of the passage, beginning with the main predicate, "was hang'd," and continuing in the description of the tapestry, both in his pictorial detour to Egypt, with its coded glances at licentious sexuality, and especially in potentially charged words such as "silk and silver," "Proud Cleopatra," "Cydnus swell'd," "press," "pride," "a piece of work." A further jab is audible in the metrical disruption of the line

Proŭd Cleŏpátră, whĕn shé mĕt hér Rómăn.

Emphasis ought to fall mainly on "met" and "Ro," on syllables 8 and 10 of the eleven syllable line, but the salacious implications of the pronouns shift the stress to "she" and "her," for Imogen is receiving *her* Roman just as Cleopatra had welcomed hers.[31] And this jest extends further, considering that this is a play in which King Cymbeline does and does not receive the Roman diplomatic and military forces.

The prepositional intrusions mentioned earlier also contribute to the density of this passage: "The roof o'th' chamber / *With golden cherubins* is fretted"; "each *on one foot* standing, nicely / Depending on their brands." In addition to the intruding or inverted phrases, two other stylistic features are apparent, the abbreviation of the first prepositional phrase ("o'th'") and the added participle that finishes the sentence. In reply to Posthumus's query about whether the diamond is actually Imogen's, Jachimo replies with "Sir (I thank her) that!" (100); and as ocular proof of his liaison, he reports that "under her breast / (Worthy her pressing) lies a mole" (134–35). Nothing need be left out.

In the finale of *Cymbeline*, Jachimo's contribution, poetically speaking, is a magnified version of the digressive function he has fulfilled from his first entrance. His appearance at the end is both necessary and redundant: his voice is required to clear Imogen of calumny, and yet, as usual, he says much more than he needs to, and much that is untrue. His re-entry into

---

[31] See J. M. Nosworthy's notes to this passage in the Arden2 edition of *Cymbeline*.

the action is, of course, withheld. He remains absent from the end of Act 2 until the second scene of Act 5, and when he does appear in the final scene, his stepping forward and delivery of the narrative of his malfeasance are noticeably delayed: he enters with the Roman prisoners, in line 68; Imogen, as Fidele, mentions the ring on his finger in line 103, declares her interest in him, and then steps aside with Cymbeline to explain herself; Jachimo obliquely resists telling his tale ("Thou'lt torture me to leave unspoken that / Which to be spoke, would torture thee" [139–40]). When he begins to recount it, he teases his principal auditor ("Wilt thou hear more, my lord?") and then seems unable to continue (" – Give me leave; I faint").

All these dramatics anticipate his extended confession, a performance in which anticipation is stimulated even further by the opening series of parallel suspensions and deviations:

> Upon a time, unhappy was the clock
> That struck the hour: it was in Rome, accurst
> The mansion where: 'twas at a feast, oh would   155
> Our viands had been poison'd (or at least
> Those which I heav'd to head:) the good Posthumus
> (What should I say? he was too good to be
> Where ill men were, and was the best of all
> Among'st the rar'st of good ones) sitting sadly,   160
> Hearing us praise our loves of Italy
> For beauty, that made barren the swell'd boast
> Of him that best could speak: for feature, laming
> The shrine of Venus, or straight-pight Minerva,
> Postures, beyond brief nature. For condition,   165
> A shop of all the qualities, that man
> Loves woman for, besides that hook of wiving,
> Fairness, which strikes the eye.
>   (5.5.153–68; Folio punctuation)

As a rejoinder to the King's query about the diamond on his finger, this isn't very helpful. According to one reader, "All is hyperbole, exclamation, digression. For every step forward in his account, Iachimo takes two sideways with parenthetical deviations."[32] Even the dim Cymbeline loses patience, interrupting with "I stand on fire. / Come to the matter" (5.5.168–69), and complaining again ten lines later with "Nay, nay, to th' purpose" (5.5.178). Jachimo has yet to give details of Posthumus's

---

[32] Judiana Lawrence, "Natural Bonds and Artistic Coherence in the Ending of *Cymbeline*," *Shakespeare Quarterly*, 35 (1984), 457.

praise of Imogen, the wager over her chastity, his own journey to Britain, his rejection by Imogen, his "practice" in securing the evidence against her, and his presentation of the proof and winning of the ring.

His resumption of the narrative is another showcase of digressively organized sentences (the one beginning "This Posthumus" in line 170 and running through line 178 is especially knotty), parenthetical insertions, inversions of the normal order of subjects and verbs or nouns and adjectives, and elliptical phrases giving the impression of speed and yet at the same time adding length and complexity. These properties also animate his last protracted speech, with its opening joke about narrative economy:

> And to be brief, my practice so prevail'd,
> That I return'd with simular proof enough   200
> To make the noble Leonatus mad,
> By wounding his belief in her renown,
> With tokens thus, and thus: averring notes
> Of chamber-hanging, pictures, this her bracelet
> (O cunning, how I got it!) nay, some marks   205
> Of secret on her person, that he could not
> But think her bond of chastity quite crack'd,
> I having ta'en the forfeit. Whereupon –
> Methinks I see him now –
> POST. [*Advancing*] Ay, so thou dost
> Italian fiend!   210
>
> (5.5.199–210)

Posthumus is transformed from a figment of Jachimo's imaginative memory to an embodied actor who arrests the wild divagation and elaboration of the narrative.

Posthumus's interruption (occurring during an interruption) amounts to a clever turn on the conflict, both syntactical and theatrical, between wandering and closure: this is Shakespeare at his wittiest and most self-conscious, a crucial moment in a scene vitally concerned with what is real and what imaginary. Jachimo produces his own antagonist and victim when a verbal illusion becomes a theatrical presence who is still nothing more nor less than a theatrical illusion, and so the romances' concern with the relation of art to life is emphasized and complicated. Looked at syntactically, the narrative structure of the ultimate scene seems to consist of a string of digressions, interpolations, and ellipses: in addition to Jachimo's narrative excursions and Posthumus's step forward, one might mention Cornelius's entrance to announce the death of the Queen; the diversion indicated by the modern stage directions *Cymbeline and Imogen talk apart* and *Cymbeline and Imogen come forward,* between which the Welsh threesome attempt to make sense of Fidele's reappearance; and Belarius's intervention to save Guiderius from execution, beginning "Stay, sir King" (5.5.301). However, the structural analogy between scenes and sentences, tempting though it is, must be postponed until a more complete catalogue of devices has been assembled.

BREAKING OFF

A verbal trick related to parenthesis and other forms of interpolation is the broken sentence, in which the speaker stops in mid-utterance. Puttenham identifies this maneuver as

> another auricular figure of defect, and is one when we begin to speake a thing, and breake off in the middle way, as if either it needed no further to be spoken of, or that we were ashamed, or afraid to speake it out. It is also sometimes done by way of threatening, and to shew a moderation of anger. The Greekes call him *Aposiopesis.* I, the figure of silence, or of interruption, indifferently.[33]

At the break, the next step may entail a change of direction, an address to the topic of the sentence from a new angle, perhaps a sudden change of subject, or even a more drastic shift:

> O, all the devils!
> This yellow Jachimo, in an hour – was't not?–
> Or less – at first? (*Cymbeline* 2.5.13–15)

> A headless man? The garments of Posthumus?
> I know the shape of 's leg; this is his hand,
> His foot Mercurial, his Martial thigh,
> The brawns of Hercules; but his Jovial face –
> Murther in heaven? How? 'Tis gone.
> (*Cymbeline* 4.2.308–12)

> There
> Require of him the hearts of lions and
> The breath of tigers, yea, the fierceness too,
> Yea, the speed also – to go on, I mean,
> Else wish we to be snails.
> (*The Two Noble Kinsmen* 5.1.38–42)

---

[33] *Arte of English Poesie,* p. 178.

Often aposiopesis is forced by the interruption of another character.

CAM. I have lov'd thee –
LEON.   Make that thy question, and go rot!
          (*The Winter's Tale* 1.2.324)

MAM. There was a man –
HER.   Nay, come sit down; then on.
          (*The Winter's Tale* 2.1.29)

Narrative or theatrical business, such as an unexpected entrance, may motivate the stop:

CLO.   . . . For, when fools shall –
    Enter PISANIO.
    Who is here? What, are you packing, sirrah?
          (*Cymbeline* 3.5.79–80)

The excerpt from *The Two Noble Kinsmen* also exhibits the additive and revisionist impulses ("yea" . . . "yea") common to the characters in these plays, another instance of a speaker's attempt to articulate an idea more precisely (". . . I mean . . .").

Shakespeare employs this figure for just the purpose that Puttenham recommends: overflow of emotion. But it is also relevant that the rhetorician, having illustrated it, indicates that

this figure is fit for phantasticall heads and such as be sodaine . . . I know one of good learning that greatly blemisheth his discretion with this maner of speech: for if he be in the grauest matter of the world talking, he will vpon the sodaine for the flying of a bird ouerthwart the way, or some other such sleight cause, interrupt his tale and neuer returne to it again.[34]

In other words, such "sodaine" breaking off is associated with flightiness or inattention. "Phantasticall heads" calls to mind Jachimo, who frequently breaks off in mid-thought, as well as Autolycus, whom the Clown describes specifically as appearing "fantastical" (*The Winter's Tale* 4.4.752). Again at the risk of jumping forward too quickly, I would point out that the organization of most of these dramas depends upon unexpected shifts in location or time. "Upon the sodaine" the playwright will "interrupt his tale" and shift the scene to Wales or Bohemia or Mytilene or another part of Prospero's island. "The figure of silence" represents the playful Shakespeare's suppression of logical connectives, his asking the audience to follow the jerks and inventions of the fable.

---

[34] *Ibid.*, pp. 178–79.

ADDITION

The syntactical "incoherence" of the late verse is attributable especially to the additive impulse Shakespeare indulges. In *Cymbeline*, "long sentences," as John Porter Houston points out, "increase in length over those of the immediately previous plays."[35] While the urge to augment manifests itself in the interpolation of clauses and phrases, an equally common and meaningful form of accumulation is the piling up of appositional or elaborative phrases, usually at the end of a sentence.

> 'Tis known, I ever
> Have studied physic: through which secret art,
> By turning o'er authorities, I have
> Together with my practice, made familiar,
> To me and to my aid, the blest infusions   35
> That dwells in vegetives, in metals, stones:
> And can speak of the disturbances that
> Nature works, and of her cures; which doth give me
> A more content in course of true delight
> Than to be thirsty after tottering honour,   40
> Or tie my treasure up in silken bags,
> To please the fool and death.
>   (*Pericles* 3.2.31–42)

Cerimon's credo, spoken as he prepares to minister to the "dead" Thaisa, represents both the digressive and the aggregative style. However punctuated, the speech amounts to a single sentence built up gradually by the addition of prepositional phrases (the interpolated "Together with my practice"), relative clauses ("That dwells in . . ."), infinitives ("To please . . ."), a second predicate introduced mid-speech ("And can speak"), as well as such extenders as supplementary examples ("in vegetives, in metals, stones"), comparatives ("more content . . . / Than to be thirsty . . ."), and alternatives ("Or tie my treasure up"). Usually the additional clauses that so distend the sentence are non-restrictive, or as linguists call them, "continuative clauses." According to Charles Barber, "In PresE we distinguish the two types in speech by intonation: the non-restrictive clause forms a separate tone-group, the restrictive does not. It is likely that some such form of distinction was also made in eModE speech."[36] If Shakespeare's actors provided such a tonal signifier for each of these added grammatical units, the auditory textures of these plays would have been even more various and complex than they seem to us.

---

[35] *Shakespearean Sentences*, p. 204.   [36] Barber, *Early Modern English*, p. 209.

The series, a major component of Cerimon's autobiographical recollections, is a favorite Shakespearean strategy for extending the sentence. Occasionally the string of clauses or phrases will precede the main grammatical units, making the sentence "left heavy," to borrow the linguist's terminology: "Sitting on a bank, / Weeping again the King my father's wrack" (*The Tempest* 1.2.392–93).[37] Although such balanced, apparently periodic constructions are fairly frequent (and are considered more thoroughly in Chapter 4), the more prevalent and noticeable manifestation is the series appended to the end of a potentially completed sentence. This kind of extension carries the listener forward but promises no destination or predictable closure.

Such an articulated grammatical structure is the single sentence in which Cloten rails to Imogen about the impropriety of her passion:

> You sin against
> Obedience, which you owe your father, for
> The contract you pretend with that base wretch,
> One, bred of alms, and foster'd with cold dishes,
> With scraps o' th' court: it is no contract, none;   115
> And though it be allowed in meaner parties
> (Yet who than he more mean) to knit their souls
> (On whom there is no more dependency
> But brats and beggary) in self-figur'd knot,
> Yet you are curb'd from that enlargement, by   120
> The consequences o' th' crown, and must not foil
> The precious note of it; with a base slave,
> A hilding for a livery, a squire's cloth,
> A pantler; not so eminent.   (2.3.111–24; Folio)

Many of the features of delay and disruption mentioned above operate here: parentheses, subjoined relative clauses, frequent ellipsis, and prepositional phrases preceding the verb. In the present context, however, the crucial detail comes at the end of the passage: Cloten's list of insults expressed as objects of the preposition "with." The sputtered list trails off into "not so eminent," the elliptical comparative that lamely concludes the tirade. In this case the series may help to depict the blustering impotence of the comic suitor, but the syntactical eccentricities of the last three lines are typical of the structures that set the late style apart from Shakespeare's earlier work. Also notable in the development of the

---

[37] Laura Wright and Jonathan Hope, *Stylistics: A Practical Coursebook* (London: Routledge, 1996), pp. 99–102.

sentence as a whole is its lack of inevitability. Cloten seems to ramble as he adds more and more matter.

At the end of the sheep-shearing in Act 4 of *The Winter's Tale*, after Polixenes has intervened to stop the marriage, Camillo proposes to Florizel a scheme for winning his father's approval:

FLO.   I am bound to you.   565
    There is some sap in this.
CAM.   A course more promising
    Than a wild dedication of yourselves
    To unpath'd waters, undream'd shores; most certain
    To miseries enough: no hope to help you,
    But as you shake off one, to take another: 570
    Nothing so certain as your anchors, who
    Do their best office if they can but stay you
    Where you'll be loath to be.

                          (4.4.565–73; Folio)

The threatened scenario of desperation emerges by means of added categories and additional elements within each category, but it also displays other typical syntactical properties. The excerpt begins with a verbless construction taking the form of a comparative ("A course more promising"), the comparison then receives further elaboration ("To unpath'd waters, undream'd shores"), and when it seems to conclude, the speaker inserts another unexpected unit, with preliminary adverbial modifiers ("most certain / To miseries enough"). The idea is further extended by means of the elliptical "[with] no hope to help you," and in its final movement the sentence shifts to address its subject by means of its opposite, the ironically hopeless "anchors," whose negative contributions are enumerated through three additional relative clauses.

This penchant for adding clauses and phrases – like the tendency to interrupt – often produces another diversion, the unusual positioning of the added material. Speakers may refine an idea or extend a thought by introducing material very loosely related, grammatically speaking, to the principal parts of the sentence. For example, a relative clause may lag behind its antecedent and thus strain the expected connection between the noun and the clause to which it is subordinated: "This *island's* mine by Sycorax my mother, / *Which thou tak'st from me*" (*The Tempest* 1.2.333–34). (In Present English, of course, the "which" clause, modifying "island," would immediately follow the noun, but Early Modern English is less prescriptive about placement.) Jonathan Hope calls this slight distortion a "movement of the relative away from the head," or "head-shifting."[38] The frequency of this syntactical transference becomes apparent when we recall some memorable examples, such as Marina's "My *mother* was the daughter of a king, / *Who died the minute I was born*" (*Pericles* 5.1.157–58) or one of Hermione's many uses: "My *life* stands in the level of your dreams, / *Which I'll lay down*" (*The Winter's Tale* 3.2.81–82). Given early modern conventions, these head-shifted relatives occur throughout the canon, but in the late plays they contribute to the impression of a loose, casually regulated syntax.

ASYNDETON

The abundant "continuative clauses" frequently represent a speaker's attempt at redefinition or more precise articulation, an effort that also accounts for the high degree of asyndeton throughout the late phase. As I indicated in Chapter 2, *Cymbeline* contains a multitude of such constructions, far more than the tragedies that precede it.[39] One of the simplest examples is Imogen's speech to her servant just before retiring: "I have read three hours then; mine eyes are weak, / Fold down the leaf where I have left: to bed. / Take not away the taper, leave it burning" (2.2.3–5). Obviously the absence of conjunctions suggests a kind of fatigue, as if the character tries not to waste breath on extra words. But asyndeton is so abundant in *Cymbeline* that a more general explanation is needed. In *Coriolanus*, as my discussion in Chapter 2 argued, asyndeton served to divide, verbally suggesting Martius's isolation from family and other human interaction, especially politics. In *Cymbeline* its function is much more various.

Sometimes, for example, the want of connectives contributes to what Houston refers to as "the asyndeton of redefining,"[40] a function apparent in Posthumus's list of female iniquities ending in "All faults that name, nay, that Hell knows, / Why hers, in part, or all: but rather all" (*Cymbeline* 2.4.179–80). This corrective habit manifests itself also in the flurry of appositives encountered in all the last plays:

> A terrible child-bed hast thou had, my dear,
> No light, no fire.   (*Pericles* 3.1.56–57)

---

[38] *Shakespeare's Grammar*, pp. 112–13.
[39] Houston, *Shakespearean Sentences*, p. 198.
[40] *Shakespearean Sentences*, p. 202.

> for the harlot king
> Is quite beyond mine arm, out of the blank
> And level of my brain: plot-proof
> (*The Winter's Tale* 2.3.4–6)

> A devil, a born devil, on whose nature
> Nurture can never stick; on whom my pains,
> Humanely taken, all, all lost, quite lost.
> (*The Tempest* 4.1.188–90)

These lists of added phrases and clauses, mostly lacking conjunctions, also promote an asyndetic spareness in the late style. It seems notable that asyndeton has been described as "the conjunctional cousin of ellipsis,"[41] in other words, as an instrument of omission or condensation: in both constructions the poet tries to distill much meaning into few words in order to express the idea thoroughly and faithfully. Most of the time asyndeton would seem to contribute to pace, allowing the speaker to skip rapidly through a series of words or phrases. It is also a source of the notion that Shakespeare in his last productive years is indolent, that he hasn't bothered to polish the verse or tighten the joints among grammatical parts. In this respect it is worth remembering that Puttenham's English phrase for asyndeton is "the loose language."[42]

THE DIFFICULTIES OF DESCRIPTION

The urge to formulate some general statements about the mature Shakespeare's syntactical practice is frustrated by its immense variety, the idiosyncratic mixture of contradictory effects. The conflict of aggregation and ellipsis is typical of the mixed stylistic signals: almost any generalization about an important syntactic trait must be qualified immediately by acknowledgement of a complementary feature. Although much attention has been given in the foregoing analysis to convolution and digression, many passages are constructed with extreme simplicity, such as Imogen's bedtime speech just cited, "I have read three hours then: mine eyes are weak." Those plain lines, however, are spoken just before Jachimo emerges from the trunk to expatiate digressively on Imogen's beauty:

> That I might touch!
> But kiss, one kiss! Rubies unparagon'd,
> How dearly they do't: 'tis her breathing that

---

[41] Elam, "Early Modern Syntax and Late Elizabethan Rhetoric," p. 73. Houston, referring to the exceptional number of constructions involving asyndeton in *Cymbeline*, similarly suggests that "we might characterize its effect most generally as one of ellipsis" (p. 200).
[42] *Arte of English Poesie*, p. 185.

Perfumes the chamber thus: the flame o' th' taper
Bows toward her, and would under-peep her lids,   20
To see th' enclosed lights, now canopied
Under these windows, white and azure laced
With blue of heaven's own tinct. But my design.
                              (*Cymbeline* 2.2.16–23)

Such contrasting excerpts indicate that, for all the complexity with which the verse unfolds, no single scheme informs its organization. Lengthy, convoluted verse sentences may be strung together, or may be interspersed with brief ones, or may be broken up with exclamations, short and long, that may not be sentences at all. The range of structures is extreme, and each particular kind – long, short, simple, complex – is apt to be extreme. In a related example near the end of the play, the Jailer's blunt, earthy prose contrasts with the formal couplets of the descending Jupiter. This farrago of syntactical forms makes description uncommonly hard: any generalization must be modified immediately with a list of exceptions, but these are often so prominent and widespread as to demand a contradictory generalization.

It is tempting, for example, to speak of the late verse as "hypotactic," a useful term naturally suggested by convolution, and indeed many sentences seem to exhibit a high degree of subordination. Such an impression arises both from "left heavy" sentences, those constructions with multiple introductory dependent clauses, and from the many sentences ending in accumulated clauses and phrases, the continuative sequences examined above. At the same time, however, certain passages may proceed by means of relatively simple coordination.

                    I have inly wept,
        Or should have spoke ere this. Look down, you gods,
        And on this couple drop a blessed crown!
        For it is you that have chalk'd forth the way
        Which brought us hither.   (*The Tempest* 5.1.200–4)

Despite the abundance of such constructions, the style cannot justly be called paratactic either. For all the instances of coordination, whether copulative (*and*), adversative (*but*), or causal (*for*), the state of balance or equivalence is too often disrupted by the intrusion of an unequal element or by clauses that require subordination. Generally speaking, hypotaxis is associated with Ciceronian complexity, parataxis with Senecan plainness, and yet neither of these rubrics seems descriptively adequate. I have proposed that the late style may profitably be considered in light of the early modern taste for Ciceronian ornament and intricacy, the cultural delight in the highly wrought, the decorative, but at times the aggregation and juxtaposition of syntactic units creates a jagged and inelegant speech, even an earthy plainness, that seems to conform to the Senecan model. Mostly the late verse is so idiosyncratic and exceptional as to thwart any attempt to place it certainly within either category.

SHAKESPEARE AND FLETCHER

An efficient means of articulating the distinctively tortuous syntax of Shakespeare's late phase is to compare his habits with those of his principal collaborator at the time, John Fletcher. As I briefly indicated in the Introduction, astute readers began to notice early in the nineteenth century the presence of two poetic voices in *Henry VIII* and *The Two Noble Kinsmen*, intuitions bolstered by twentieth-century scholarship and now being confirmed by technological studies. The most persuasive arguments distinguishing between the two writers' contributions are metrical, grounded in perception of their dissimilar approaches to the pentameter line. Fletcher, for example, preserves the integrity of his line by making it end-stopped, whereas Shakespeare at this moment prefers enjambment and thus rarely ends the sentence or clause at the end of the line. Partly as an instrument for sustaining such regular lineation, Fletcher employs disyllabic and even trisyllabic endings much more frequently than Shakespeare.[43]

Even though syntax is less hospitable to such differentiation, the preferences and habits of the two dramatic poets make it possible to discriminate between their two syntactic styles. Charles Lamb's famous distinction between Shakespeare and Fletcher, quoted in the Introduction, does not mention sentence structure particularly, but it nevertheless identifies the two separate approaches in a way that includes syntax. While Fletcher, says Lamb, "lays line upon line, making up one after another," Shakespeare "mingles everything . . . runs line into line, embarrasses sentences and metaphors."[44] This commentary, capturing in a few words the essence of Shakespeare's late practice, is also helpful in studying metaphor and metrics, but for present purposes the crucial distinction is between syntactical forms: Fletcher's sentences tend to unfold smoothly and perspicuously, whereas Shakespeare's are clotted and often difficult to follow. One

---

[43] See Brian Vickers, *Shakespeare Co-Author* (Oxford: Oxford University Press, 2002), pp. 337–47, for a summary of some of the evidence and ample illustration of the differences.

[44] Charles Lamb, *Specimens of English Dramatic Poets, who lived about the time of Shakspeare*, 2nd edn. (London: John Bumpus, 1813), p. 419.

of Fletcher's primary goals is to dazzle the audience's collective ear. As Cyrus Hoy puts it, "Fletcher is clearly as much concerned with creating patterns of sound, rhythmic designs, as he is with embellishing or diversifying his blank verse."[45] The most distinctive property of Fletcher's verse is his predilection for repeated structures: parisonically arranged clauses, long strings of anaphora, and recurrent alliteration. Shakespeare knows such tricks as well, but in Fletcher's case they are proudly displayed, carefully managed, and not permitted to disrupt the iambic pattern.

A single passage of Fletcherian speech will serve to illustrate the very different sound his verse sentences produce:

BUCK.   All good people,   55
   You that thus far have come to pity me,
   Hear what I say, and then go home and lose me.
   I have this day receiv'd a traitor's judgment,
   And by that name must die; yet, heaven bear witness,
   And if I have a conscience, let it sink me,   60
   Even as the axe falls, if I be not faithful!
   The law I bear no malice for my death;
   'T has done, upon the premises, but justice;
   But those that sought it I could wish more Christians.
   Be what they will, I heartily forgive 'em;
   Yet let 'em look they glory not in mischief,   65
   Nor build their evils on the graves of great men,
   For then my guiltless blood must cry against 'em.
                   (*Henry VIII* 2.1.55–68)

The passage contains a number of features that Shakespeare might have used contrapuntally to impede the progress of the argument, such as the digressive suspension (lines 59–61) ending with the conditional clause ("if I be not faithful"), or the indirect object placed before subject and verb ("The law I bear no malice"). In Fletcher's hands, however, these twists barely disturb the smooth unfolding of the plea. That polished surface is also secured by Fletcher's determination to maintain congruity between phrase and line: almost all the lines are end-stopped, a practice that Shakespeare by this time deliberately flouts.[46]

---

[45] Cyrus Hoy, "The Language of Fletcherian Tragicomedy," in *Mirror up to Shakespeare: Essays in Honour of G. R. Hibbard*, ed. J. C. Gray (Toronto: University of Toronto Press, 1984), p. 107.

[46] See George T. Wright, *Shakespeare's Metrical Art* (Berkeley: University of California Press, 1988), pp. 213–18, and Ants Oras, *Pause Patterns in Elizabethan and Jacobean Drama: An Experiment in Prosody* (Gainesville: University of Florida Press, 1960), pp. 15–16. For nineteenth- and twentieth-century responses to these differences, see Vickers, *Shakespeare, Co-Author*, especially Chapters 6 and 7.

This Fletcherian speech to the crowd is especially instructive because it sounds so manifestly different from the Shakespearean lines the same Duke utters at the moment of his arrest. I have already quoted a few lines of it in another context, but it is worth reproducing the whole so as to emphasize its differences from the Fletcherian style:

> Pray give me favor, sir: this cunning Cardinal
> The articles o' th' combination drew
> As himself pleas'd; and they were ratified   170
> As he cried, "Thus let it be!" to as much end
> As give a crutch to th' dead. But our count-cardinal
> Has done this, and 'tis well; for worthy Wolsey
> (Who cannot err), he did it. Now this follows
> (Which, as I take it, is a kind of puppy   175
> To th' old dam, treason), Charles the Emperor,
> Under pretense to see the Queen his aunt
> (For 'twas indeed his color, but he came
> To whisper Wolsey), here makes visitation –
> His fears were that the interview betwixt   180
> England and France might through their amity
> Breed him some prejudice; for from this league
> Peep'd harms that menac'd him – privily
> Deals with our Cardinal, and, as I trow –
> Which I do well, for I am sure the Emperor   185
> Paid ere he promis'd, whereby his suit was granted
> Ere it was ask'd – but when the way was made
> And pav'd with gold, the Emperor thus desir'd,
> That he would please to alter the King's course,
> And break the foresaid peace. Let the King know   190
> (As soon he shall by me) that thus the Cardinal
> Does buy and sell his honor as he pleases,
> And for his own advantage.   (1.1.168–93)

Buckingham's account serves as a kind of showcase for the late Shakespearean style, displaying most of its hyperbatonic properties: intrusions, elliptical phrases, embedded clauses, loose connections among grammatical elements, regular enjambment, numerous light and weak endings, playfulness with caesurae, stops near the end of the line, all this amounting to a kind of jagged music, but music nonetheless.

A century and a half ago James Spedding, pressing his claim that Shakespeare could not have written certain passages in *Henry VIII*, at least not at the end of his career, picked out the speech of Buckingham now regularly assigned to Fletcher, the speech I quoted above. Spedding shows how the smoothness could not have been authentically Shakespearean even in an earlier phase, and certainly not at the end of the career.

In his earlier plays, when his versification was regular and his language comparatively diffuse, there is none of the studied variety of cadence which we find here; and by the time his versification had acquired more variety, the current of his thought had become more gushing, rapid, and full of eddies; and not to add that at no period whatever in the developement [*sic*] of his style was the proportion of thought and fancy to words and images so small as it appears in this speech of Buckingham's.[47]

Although Spedding seems to be talking mainly about prosody, his comments apply nonetheless to sentence structure. Moreover, that last little phrase, concerning "the proportion of thought and fancy to words and images"– very high for Shakespeare, very low for Fletcher – constitutes one of the most valuable insights about the distinctiveness of Shakespeare's late verse ever written. This high proportion, the source of perceived richness and profundity, is the direct product of the grammatical and syntactical maneuvers I have been surveying. Most of them amount to shortcuts to meaning.

MEANDERING AND MEANING

Cooper's *Latin Thesaurus* (1573) defines "syntaxis" as "Order of construction." The earliest uses of the English form are those of Francis Bacon, who speaks in *The Advancement of Learning* about "the Syntax and disposition of studies, that men may know in what order or pursuite to reade" (*OED* 1.a), and of Robert Cawdrey, who in the *Table Alphabeticall* (1613) defines it as "construction and order of words." The second *OED* definition is especially illuminating: "physical connexion, junction," with a citation from Helkiah Crooke's *Mikrokosmographia* (1631). In the sixteenth and seventeenth centuries, before the noun acquired its modern, exclusively grammatical sense, its application was far more general, pertaining to systems of organization, particularly those involving connections among parts. Most frequently the human body was the primary example, specifically the junctions of bones. Crooke's usage ranges from the joining of three small bones in the ear to larger osseous structures: "the universall compage or coagmentation of the bones is called a *Syntaxe*, and the packe of bones so fitted together

---

[47] James Spedding, "Who Wrote Shakespeare's *Henry VIII*?," *Gentleman's Magazine*, August 1850, 121.

is called a *Sceleton*.'[48] Marjorie Garber, commenting on this passage, points to the discursive intersection: "A 'compage' is a framework or system of conjoined parts, a complex structure, a means of joining. So *syntax*, in modern usage most frequently considered an aspect of grammar, and *articulation*, frequently regarded as an aspect of speech, thus each inhabit, in their early modern forms, an intellectual and conceptual space modeled on the body, and, quite specifically, on its 'connexions' or 'joints.' "[49]

These historical observations help us to think productively about the resemblance between the structure of the human body, the framework of the English sentence, and the narrative bones of the textual body. The general critical agreement on the "loose parenthetical syntax" of Shakespeare's late period is again pertinent in this physical context.[50] We might say that in this difficult late verse the grammatical "coagmentation," Crooke's word for cementing or fastening together, is weak: a determining feature of the late syntax is tenuous or broken connections among parts of sentences. In constructing speech for his characters, the mature Shakespeare ignores or elides the expected joints, carrying the listener forward roughly and even carelessly, inserting qualifiers, adding yet more semantic material, reversing direction, or simply breaking off and beginning afresh. The "sceleton" of the sentence is hard to discern from within. Sometimes an especially circuitous speaker will reach a satisfying end to a digressive construction, a feature examined more specifically in the next chapter, but when no such conclusion is promised or finally supplied, the audience is thrust forward into the further development of an idea or the introduction of a different or contrary line of thought. In the circumlocutions of Jachimo or Antonio, or in the jagged stopping and starting of Leontes or Posthumus, even attentive listeners risk losing their way. Conventional guides, the normal formations of syntax and grammar, are sometimes unhelpful, especially when the speaker indulges additive or revisionary impulses.

This neglect of logical connections is perhaps the most helpful stylistic pointer to the congruity between the arrangement of the verse sentences and the larger structural principles: the organization of events in a play like *The Winter's Tale* or *The Two Noble Kinsmen* is "loose" or even

[48] Helkiah Crooke, *Mikrokosmographia, A Description of the Body of Man* (London, 1631), p. 930.
[49] Marjorie Garber, "Out of Joint," in *The Body in Parts: Fantasies of Corporeality in Early Modern Europe*, ed. David Hillman and Carla Mazzio (New York: Routledge, 1997), pp. 34–35.
[50] J. H. P. Pafford, Introduction to *The Winter's Tale* (London: Methuen, 1963), p. lxxxv, n.2.

"parenthetical." The comparison between sentences and stories, especially how such a resemblance functions or what it signifies about artistic aims and effects, has thus far been mostly confined to studies of prose narrative. The stylistic convolutions, reversals, ellipses, delayed grammatical units, repetitions, additives, and other features to which the ear must become accustomed have their narrative counterparts in the unstable realm of romance fiction. The characters' wanderings, whether geographical, as in the case of Pericles, or geographical and psychological, as in *Cymbeline* or *The Winter's Tale* or *The Tempest*, take the same unpredictable shape as the sentences uttered.

Pericles immediately suggests a fundamental correlation between grammatical parts and narrative episodes, or syntactical arrangement and dramatic architecture. It begins with what we might call a strong statement, a kind of nominative introduction of the young hero: with little exposition or preparation, he must answer the riddle concerning Antiochus and his daughter. The subsequent movement of the action seems additive, neither inevitable or predictable. From this opening narrative "clause" the plot begins to unfold in its episodic, surprising, and yet mysteriously shapely way, comprising both logical and inexplicable action: Pericles' flight across the Mediterranean from Thaliard the assassin, his arrival in Tharsus and relief of its starving citizens, the uncanny recovery of his ancestral armor on the seashore at Pentapolis, the winning of the tournament and marriage to Thaisa, the violent storm, her "death" in childbirth followed by her resuscitation, the leap over sixteen years, the attempted murder of Marina and her sudden rescue, her frustrating sojourn in the brothel, the arrival of Lysimachus, Marina's ministrations to the desolate Pericles and the ensuing recognition, the playing of heavenly music and divine direction to Ephesus, the discovery of Thaisa in the temple and the reunion of the family. This sequence of incidents is both incoherent and coherent, sprawling and disconnected but structured by an underlying pattern of parallels and repetitions.

In the denouement of *Cymbeline*, the king asks his daughter for the details of her adventures, wondering about what else "should be demanded, / And all the other by-dependances, / From chance to chance" (5.5.389–91). The diction of his query ("by-dependances") helps to point the analogy between the articulation of the sentence and the unfolding of narrative: in asking about the sequential and logical connections between events, he employs language connoting syntax and subordination. His inquiry has to do with the *circumstances* of Imogen's reunion with her brothers, and while that noun does not appear in this passage, it helps us to see the links between geography and grammar, or plot and syntax. "Circumstance" is "an event viewed as a detail of some narrative, or history, or of the general course of events; an incident, an occurrence" (*OED* III.10); in early modern usage, it could also signify "circumstantiality of detail; detailed and . . . circuitous narration, circumlocution, beating about the bush, indirectness" (*OED* II.6). This is the sense Iago invokes in disparaging the "bombast circumstance" with which Othello has rejected Iago's professional sponsors. Even the common stylistic metaphor "beating about the bush" implies the identity of story and sentence, and "circumlocution" implies travel, especially the kind experienced by characters in romance fiction. Yet another sense of "circumstance" may be relevant. In *Othello*, Bianca, thwarted by an ambiguous answer from Cassio about his plans, responds by saying "Very good. I must be circumstanc'd." She may mean "content with her circumstances as a sometime girlfriend," or she may mean "subject to or governed by circumstances," i.e. not a free agent. All these senses are relevant to the circumlocutory style and the circuitous structure of the romances.

William Hazlitt remarked of *Cymbeline* that "The *reading of this play* is like going a journey with some uncertain object at the end of it," and his comment has stylistic as well as narrative ramifications.[51] Treating the sentence as a plot and the plot as a sentence is justified particularly in the late plays by the centrality of the journey as a structural device. Traditionally the quest was the backbone of romance fiction, a feature so common that it represents what Helen Cooper has described as "a 'meme', an idea that behaves like a gene in its ability to replicate faithfully and abundantly, but also on occasion to adapt, mutate, and therefore survive in different forms and cultures."[52] Characters in other modes do not invariably stay at home, of course, but travel forms the skeleton of romance in ways that it does not for the other major dramatic kinds. Indeed, the "adventure" upon which romance is structured is a term etymologically derived (*ad-venire*) from the Latin for "travel." Tyre, for example, sees little of its Prince: *Pericles* is almost all journey, beginning with the hero's visit to Antioch, moving throughout the Mediterranean, and ending in the temple of Diana at Ephesus. Often, of course, the travel is both literal and figurative. In *Cymbeline*, for instance, Jachimo's attempted corruption of Imogen requires a physical journey from Rome

---

[51] William Hazlitt, *Characters of Shakespear's Plays* (London: C. H. Reynell, 1817), p. 1 (italics added).
[52] Helen Cooper, *The English Romance in Time: Transforming Motifs from Geoffrey of Monmouth to the Death of Shakespeare* (Oxford: Oxford University Press, 2004), p. 3.

to Britian, but the scheme is described by Posthumus as a "voyage upon her" (1.4.158); he hopes to "get *ground* of [Posthumus's] fair mistress" (1.4.104); her chastity is described as a distant "prize," a "jewel"; he schemes to make it appear that he has "pick'd the lock and ta'en / The treasure of her honor" (2. 2. 41– 42).[53]

The spatial limitation for which *The Tempest* is famous reveals immediately that the most significant movement, the travel of which the various journeys are physical manifestations, is internal. The psychological or spiritual adventures of the major characters, most obviously Posthumus, Leontes, and Prospero but others as well, propel them along a line from innocence to experience. Many of them enact a pattern of fall and rise, a descent into something like madness from which they are ultimately rescued by a mix of penitence and providential intervention. Depending on the tale, the theatrical representation of the possible stages in such a journey will vary. Whether or not Leontes feels and conceals jealousy at the beginning of scene 2,[54] his earliest interchanges (1.2) with Polixenes and Hermione would seem to depict a state of contentment, and the audience is usually shocked by his sudden passage into emotional torment, a journey into madness that inflicts great suffering and delivers him, only after much pain, through penance to a kind of recovery.[55] Prospero's course is dramatized more economically: the audience, having heard his confession of neglected duty and the political fall it provoked, sees only his transformation from vengeful victim to gracious harmonizer.

The representation of these psychological journeys, in other words, is elliptical, sketchy, oblique. The audience is granted an occasional look-in and invited to fill in the blank spaces in the character's mental or spiritual progress: Posthumus leaves the stage ranting misogynistically about

---

[53] See Patricia Parker, *Literary Fat Ladies* (London: Methuen, 1987), pp. 132–40. As she points out, the vehicle "getting ground" is originally from fencing, "but it suggests both the acquisition of territory and its sexual counterpart" (p. 134).

[54] The debate over the depiction of Leontes' madness as nursed or new is revived from time to time: some representative pieces include Nevill Coghill, "Six Points of Stage-Craft in *The Winter's Tale*," *Shakespeare Survey 11* (1958), 31–41, and Howard Felperin, "'Tongue-tied, Our Queen?' The Deconstruction of Presence in *The Winter's Tale*," in *Shakespeare and the Question of Theory*, ed. Geoffrey Hartmann and Patricia Parker (London: Methuen, 1985), pp. 3–18.

[55] The usual equation of tortured syntax and tortured mind is represented in remarks by Ifor Evans and J. H. P. Pafford respectively. "The rough and abrupt phrases, which huddle upon one another so as almost to break the texture of the line, represent the mind of Leontes maddened by the distemper of jealousy." *The Language of Shakespeare's Plays* (London: Chatto and Windus, 1952), p. 181. "He is at times incoherent as a jealous man in a state of mad uncertainty must be. His speech is tangled because his mind and emotions are tangled." Introduction to *The Winter's Tale*, pp. lxxxiv–lxxxv.

Imogen's treachery, and when he finally re-enters, castigating himself for his own folly, some fourteen hundred lines, well over a third of the text, have been spoken. Considered in syntactical terms, *Pericles*, *Cymbeline* and *The Winter's Tale* exhibit the linear, additive structure of the complicated sentences that so many of the characters speak. *The Tempest* is not long or episodic, but it does expand from within by virtue of narrative interpolation: grammatically speaking, Antonio's attempt to assassinate his brother and the clowns' alliance with Caliban behave like modifying clauses, inserted within the conventional structure to illuminate the main thematic concerns or restate the idea from another angle.

Whether physical or spiritual, travel involves chance, and even when characters are not in danger of losing their lives they risk losing their way:

CAM.   Have you thought on
     A place whereto you'll go?
FLO.   Not any yet:
     But as th'unthought-on-accident is guilty
     To what we wildly do, so we profess
     Ourselves to be the slaves of chance, and flies   540
     Of every wind that blows.
                    (*The Winter's Tale* 4.4.536–41)

The phrase "slaves of chance" has a wide applicability, related as it is to the uncertainties of direction and outcome felt by many of the wanderers. Shakespeare repeatedly emphasizes the limits on human agency or the inefficacy of most attempts at control, as in Autolycus's claim that "Fortune . . . drops booties in [his] mouth" (*The Winter's Tale* 4.4.831–32), or Pisanio's "Fortune brings in some boats that are not steer'd" (*Cymbeline* 4.3.46). Many of these fortunate accidents send the characters on their way elsewhere: the shepherd and clown on the ship to Sicilia, the disguised Imogen fetching up at the Welsh cave of Belarius and her brothers, or the route of Alonso's vessel returning from Tunis. In *The Tempest*, the several journeys that have brought the cast to the spot are meaningfully related. Even when the travel ends safely or with unanticipated joy, the experience along the way is fraught with pain and fear. Such apparent perils are embodied in the storm that leads to Thaisa's being thrown overboard, generates the chaos in the first scene of *The Tempest*, or drowns the mariners off the seacoast of Bohemia. In *Henry VIII*, the travel is figurative rather than literal: the Henrician court is represented as a frightening, perilous realm through which the pilgrim – courtier or wife or prelate – must navigate. The shape and result of the travels in the romances are useful for thinking about the progress of the audience through the dramatic action and, more specifically, about its difficult journey through the verbiage.

"Motivation is not the strong point of most romancers," Stanley Wells reminds us,[56] and the romancer's typical reticence about explanations reflects the poet's casual approach to syntactical guidance. The suppression of motive affects the narrative ordering in the same way that the elision or suspension of grammatical units determines the arrangement of sentences. In Shakespeare's late work, such withholding governs not only the irrational jealousy of a Leontes or the sudden treachery of a Dionyza but also the disparately occurring actions, the nebulous relations among plots, the entrance of supernatural figures, and the unlikely endings. The overriding influence of chance in romance fiction seems to create a mysterious, apparently random universe, but some force is usually credited with arranging events or at least guiding characters toward reunion and fulfillment, as when Jupiter appears to the ghostly family of Posthumus. The plays abound in actions that surprise the audience or suddenly torque the plot in a new direction, narrative turns that are magnified by the extraordinary self-consciousness of their presentation. These are "turns" in more than one sense – not only twists of plot but theatrical showpieces spotlighting the playwright. The dramatist presents characters and their behavior in ways that sometimes seem haphazard or ill-considered, and in this respect especially the ordination of events mimics the apparently random, jerky movement of the verse sentence.

Hyperbaton, Puttenham's term for syntactical "figures of disorder," applies handily to the distribution of persons and events in the world of romance. Jachimo himself is a "figure of disorder," or, to return to Puttenham's English translation of the Greek term, a "trespasser" into Imogen's chamber, one whose audacious behavior and surprising movements disrupt and complicate the action just as such a verbal trope does to the sentence. Moreover, his disorderly contribution to the plot narratively replicates the theatrical, convoluted patterns of his speech. His emergence from the trunk is a spectacular interpolation, a theatrical parenthesis that is not only surprising but also significantly modifies the subsequent action. In *The Tempest*, as Stephano, Trinculo, and Caliban enact a parodic version of their political superiors' conspiracy, they create a digression that distracts the audience temporarily from the main movement of the action. The Masque of Ceres offers a similar diversion,

---

[56] Stanley Wells, "Shakespeare and Romance," in *Later Shakespeare*, ed. John Russell Brown and Bernard Harris (London: Edward Arnold, 1966), p. 65.

shifting the direction of the play and beguiling the audience with unexpected pleasures in the midst of a plot to which it is only loosely related. Shifts in direction may be temporary, or gradual, or violent, and often in the romances the audience is shocked or puzzled by such a narrative alteration.

The most striking of these might be called narrative *aposiopesis*, in the sense that the narrative breaks off and resumes in a new direction.

Enter certain Reapers, properly habited: they join with the Nymphs in a graceful dance, towards the end whereof Prospero starts suddenly, and speaks; after which, to a strange, hollow, and confused noise, they heavily vanish.

PROS. (*Aside*) I had forgot that foul conspiracy
Of the beast Caliban and his confederates
Against my life.

              (*The Tempest* 4.1.139–41)

This famously clunky moment is especially instructive because it is the narrative equivalent of breaking off a speech in order to resume in another direction. The effects of this habit of interruption are far-reaching, as Brian Gibbons points out:

in *The Tempest* interruption is the expression of power. It is Prospero, directly or via Ariel, who effects all the interruptions in the play. Art, like magic, is characterized by an arresting and reordering of natural events. Prospero is a dramatic artist as well as a magician – he is a composer of human events, and it is his continuous manipulation of the action which commands the spectators' interest, intrigues them, frequently wrong-foots them. Interruptions – even scripted ones – in live performance are exciting, tantalizing, because they put the dramatic illusion at risk: interruptions in *The Tempest* are also metatheatrical, they make a spectator self-consciously aware of theatre as a metaphor for life.[57]

Shifts of place are the rule in the romances: Antioch, Tyre, Tharsus, Mytilene, Sicilia, the road from Delphos, Bohemia, etc. In the modern theater, directors of *Cymbeline* – or perhaps more accurately their designers – usually emphasize the scenic shift between 1.3 and 1.4 by giving the Roman scenes a distinctly different feel from the British setting to which the audience has become accustomed, and then doing so again when we arrive in Wales.

The most memorable dislocations are temporal, those authorial shifts that disrupt the time scheme in *Pericles* and *The Winter's Tale*. Since Gower has served the audience as guide from the beginning of *Pericles*,

---

[57] Brian Gibbons, "*The Tempest* and Interruptions," *Cahiers Elisabethains*, 45 (1994), 47–48.

making the storytelling unusually self-conscious, his ironically under-stated announcement that the passage of time ("our fast-growing scene") has brought Marina to adulthood is perhaps not shocking, but it never-theless implies a casual mode of narrative and requires that the audience stretch the rules normally pertaining to dramatic plots. In *The Winter's Tale*, where the narrative syntax is disordered and loosely connected from start to finish, the most violent shift comes with the entrance of Time, the Chorus, whose speech wrenches us into new chronological territory. As for actual territory, we have already been transported, with Antigonus and his bundle, from Sicilia to Bohemia in the middle of the third act. That shift follows a series of narrative jerks – the blunt words of the oracle contradicting Leontes' charges, the servant's entrance announcing the death of Mamillius, Leontes' confession of error, and Paulina's return to declare the death of Hermione. All these turns proceed narratively from what has gone before, but the connections are relatively loose and, like the realm of romance generally, mysterious. The Bohemian scenes, taken together, constitute an enormous narrative interpolation: framed by the Sicilian events they interrupt, this series of episodes depends upon, refers to, and modifies the story that has preceded and will follow it. As for narrative hyperbaton, what better figure of disorder than the bear that dashes into the tale and out again?

RELAXATION

The "loose" syntax I have been describing has prompted complaint that the structure of the late verse signifies a relaxation of Shakespeare's poetic intensity, taking "relaxation" in the negative sense of inattention or lack of persistence. James Sutherland's claim that Shakespeare suffered artistic "fatigue" is a version of this view.[58] Especially after the compressed and tightly organized speeches delivered by the tragic heroes, such scarcely-knit passages can sound flaccid or ill-thought-out, as if the poet couldn't be bothered to tidy up the syntactical loose ends. But the parallels between syntax and larger elements of structure suggest unity of inspiration. Other artistic choices, for example, confirm the new, casual approach implied by relaxation of the syntactical framework. In choosing a source for *The Winter's Tale*, for example, Shakespeare eschews Roman or British history

---

[58] See James Sutherland, "The Language of the Last Plays," in *More Talking of Shakespeare*, ed. John Garrett (London: Longmans, 1959), p. 152. Ifor Evans, in *The Language of Shakespeare's Plays*, exhibits similar impatience.

and turns instead to Robert Greene for an old tale that, at least on its surface, seems considerably less demanding or less historically important than Plutarch or Holinshed. Similarly, his protraction and dispersal of the stories that finally cohere in the virtuosic final scene of *Cymbeline* signify an apparently casual or playful approach to dramatic structure, compared, for example, to the directness of *Macbeth* and *Coriolanus*. Not "bored" but confident and unconcerned with spelling out connections, Shakespeare has taken a deliberately "careless" approach to construction and explanation, an insouciance in which the audience is invited to share. Words, phrases, clauses, and sentences are less significant than the meanings behind them, and we are able, paradoxically, to approach and ultimately to apprehend those meanings by not trying too hard.

CHAPTER 4

Syntax (II): suspension

And therefore it is easie to observe, that in all Metricall composition,
. . . the force of the whole piece, is for the most part left to the
shutting up; the whole frame of the Poem is a beating out of a piece
of gold, but the last clause is as the impression of the stamp, and that
is it that makes it currant.

John Donne, *Sermons*

Make 'em laugh; make 'em cry; make 'em wait.

Wilkie Collins

This chapter develops the correspondence, begun in Chapter 3, between
the structure of the verse sentence and the disposition of dramatic action in
the romances. The audience's journey through the syntactical thicket of the
late style produces both frustration and pleasure, and having concentrated
on the baffles and complications within the sentence, here I turn to the
payoff, the expectation and achievement of closure. The aggressively digressive syntax carries the listener on a winding and difficult semantic course, a
congeries of grammatical inversions, accumulated clauses, interpolations,
unexpected breakings off, and other such obstacles and sidetracks. But in a
striking number of instances, essential elements of grammar, particularly
the verbal phrase, often the direct object, and sometimes even the
subject, are withheld until the very end of the sentence. We might say,
speaking not as Latinists but as literary critics, that such sentences are
organized periodically, since semantic gratification is withheld until just
before the full stop or period. This combination of digressive and
climactic strategies creates a crucially valuable tension between ending and
not ending, between the pleasure of expectation and the reward of semantic
completion.

It must be meaningful that Shakespeare should resort to such a style for
plays in which the narrative middle is flagrantly digressive and the shape
and meaning of the action become apparent only in the final moments.

149

At the end of the last chapter, I cited Hazlitt's response to *Cymbeline*, "The reading of this play is like going a journey with some uncertain object at the end of it," and that passage continues as follows:

. . . the suspense is kept up and heightened by the long intervals between each action. Though the events are scattered over such an extent of surface, and relate to such a variety of characters, yet the links which bind the different interests of the story are never entirely broken. The most straggling and seemingly casual incidents are contrived in such a manner as to lead at last to the most complete development of the catastrophe. The ease and conscious unconcern with which this is effected only makes the skill more wonderful.[1]

Hazlitt's last adjective is especially apt. The wonder that marks the end of these dramas – "such a deal of wonder has broken out within this hour that ballad-makers cannot be able to express it" (*The Winter's Tale* 5.2.23–25) – is a product of Shakespeare's gift not only for theatrical but also for grammatical arrangement.

ARE WE THERE YET?

The audience's struggle with the obstacles and byways of the late style is a source of considerable pleasure. Early definitions of the verb "digress" signify this effect by associating deviation with straying or error, as in Bacon's statement, in *The Advancement of Learning*, that "man, while he aspired to be like God in knowledge, digressed and fell" (*OED* 3). Both "deviation" and "digression" derive etymologically from roots having to do with a road (*via*) or step (*gradus*), and the temptation to stray from the main path is one of the inherent dangers and one of the inherent pleasures of travel. The wayward, convoluted verbal structures through which the audience must move in processing meaning are both frustrating and exhilarating. In the sentence, the verse paragraph, the speech, or the dialogue among speakers, the listening mind finds itself pushed in various directions by multiple and conflicting grammatical indicators, and the same is true of narrative and its affective cues.

Imogen's outburst in the middle of *Cymbeline*, when she believes she is to meet Posthumus at Milford Haven, exhibits with unusual clarity the tension between linearity and digression:

O, for a horse with wings! Hear'st thou, Pisanio?
He is at Milford-Haven. Read, and tell me

---

[1] From William Hazlitt, *Characters of Shakespear's Plays* (London: C. H. Reynell, 1817), p. 1.

How far 'tis thither. If one of mean affairs   50
May plod it in a week, why may not I
Glide thither in a day? Then, true Pisanio,
Who long'st like me to see thy lord; who long'st,
(O let me bate!) – but not like me – yet long'st
But in a fainter kind – O, not like me,   55
For mine's beyond beyond – say, and speak thick
(Love's counselor should fill the bores of hearing,
To th' smothering of the sense), how far it is
To this same blessed Milford. And by th' way
Tell me how Wales was made so happy as   60
T' inherit such a haven. But first of all,
How we may steal from hence; and for the gap
That we make in time, from our hence-going
And our return, to excuse. But first, how get hence.
Why should excuse be born or ere begot?   65
We'll talk of that hereafter. Prithee speak,
How many score of miles may we well rid
'Twixt hour and hour?   (*Cymbeline* 3.2.48–68)

Imogen asks questions that imply an end, makes a plan, and yet modifies those questions and plans as she proceeds, thus delaying her own and the auditor's satisfaction. Her speech also illustrates the way that, throughout the late verse, the syntax pleasurably diverts the listener even as it puzzles. The apprehension of meaning in dramatic speech demands that we follow the speaker along a winding grammatical path, an experience that, putting it crudely, represents an aural equivalent of the reversals and deviations of the wager plot.

Shakespeare glances rather specifically at the analogy between grammar and travel in the middle of Imogen's speech ("And by th' way / Tell me"), and throughout the passage the audience must hold in balance the conflicting impulses of wandering and arrival, development and completion. Having finished reading the letter, now imagining the reunion with Posthumus, Imogen finds her brain crowded with joy, anxiety, and a series of practical questions. The expression of these disparate ideas is loosely organized and proceeds rapidly, so much so that her thought seems joyfully scattered. The familiar Shakespearean habit of proceeding by means of antithesis makes itself felt, initially in the opposition between the normal pace of "one of mean affairs" versus "I" (lines 50–51); "plod" versus "glide" (lines 51–52); "a week" versus "a day" (lines 51–52). But then the comparison between the respective relationships begins to break down under further scrutiny: "like me . . . but not like me . . . O, not like me" (lines 53–55). The audience's perception of meaning is enhanced, and its experience enriched, by multiple patterns, repetitions, evanescent metaphors, and other poetic delights: "who long'st . . . who long'st . . . yet long'st"; "like me . . . / . . . but not like me . . . / . . . O, not like me"; "beyond beyond"; "speak thick"; "To th' smothering of the sense"; "how Wales was made"; "so happy as / I' inherit such a haven." The self-consciousness of the confused expression increases our sense of pleasure, notably in the intrusion of "O let me bate!" and the ironic introduction, at the end of the speech and twice over, of "But, first of all . . . But first." The tension between end and middle is effected specifically by ellipses – "But first of all, / [tell me] How we may steal . . ." – and by delayed verbs: "and for the gap / . . . / . . . to excuse." Progress is also impeded as the metaphor of sealing wax appears momentarily and then shifts to the image of ear wax. Finally, the entire passage is colored by our ironic awareness, shared with Pisanio, of the actual intent of the letter: that Imogen is being lured to Milford Haven to be murdered for supposed infidelity compromises our wholehearted participation in her excited state.

The conflicts within and between the grammatical and poetic texture of Imogen's speech are typical not only of the verse that Shakespeare has developed for these plays but also of his plots. Helen Cooper points to this tension between digression and shapeliness in the organization of *Pericles*:

> This sprawl of place and time and the irrelevance of human intention is offset by the precision of its symmetries of structure. The play heightens what is already found in the *Apollonius* and Gower as a pattern of repetitions in which each recurrence recasts our understanding of what has gone before. Its outermost form is that of the exile-and-return romance, in which Pericles abandons and resumes his kingship. The relationships of father and daughter, husband and wife, are more central in every sense, from the incest with which the play opens, through the "good" wooing of Thaisa that concludes with the report of the deaths of Antiochus and his daughter, to the reunion of the family at the end, when marital and paternal and filial love are separated out and celebrated with an intensity greater than the condemnation of the abhorrent affinities of the opening. This is not just plot progression, but a process of commentary, or rather overwriting: aberration, deviance, is replaced by what is good in both human and divine terms.[2]

Cooper catalogues similar instances of mirroring and repetition in *The Tempest*, and readers will immediately recognize the pertinence of her observations to *The Winter's Tale* and *Cymbeline*. Although *Henry VIII*

---

[2] Helen Cooper, *The English Romance in Time: Transforming Motifs from Geoffrey of Monmouth to the Death of Shakespeare* (Oxford: Oxford University Press, 2004), p. 65.

seems not to adhere to such a model, lacking as it does the mythic wandering or homecoming, it coheres structurally by similar means: the serial episodes of fall and rise at the Tudor court create a recurring pattern that implies some controlling force. The birth of Princess Elizabeth, the rise that proceeds from the political fall of Katherine and the physical "fall" of Anne Boleyn, is the period – the Tudor period – towards which the convoluted actions move. And what Cooper concludes about *Pericles* seems relevant to *Henry VIII* also, if in a less obvious way: "dramatic irony becomes a kind of structural parallelism within the play, as audience expectations implicitly provide a running commentary on his own tragic text, rewriting and correcting it for good."[3] In all the romances such symmetrical episodes ground the divagatory narratives and guide the audience through the chaotic realm, functioning in the same way that alliteration, reiterated words, duplicated rhythms, and indeed the basic pattern of blank verse protect the audience against the syntactical vagaries of tangled speeches.

THE PLEASURE TRIP

The frustrations and difficulties of the syntactical route notwithstanding, we should also acknowledge the delights of not arriving. The delays, diversions, and postponements encoded in the linguistic structures of these works cause us to experience directly the vicissitudes of their stories, requiring that we participate in the challenges to patience and expectation that the characters endure. But at the same time the stylistic and narrative journey gives immense theatrical and poetic satisfaction, pleasure built on the distance from the characters' plight. The phenomenon of postponement and perspective that Peter Brooks describes is relevant here: speaking of Shahrazad and her thousand and one stories, he proposes that "narration, in this allegory, is seen to be life-giving in that it arouses and sustains desire, ensuring that the terminus it both delays and beckons toward will offer what we might call a lucid repose, desire both come to rest and set in perspective."[4] In Shakespearean romance, expectations of order are met by the blank verse and by the grammatical conventions that underlie the transmission of meaning in all communication, but the threats to such coherence and clarity are formidable. The conflict in each

[3] *Ibid.* p. 66.
[4] Peter Brooks, *Reading for the Plot: Design and Intention in Narrative* (New York: Alfred A. Knopf, 1984), p. 61.

sentence between progression and digression, achievement and diversion, helps to acclimate the audience to the difficulties of the stage world. Brooks's term "perspective" is especially pertinent in a stylistic context. Since the value of perspective is perhaps the major thematic imperative of these last works, an awareness of how the poetry helps to promote this ideal augments our understanding of these texts in ways that critics have hitherto gestured at but not really demonstrated.

Perspective implies security, the safety of a standpoint permitting a broad view, and Providence is the guarantor of that security.[5] The audience enjoys a sense of exhilaration in following a speaker through convoluted, hyerbatonic speeches, and the pleasures of such a semantic challenge are magnified by the sense of insured risk. The confusing sentences give aural being to the breadth of the romance universe, the excitement of the adventure narrative, and the providential guidance the form implies. The audience is obliged to relax and not to relax, to attend carefully but not too carefully. Listeners must believe that the sentence will ultimately deliver its meaning, just as they believe that the plot will eventually produce a happy ending. Such belief implies confidence in a controlling power, a willingness to hang on until the semantic unit is completed. The verse and the narratives represent an odd mixture of the casual and the careful on the part of the poet, engagement and detachment on the part of the audience.

Such a tension between delight and perplexity, chaos and comprehension, informs the most outlandish, self-conscious passages:

2.   QUEEN   Honored Hippolyta,
     Most dreaded Amazonian, that hast slain
     The scythe-tusked boar; that with thy arm, as strong
     As it is white, wast near to make the male   80
     To thy sex captive, but that this thy lord,
     Born to uphold creation in that honor
     First Nature styl'd it in, shrunk thee into
     The bound thou wast o'erflowing, at once subduing
     Thy force and thy affection; soldieress   85
     That equally canst poise sternness with pity,
     Whom now I know hast much more power on him
     Than ever he had on thee, who ow'st his strength,
     And his love too, who is a servant for

[5] Patricia Parker, writing of *The Faerie Queene*, suggests that the physical, spiritual, and stylistic wanderings of that poem are "sustained by, and grounded in, the permanent and the eternal, that ordering frame which enables divagation to be a species of delight." *Inescapable Romance: Studies in the Poetics of a Mode* (Princeton: Princeton University Press, 1979), p. 10.

The tenor of thy speech; dear glass of ladies,   90
Bid him that we, whom flaming war doth scorch,
Under the shadow of his sword may cool us;
Require him he advance it o'er our heads;
Speak't in a woman's key – like such a woman
As any of us three; weep ere you fail;   95
Lend us a knee;
But touch the ground for us no longer time
Than a dove's motion when the head's pluck'd off;
Tell him, if he i' th' blood-siz'd field lay swoll'n,
Showing the sun his teeth, grinning at the moon,   100
What you would do.
                (*The Two Noble Kinsmen* 1.1.77–101)

I quote this astonishing sentence without explication, allowing it to serve as a kind of introduction to the following discussion: the reader will have noticed the profusion of digressions, resumptions, parentheses, ellipses, repetitions, and other typical poetic features. As a prayer to the Amazonian Queen, it is clearly a performance, a structural tour-de-force, a kind of litany unresolved until the long-delayed arrival of the final noun clause that serves as the direct object: "Honored Hippolyta . . . Bid him . . . Require him . . . Tell him . . . What you would do." But the star performer, though the words are put in the mouth of a secondary character, is Shakespeare.

The romance audience anticipates that the performing playwright will arrange a harmonious ending, but the pleasures of the dramatic experience derive also from the challenge of getting there. In *Pericles*, for example, the main business of the play consists of the deviations and adventures encountered along the way, notably the tournament in Pentapolis, the magical revival of Thaisa, and the perils of Marina in both Tharsus and Mytilene. In David Thacker's 1989 RSC production, as Leonine gathered his courage to murder Marina – on the orders of Dionyza, itself an unexpected turn – and she eloquently resisted, suddenly pirates descended on pink ropes from the flies of the Swan Theatre, a directorial stroke that aptly exaggerated the inherent surprise of the plot device. The piratical hijack shifts Marina and the audience to the brothel, and this new location, with its vivid, grotesque characters, protracts the adventures and trials of virtue in unexpected ways. Such a tonal shift might also be said to extend the adventures vertically rather than lineally, moving us as it does from potential tragedy to the precincts of low comedy. Surprising actions and new narrative directions challenge the attention and expectations of the audience in the same way that elements of the protracted, complex verse sentences do. The audience is diverted by being diverted.

A PERFIT SENCE AND FULL PERIODE

Every sentence is to some extent periodic, obviously, and as Northrop Frye and others have taught us, the ending of every play might be considered the primary determinant of its meaning.[6] In both respects, however, the romances are distinctive. Shakespeare regularly exaggerates the grammatical means of suspension so that sentences or passages in these late works engage, frustrate, and then finally satisfy the listener, often in an unexpected fashion. Likewise, in each case the significance of complex acts, whether linguistic or dramatic, is altered and clarified by a highly theatrical conclusion, sometimes even a surprise ending. The romances offer a parallel between syntactical and narrative satisfaction, between small and large units of dramatic structure, and the nature of that correspondence is attributable to the altered conception of human experience determining Shakespeare's choice of stories and management of style.

The method of syntactical or semantic postponement is one of the most revealing stylistic traits of the late work. It sounds most prominently in *The Winter's Tale*, as in this example from Leontes' interrogation of Camillo:

> Ha' not you seen, Camillo
> (But that's past doubt; you have, or your eye-glass
> Is thicker than a cuckold's horn), or heard
> (For to a vision so apparent rumor   270
> Cannot be mute), or thought (for cogitation
> Resides not in that man that does not think)
> My wife is slippery?   (1.2.267–73)

Leontes begins by posing a question, but before disclosing its substance he leads the auditor through a maze of parenthetical elements and qualifying material: a series of three verbs, "seen," "heard," and "thought," alternates with a corresponding series of lengthy clauses asserting that Camillo must have seen, heard, and thought. The interruptions here are comparatively regular, imposing a complementary or contrapuntal pattern of their own rather than simply deranging the sentence.

---

[6] See, most obviously, Northrop Frye's *The Anatomy of Criticism* (Princeton: Princeton University Press, 1957) as well as his other works on romance and comedy. The other indispensable discussion is that of Frank Kermode, *The Sense of an Ending: Studies in the Theory of Fiction* (New York: Oxford University Press, 1967).

The most telling feature is that Shakespeare has scrupulously controlled the grammar of the sentence to augment the force of the final clause. Without the last four words the sentence is meaningless, and yet getting to the end is no easy matter. The effect is that of a grammatical labyrinth in which we make our way through a series of baffles, then turn a corner, and find ourselves faced with the beast – "My wife is slippery." The mechanics of this construction leave us suspended in air, dangling through six circumlocutory lines, until we land with a jolt on the final clause. Sylvia Adamson points out that such constructions can be dangerous in English: "The postponement of the main clause within the clause group is prob- lematic, because the rhythmic bias of English is towards right-heavy rather than left-heavy structures and the effect of a left-heavy Period is likely to be bathos rather than resolution."[7] Leontes' question comes close to bathos: the audacity of the construction is clearly calculated to indicate the extent of his lunacy.

Semantic suspension is rarely as ostentatious as in the preceding example, but the frequency with which it appears sustains the aural effect of delayed completion. Simple inversions, for example, can create such an impression.

> Bravely the figure of this harpy hast thou
> Perform'd, my Ariel; a grace it had, devouring.
> Of my instruction hast thou nothing bated   85
> In what thou hadst to say; so with good life,
> And observation strange, my meaner ministers
> Their several kinds have done.
>   (*The Tempest* 3.3.83–88)

>   But the whole week's not fair
> If any day it rain. Their valiant temper
> Men lose when they incline to treachery,
> And then they fight like compell'd bears, would fly
> Were they not tied.
>   (*The Two Noble Kinsmen*, 3.1.65–69)

>   Let not conscience,
> Which is but cold in flaming, thy lone bosom
> Inflame too nicely, nor let pity, which
> Even women have cast off, melt thee, but be
> A soldier to thy purpose.   (*Pericles*, 4.1.4–8)

---

[7] Sylvia Adamson, "Literary Language," in *The Cambridge History of the English Language, vol. III, 1476–1776*, ed. Roger Lass (Cambridge: Cambridge University Press, 1999), p. 588.

Each of these passages contains more than one reversal, the most common being that in which the object precedes the verb and sometimes the subject as well. John Porter Houston has identified "a great variety of inversions" in the grammar of *The Tempest*:

OVS [Object, Verb, Subject] patterns and their analogues, for example, which are often as few in number as five or eight in longer plays, add up to twelve in *The Tempest*, which has only about 1,600 lines of verse. While there are only seventeen SOV [Subject, Object, Verb] constructions, nineteen analogous ones reinforce them. Six hyperbatic *of* phrases, almost as many as in *Antony and Cleopatra*, are also present, along with every other kind of inversion Shakespeare had used.[8]

Such minor alterations of normal word order can serve different functions at particular moments, as some of the examples in Chapter 3 indicated – heightening the level of formality, for example. But whatever the immediate effect, such an inversion always produces a slight cognitive hesitation, a moment of withholding that augments the semantic impact of the concluding phrase.

The grammatical suspension may be as familiar as a simple conditional sentence. The first line of *The Winter's Tale*, "If you shall chance, Camillo, to visit Bohemia . . .," is just such a construction, establishing the tone of conditionality characteristic of the mode in general and of this play in particular. According to the familiar form of such semantic structures, the mind's ear requires that the conditional beginning be resolved. Even the simplest construction beginning with an "if" clause engages the listener in a rhythmic process of tension and release. In these last plays Shakespeare regularly elaborates and protracts the first term to such a degree that we risk losing our way before receiving syntactical and semantic satisfaction.

The conspicuously suspended sentence, we might say, represents a kind of gamble, and Shakespeare's magnification of introductory phrases and clauses to extreme lengths entails a kind of authorial risk. He seems to be testing the listener's patience and acuity, pressing towards the limits of comprehensibility, and what is more, he seems to be doing so playfully, as if the verbal medium were a kind of athletic bar to be continually raised. A sense of dare underlies the complexity of the style, as if the author is urging the reader on to a difficult task with the promise of reward. That playful attitude towards style seems to inform *Cymbeline* especially, where

[8] John Porter Houston, *Shakespearean Sentences: A Study in Style and Syntax* (Baton Rouge: Louisiana State University Press, 1988), pp. 210–11.

it also governs the ironic and audacious handling of the complex action and resolution, notably in the finale. Many of Shakespeare's dramatic choices in this phase seem determined by an attraction to conditionality, a willingness to entertain the possibility of the unlikely, to suspend disbelief for the purposes of play.

In the first Roman scene in *Cymbeline*, the wager between Jachimo and Posthumus is so constructed, offering a prose instance of the structural principles so far illustrated mainly in verse:

JACH. If I bring you no sufficient testimony that I have enjoy'd the dearest bodily part of your mistress, my ten thousand ducats are yours, so is your diamond too. If I come off and leave her in such honor as you have trust in, she your jewel, this your jewel, and my gold are yours – provided I have your commendation for my more free entertainment.

POST. I embrace these conditions, let us have articles betwixt us. Only, thus far you shall answer: if you make your voyage upon her and give me directly to understand you have prevail'd, I am no further your enemy; she is not worth our debate. If she remain unseduc'd, you not making it appear otherwise, for your ill opinion and th'assault you have made to her chastity, you shall answer me with your sword.

(1.4.148–63)

The two "if" clauses proposed by each speaker are emblematic of the fairy-tale world of *Cymbeline* and of the late plays in general. The subject here is a bet – or more appropriately, since the point of contention is Imogen's chastity, a "lay" (147) – and it is this inherently dramatic contest that drives the plot. Playful impulses also express themselves in the stylistic gambles of such extraordinary suspensions. We feel a physical tension between the impetus to expand, to digress, to increase the stakes, on the one hand, while on the other, we enjoy the grammatical comforts of control and the expectation of winning.

A variant of the flashy suspension is the extended sentence that changes direction.

> This entertainment
> May a free face put on, derive a liberty
> From heartiness, from bounty, fertile bosom,
> And well become the agent; 't may – I grant.
> But to be paddling palms and pinching fingers,   115
> As now they are, and making practic'd smiles,
> As in a looking-glass; and then to sigh, as 'twere
> The mort o' th' deer – O, that is entertainment
> My bosom likes not, nor my brows!
> (*The Winter's Tale* 1.2.111–19)

Such a grammatical structure is effectively periodic and representative of the way Shakespeare's syntactic choices function throughout the romances. Leontes begins with a possibility (that intimate cordiality might be innocent), enumerates in a string of verbal and prepositional phrases the ways in which it could be construed as proper, summarizes this interpretation in a conditional clause calculated to prepare for its rejection, then demolishes the case for purity in the massive infinitive phrase beginning with "But," and finally recapitulates his conclusion in the appended clause that taints the sense of "entertainment." Technically speaking, the sentence owes its effect to the rhetorical device known as anacoluthon, a statement that begins in one direction, shifts in the center, and concludes in the opposite direction. The *Riverside* text, quoted here, divides the passage into two sentences, whereas the Folio prints a colon instead of the period after "I grant." In either case, the conjunctive "But" signifies the reversal.

My use of the term "periodic" perhaps demands some explanation, especially since it is here applied to poetry, and not only to sentences but also to whole speeches. The sentences examined in this chapter mostly lack the tight grammatical joinery of a conventionally "periodic" prose style: in fact, as I have spent some time establishing, the syntactical arrangement of most sentences in Shakespeare's late verse is loose and digressive. The typical lengthy sentence is made up of tenuously connected phrases and clauses, and these are frequently interrupted by parentheses, dashes, and shifts in direction. Moreover, the frequent resort to ellipsis compels the listener to labor at making connections that the polished Ciceronian style, often described as periodic, would normally supply. But the term "period" was regarded more loosely than we have come to think. As Sylvia Adamson points out, "renaissance writers, like their classical mentors, regarded the Period as a category of *rhetoric* rather than *grammar*, to be discussed primarily in terms of meaning and effect."[9] And in Shakespeare's hands the digressive strategies do not make the lengthy, convoluted sentences in which they appear seem less dependent upon the material placed immediately prior to the full stop. In fact, their length and complexity serve to delay the anticipated resolution and so to increase the semantic payoff.[10]

---

[9] "Literary Language," p. 584.
[10] Adamson demonstrates that early modern writers used a range of tactics to create the effect of a delayed conclusion. "The aim in all cases is to find a means of postponing the reader's grasp of the Period's unity until its close. In other words, the unified composition and the sense of an ending

Puttenham recognizes this pattern of frustration and release when he describes the auricular figure known as "*Irmus, or the long loose.*"

Ye haue another maner of speach drawn out at length and going all after one tenure and with an imperfit sence till you come to the last word or verse which concludes the whole premisses with a perfit sence and full periode, the Greeks call it *Irmus*, I call him the [long loose] thus appearing in a dittie of Sir *Thomas Wyat* where he describes the diuers distempers of his bed.

> *The restlesse state renuer of my smart,*
> *The labours salue increasing my sorrow:*
> *The bodies ease and troubles of my hart,*
> *Quietor of mynde mine vnquiet for:*
> *Forgettor of paine remembrer of woe,*
> *The place of sleepe wherein I do but wake:*
> *Besprent with teares my bed I thee forsake.*

Ye see here how ye can gather no perfection of sence in all this dittie till ye come to the last verse in these wordes *my bed I thee forsake.* And in another Sonet of *Petrarcha* which was thus Englished by the same Sir *Thomas Wyat.*

> *If weaker care if sodaine pale collour,*
> *If many sighes with little speach to plaine:*
> *Now ioy now woe, if they my ioyes distaine,*
> *For hope of small, if much to feare therefore,*
> *Be signe of love then do I love again.*

Here all the whole sence of the dittie is suspended till ye come to the last three wordes, *then do I loue againe,* which finisheth the song with a full and perfit sence.[11]

"Loose" is an early modern term for "conclusion" or "close," the upshot or end of a matter; it is related to the use of the term in archery, where the "loose" or release of the bowstring signified the accomplishment of the shot.[12] "Speach drawn out at length," "perfection of sence," "sence . . . suspended" – the rhetorician's vocabulary illuminates the theatrical, poetic, and thematic effects of semantic postponement. It also bears comparison with the modern critic Eric Rabkin's description of how

---

are not separate but interdependent ideals. The Period is a teleological construct whose author works in the same spirit as the divine creator, foreseeing the end and directing the unwitting reader/hearer towards its final disclosure." ("Literary Language," p. 590).

[11] *The Arte of English Poesie,* a facsimile reproduction ed. Edward Arber, with an Introduction by Baxter Hathaway (Athens, Ohio: Kent State University Press, 1988), pp. 186–87.

[12] As Puttenham explains earlier in his definition of "vulgar rhyme," or "omoioteleton," according to the Greeks, "We call this figure following the originall, the [*like loose*] alluding to th'Archers term who is not said to finish the feate of his shot before he give the loose, and deliver his arrow from the bow, in which respect we use to say marke the loose of a thing for marke the end of it" (*Arte,* pp. 184–85).

certain fiction writers contrive for their sentences to "discharge."[13] The diction of the two commentators is analogous – Puttenham's implies the shooting of arrows, Rabkin's the firing of guns – and both emphasize the contrast between the accumulated pressure at the beginning of the sentence and the climactic release of that syntactical frustration.

The accumulation of subordinate clauses is vital to Imogen's description, at the beginning of *Cymbeline*, of how her farewell to Posthumus was interrupted:

> I did not take my leave of him, but had   25
> Most pretty things to say. Ere I could tell him
> How I would think on him at certain hours
> Such thoughts and such; or I could make him swear
> The shes of Italy should not betray
> Mine interest and his honor; or have charg'd him,   30
> At the sixt hour of morn, at noon, at midnight,
> T'encounter me with orisons, for then
> I am in heaven for him; or ere I could
> Give him that parting kiss which I had set
> Betwixt two charming words, comes in my father,   35
> And like the tyrannous breathing of the north
> Shakes all our buds from growing.   (1.3.25–37)

The grammatical subject ("my father") does not arrive until the third line from the end, and when it finally enters it comes as part of an inverted clause, with one verbal phrase preceding it ("comes in") and one – preceded by an extended simile – following it ("Shakes"). In other words, the grammatical key to the structure, the main clause for which the ear is trained to wait, is deferred for some nine lines, preceded by four enormous prepositional phrases, all based on "ere" or "or [ere]." The third of these, having to do with their simultaneous prayers, includes a digressive and gratuitous explanatory clause: "for then / I am in heaven for him" (32–33). The poet has controlled the structure of the sentence, kept it in balance, by emphasizing the parallel form of the extended and unwieldy introductory phrases. It is also worth remarking that the wished-for conditional state detailed in the four-part introduction is demolished by the violent entrance of the king: that is, the grammar of the sentence performs the action that Imogen reports.

---

[13] Eric Rabkin, *Narrative Suspense* (Ann Arbor: University of Michigan Press, 1973), pp. 54–58; 87–89. My use of the term "discharge" is somewhat less specific and subtle than Rabkin's.

Shakespeare's mischievous pleasure in grammatical deferral and surprise governs one of the crucial moments in *The Winter's Tale*, Paulina's
entrance at the end of the trial scene to announce the demise of the queen:

> What studied torments, tyrant, hast for me 175
> What wheels? racks? fires? What flaying? boiling
> In leads or oils? What old or newer torture
> Must I receive, whose every word deserves
> To taste of thy most worst? Thy tyranny,
> Together working with thy jealousies, 180
> (Fancies too weak for boys, too green and idle
> For girls of nine), O, think what they have done,
> And then run mad indeed – stark mad! for all
> Thy by-gone fooleries were but spices of it.
> That thou betrayedst Polixenes, 'twas nothing – 185
> That did but show thee, of a fool, inconstant,
> And damnable ingrateful; nor was't much
> Thou wouldst have poison'd good Camillo's honor,
> To have him kill a king – poor trespasses,
> More monstrous standing by; whereof I reckon 190
> The casting forth to crows thy baby-daughter
> To be or none or little – though a devil
> Would have shed water out of fire ere done't;
> Nor is't directly laid to thee, the death
> Of the young Prince, whose honorable thoughts 195
> (Thoughts high for one so tender) cleft the heart
> That could conceive a gross and foolish sire
> Blemish'd his gracious dam; this is not, no,
> Laid to thy answer: but the last – O lords,
> When I have said, cry "Woe!" – the Queen, the Queen, 200
> The sweet'st, dear'st creature's dead, and vengeance for't
> Not dropp'd down yet.   (3.2.175–202)

Dramatically crucial as a counterweight to the monstrosity of Leontes'
fantasy, Paulina's obloquy is a masterpiece of suspenseful calculation. The
speech throws all its force upon the "fact" of death. In the indirect and ironic
beginning, Paulina delivers herself of a string of questions about how Leontes
plans to torture her (175–79). Although this gambit is initially mystifying, it
coheres logically with the theme it introduces, for torturing the faithful old
woman would be consistent with the errors and harms the king's "Fancies"
have visited upon those who love and serve him. Moreover, the violent
images with which she begins attest to the damage already inflicted. As the
tirade unfolds, it becomes clear that Paulina's joint purposes are intertwined:
she will simultaneously condemn Leontes and expose his most appalling

crime. But her secret – Hermione's death – remains concealed until the end of the speech. Every line looks forward explicitly or implicitly to this climax, for every act of folly and cruelty must be judged from the perspective – the viewpoint – of Leontes' last incomparable outrage.

Not only is the execration constructed periodically, but it also advertises and relishes its periodicity. Just after the initial questions, Paulina ticks off the specific harms inflicted so far, proclaiming that each must be diminished by what she will announce. It might be said also that the shape of her disclosure is fundamentally and pleasingly theatrical. The speaker aims for the tirade to create a powerful effect upon her main auditor, Leontes, and has tailored it for and addressed it directly to him. But it works similarly upon the stage spectators, acknowledged in "O lords," and also upon the theatre audience. The listener is made to wait, to attend closely in anticipation of horror. This affective aim is typical of Paulina's theatrical manner elsewhere. Pafford speaks of "the calculated tactlessness which is her favourite weapon,"[14] and her directorial role in the final scene is an expansion of her rhetorical strategy in this crisis.

The emotion and energy of the attack make themselves felt in its violent music. The syncopated effect of one rhythm superimposed upon another is especially audible here. The lines teem with spondees – "what wheels" (176), "most worst" (179), "stark mad" (183), "cry 'Woe!' " (200) – pairs of sounds that threaten the iambic order. Another kind of syncopation is discerned by F. E. Halliday, who notes that "Shakespeare, particularly in his later plays, imposes a secondary rhythm on the primary iambics" by integrating "natural trochees" into the familiar pattern. This practice accounts for the richly polyphonic texture of Paulina's speech. A third of the lines contain at least two such falling disyllables, and many of these are connected, as Halliday shows they often are, by alliteration and assonance: "NEWer TORture" (177), "MONstrous STANDing" (190) "LITtle … DEVil" (192), "BLEMish'd … GRACious" (198). In each case the rhetorical impetus of the sentence strains against the fundamental beat of the verse, such tension enriching the musical texture and charging the lines with emotional power.[15]

Tempo also fortifies Paulina's speech, for she increases velocity as she proceeds. After the broken rhythms of the preliminary interrogatives, the

---

[14] "Introduction" to the Arden edition of *The Winter's Tale* (London: Methuen, 1963), pp. lxxiv–v.

[15] F. E. Halliday, *The Poetry of Shakespeare's Plays*, pp. 31–32: Halliday illustrates the method with a well-known line from *The Tempest*, Alonso's "I'll SEEK him DEEPer than e're PLUMmet SOUNDed." "This combination of rhythm and assonance, each emphasizing the other, adds another quality to the later poetry, in which whole speeches are integrated and harmonized by the complex contrapuntal interweaving of a double rhythm with a melodic theme."

passage accelerates through the recitation of the king's crimes and moves purposefully toward its fearsome close. This swift pace is not easily or immediately achieved: for example, the retrospective survey (lines 179–84) of the king's "tyranny" and "fancies," a speech with halts and jerks, repetitions and appositives and interjections, necessarily retards the speaker. The specific catalogue of crimes that follows unfolds in a sentence extending to seventeen lines. That quickening tempo is impeded by brief stops and a set of obstacles just prior to the conclusion: "but the last – O lords, / When I have said, cry 'Woe!' – the Queen, the Queen . . . " Paradoxically, however, the collision of such intrusive clauses with the achieved momentum of the sentence propels the listener even more rapidly and irresistibly toward the revelatory end. Paulina delays slightly with the repetition of "the Queen," and her sibilants and elisions in the penultimate line thrust us toward the ugly monosyllable "dead." But this is still not the end of the speech: the remainder, that anti-climactic final clause, "and vengeance for't / Not dropp'd down yet" (201–2), records a fitting conclusion that has not occurred, and so the words "drop down" with a monosyllabic flatness, alliteration and assonance establishing acoustically the hollowness denoted. It is probably significant, moreover, that the queen's "death" is neither the end of the sentence nor the end of the play.

Paulina bewails disorder in poetry that, crowded with words, threatens to burst out of its formal limits. Syntactical complexity tends to elongate the lines, as in the repeated questions needing a pause after each: "What wheels? racks? fires? what flaying? boiling . . .?" Extra syllables abound: ten of the twenty-seven lines end with a soft syllable. One line, "Thy by-gone fooleries were but spices of it" (184), contains twelve syllables, and even though *fooleries* is compressed into two ("fool-ries"), the end of the line is loaded with an additional beat, in *spices of,* thus throwing the emphasis on the still-nebulous "it." Elision is frequent: "That thou betray'dst Polixenes, 'twas nothing" (185); "The sweet'st, dear'st creature's dead" (201). Metrical order is barely maintained.[16] Crowded lines and weak endings appear most prominently at the opening of the passage, and as Paulina moves more swiftly toward her end, the line endings become more regular, the iambic beat more audibly

[16] Dorothy L. Sipe, *Shakespeare's Metrics,* Yale Studies in English 166 (New Haven: Yale University Press, 1968), objects to the critical emphasis on irregularity in Shakespeare's verse, particularly to the study of contrapuntal rhythm suggested by Halliday and others. Her unshakable purpose is to establish "that Shakespeare was in fact greatly concerned about preserving the regularity of his verse" (p. 6), an aim that deafens her to the subtlety and variety of Shakespeare's rhythmic experiments. See Brian Vickers's perceptive review of her book, *The Yearbook of English Studies* 1 (1971), pp. 241–43.

insistent. "More regular" is a relative term, to be sure: there are interruptions and metrical kinks aplenty. But Paulina's periodic manner, her fashioning of an ordered and histrionically efficient whole from a mysterious and chaotic beginning, is assisted by the increasing regularity of the verse.

Shakespeare embellishes this poetic frame with musical devices that reinforce the hearer's sense of its complexity. The introductory lines foster a mood of incantation, particularly with the repetition of *l* sounds in lines 176 and 177 ("wheels," "flaying," "boiling," "leads," "oils," "old"). Indeed, the entire passage seems exceptionally alliterative, even for the highly ornate verse of this phase of Shakespeare's career: "What wheels?"; "To taste of thy most worst"; "green and idle / For girls of nine"; "kill a king"; "More monstrous standing by"; "casting forth to crows"; "thee the death"; "could conceive a gross and foolish sire / Blemish'd his gracious dam"; "sweet'st, dear'st creature's dead." Similarly, internal rhyme creates color: "newer torture"; "every word deserves . . . worst"; "Together working"; "damnable ingrateful." Similar sounds often conspire to create extraordinary aural effects: "O, think what they have done, / And then run mad indeed. . ." My devotion to the smallest acoustic details has probably tried the reader's patience and may appear to have removed us from the main topic, the periodic structure of Paulina's announcement, but all these poetic tactics enrich and fortify the verbal construction, adding weight and difficulty that make the resolution all the more meaningful.

The theatrical withholding of information, here brilliantly exploited by Paulina, is also characteristic of Leontes and Jachimo and Prospero: as possessors of secrets, they consciously dramatize the revelation of what they "know" by building suspense and stimulating the anticipation of the audience. But this tactic should not be regarded chiefly as a form of characterization. It is not, to return to Todorov on James, chiefly a result of "a referential (for instance, psychological) complexity."[17] Rather, such arrangement is a formal concomitant of the playwright's style manifested throughout the last plays, a style that bespeaks an altered sense of the theatrical enterprise itself.

SYNTAX AND STORY

The formal contribution of these stylistic properties is not difficult to discern: the loose and periodic shape of the sentences in the last plays replicates the distinctive form of the romance. Form, as Kenneth Burke

---

[17] Tzvetan Todorov, "The Secret of Narrative," in *The Poetics of Prose*, tr. Richard Howard (Ithaca: Cornell University Press, 1977), p. 148.

argues, is "the creation of an appetite in the mind of the auditor, and the adequate satisfying of that appetite,"[18] so that the act of beginning and completing a sentence creates and satisfies desire just as narrative does. And Norman Bryson urges that we "try to conceive of form . . . in dynamic terms, as matter in process, in the sense of the original, pre-Socratic word for form: *rhuthmos*, rhythm, the impress on matter of the body's internal energy, in the mobility and vibrancy of its somatic rhythms."[19] Romance is characterized by its power to entrance, to engage the attention of the reader or spectator through a series of adventures that seem to promise fulfillment but that postpone its delivery. "Attention" is a function of narrative tension – as the etymology of both words implies, we are left hanging, suspended in a world of illusion and expectation. In the greatest examples of literary romance, the operation of the medium reinforces the effects of the narrative action. Hazlitt, in his lecture on Spenser, describes the poetry as "a labyrinth of sweet sounds, 'in many a winding bout of linked sweetness long drawn out' – that would cloy by their very sweetness, but that the ear is constantly relieved and enchanted by their continued variety of modulation . . . it is the perfection of melting harmony, dissolving the soul in pleasure, or holding it captive in the chains of suspense."[20] Shakespeare's practice is not exactly like that: given the temporal limits of theatrical performance, the end presses more insistently on the consciousness of the spectator than on the reader of narrative romance. But the tangle of clauses and pauses and interruptions that precedes the period entraps the auditor in a histrionic version of Spenser's "chains of suspense."

Thorough and suggestive accounts of the structure of romance are available in the work of Patricia Parker, Helen Cooper, and others who have extended and clarified earlier treatments by W. P. Ker, Eugène Vinaver, and Northop Frye.[21] I want to concentrate on one significant

---

[18] Kenneth Burke, "Psychology and Form," in *Perspectives by Incongruity*, ed. Stanley Edgar Hyman with the assistance of Barbara Karmiller (Bloomington: University of Indiana Press, 1964), p. 21.

[19] Norman Bryson, *Vision and Painting: The Logic of the Gaze* (New Haven: Yale University Press, 1983), p. 136.

[20] *The Complete Works of William Hazlitt*, ed. P. P. Howe, after the edition of A. R. Waller and Arnold Glover, vol. v (London: J. M. Dent and Sons, 1930), p. 44.

[21] See Parker, *Inescapable Romance*; Howard Felperin, *Shakespearean Romance* (Princeton: Princeton University Press, 1972), especially chapter 1; Frye, *The Secular Scripture* (Cambridge, Mass.: Harvard University Press, 1976); Vinaver, *The Rise of Romance* (New York: Oxford University Press, rpt. 1971); and Ker, *Epic and Romance* (London: Macmillan, 2nd. edn. 1908). Felperin's book, as its title suggests, is most directly related to Shakespeare; the others' are more general studies.

feature of the form – the particular kind of suspense the romancer is able to generate. According to Parker, " 'Romance' is characterized primarily as a form which simultaneously quests for and postpones a particular end, objective, or object, a description which Fredric Jameson approaches from a somewhat different direction when he notes that romance, from the twelfth century, necessitates the projection of an Other, a *projet* which comes to an end when that Other reveals his identity or 'name.'"[22] This paradoxical tendency to project a goal or ending and at the same time to defer attainment of that goal is one of the keys to the attraction of such stories. Most examples of literary romance look towards a predictable and desired conclusion, usually a reunion of some kind, and for the most part the audience (or reader, depending on the genre) receives assurances that such a positive end will be attained. Prior to that joyous reunion, however, the audience must accompany the characters through a series of obstacles that make the ending seem increasingly distant – shipwrecks, stolen infants, imprisonment or slavery, threats of incest, mistaken identity, savage landscapes, angry gods, treacherous monarchs, pirates, poisonings, banishment, attempted rape, a voracious bear, and other such threats to life and happiness. This relation between obstacles and completion, between frustration and release, is the desirable tension that gives most examples of romance their peculiar flavor. As Cecily puts it in *The Importance of Being Earnest*, a play that knows something about romance, "The suspense is terrible. I hope it will last."

A fundamental appeal of romance for the audience, then, is suspension in a virtual world of danger, a controlled environment in which the perils are gratifying because a happy end is foreseeable and assured. It is the pleasure offered by roller coasters, by horror films, by the peeled grapes (eyeballs) and spaghetti (intestines) in the haunted house got up for Halloween. Although the characters find the obstacles so formidable that existence itself seems imperiled, the audience benefits from the security of the formal contract, knowing as it does that the hero will not only survive but also receive unexpected and joyous rewards. The physical and spiritual quests that structure most romances are the source of pain and confusion for those who undertake them, but at the same time such wanderings make up the framework of the complex narrative that gratifies the theatre audience. When the quest is accomplished, the fiction will be finished, and we will have to go home. This simultaneous desire for and resistance to closure accounts for both the audience's pleasurable experience in the

---

[22] *Inescapable Romance*, p. 4.

theatre as well as for the structure of the form itself. Romances try not to end because their audiences and readers want to sustain the pleasurable suspension, to enjoy indefinitely the satisfactions of virtuality. To quote Dr. Johnson, "In romance, when the wide field of possibility lies open to invention, the incidents may easily be made more numerous."[23] Hence the tendency to digress, to add further adventures, to include one more episode.

Throughout the late verse, particularly in the most difficult passages, the sentence itself becomes a kind of miniature romance narrative. The complex syntactical structures are animated by the same tension that obtains in the larger tale, the conflict between a desire for meaningful closure on the one hand and the stimulation of process on the other. Shakespeare seems to explore the limits of inclusiveness and linearity, approximating stylistically the protraction of the entire narrative. Modern interest in structural linguistics has focused attention on the temporal and linear qualities of all speech: as Robert Scholes explains the principle, derived from Saussure, "not only is each sign linear, each utterance is even more obviously so. Unlike the picture, which can display various significant elements simultaneously, the elements of a verbal narrative must be delivered in an order which is itself significant. The sign, then, as well as the sentence and all larger units of discourse, is primarily narrative."[24] The linearity of speech causes understanding to occur gradually, as the syntagmatic structure establishes itself: units of language modify one another, meaning is altered, until completion and comprehension are finally achieved. The auditor is drawn into complex verbal structures without being able to predict their destination, propelled in one direction and then another by unexpected, contradictory clauses, and finally delivered to clarity by a conclusion that makes sense of all that has gone before.

Much the same is true of the plot of a play like *The Winter's Tale*.[25] The great syntactical suspensions replicate grammatically the deferrals in the

---

[23] Quoted in Stanley Wells, "Shakespeare and Romance," in *Later Shakespeare*, ed. John Russell Brown and Bernard Harris (London: Edward Arnold, 1966), p. 55.

[24] Robert Scholes, *Structuralism in Literature: An Introduction* (New Haven: Yale University Press, 1974), p. 17.

[25] The sort of stylistic and narrative coherence I have in mind here has been discerned in the work of a number of authors by a number of critics. Apart from Todorov, cited above, some of the most persuasive of such analysis has been performed by Eric Rabkin. Quoting a long sentence from *Absalom, Absalom!*, he shows how the syntax recreates narrative structure and suggests that "the structural similarities between the manner of multiple narration and the style may be called, in opposition to image-structure, syntax-structure. Both image-structure and syntax-structure cooperate to foist the fictional reality subliminally on the reader" (*Narrative Suspense*, p. 56).

action, the withholding of information that will, in Puttenham's words, "conclude . . . the whole premisses with a perfit sence and full periode." As listeners and spectators, we are forced to wait, left suspended, denied immediate understanding of a jarring phrase or a surprising event until the end of the sentence or the end of the play. The binary form of many sentences, such as the "if-then" construction, is equivalent to the tragicomic structure of the whole work. The second half modifies and illuminates the opening, incomprehensible without the final segment. Dramatically and grammatically, the conflicts of the first unit are not canceled by the resolution of the second; rather, each term qualifies the other, and the meaning of the conclusion is enriched by the difficulties preceding it. And the choppy and hypotactic properties of the syntax derive from the same sensibility that protracts and tangles the narrative.

In *The Winter's Tale* the plot begins in one direction, with Leontes' jealousy; becomes more complex with the flight of Camillo and Polixenes, the illness of Mamillius, and the banishment of Perdita; reverses itself with Hermione's divine vindication and Leontes' epiphany; is intruded upon unexpectedly by the entrance of Time; begins afresh with the pastoral romance of Florizel and Perdita; changes course when Polixenes interferes (in a conversation with a surprise ending [*Discovering himself*]); and finally achieves coherence in the return of the young lovers to Sicilia, the reconciliation of the kings, the reunion of father and daughter, and the restoration of the queen. More specific parallels suggest themselves. Just as devices such as alliteration and internal rhyme impart cohesion and music to the poetry, so repeated elements of action and character create emotional discord and harmony in the progress of the story. The varied repetition of character types contributes a kind of narrative alliteration: Mamillius and Florizel, or Camillo and Antigonus. As I indicated in Chapter 2, the combination of ellipsis and pleonasm in the style corresponds to the notorious omissions in the plot, the gap of sixteen years, the reported deaths, the voyage to Bohemia and back, the endlessly described (and undramatized) reunion of fathers and children. The plot itself might be considered an enormous dramatic anacolouthon: its initial movement is negative, Time is the dash signifying a shift in direction, and the final movement is affirmative.

The auditor's mixed response to particular sentences – uncertainty or confusion accompanied by ironic confidence – constitutes a stylistic version of the pleasurable anxiety stimulated by various narrative devices. Suspense and irony can be mutually exclusive, as Wayne Booth has demonstrated in his analysis of narrative technique: the author who wishes to create suspense usually must suppress information, and this tactic is incompatible with irony, which affords the reader superior insight. Dramatically, Shakespeare contrives to furnish his audience the advantages of both techniques. When Booth claims that "the author must, then, choose whether to purchase mystery at the expense of irony,"[26] he identifies what becomes in the hands of the romancer a tension between continuation and closure, uncertainty and revelation. Our confidence in eventual clarification, whether grammatical or narrative, allows us to savor the temporary pleasures of confusion. This is the delight of the maze, the teasing difficulty of the unfinished puzzle. We are disoriented but safe, uncertain and certain at the same time.

As he has done throughout his career, Shakespeare at this late point tends to cultivate in his audience the benefits of the ironic advantage. His practice in this respect resembles his positioning of the audience in a play like *Twelfth Night*, where the main pleasure derives from our awareness of the potential remedy for Olivia's "fruitless sighs," since the truth of Sebastian's survival is revealed to the audience relatively early.[27] In all the romances the audience possesses information, and therefore enjoys a kind of emotional insulation, that the characters lack: Thaisa's revival and Marina's survival, Posthumus's instructions to Pisanio to murder Imogen at Milford Haven, the existence of Cymbeline's stolen sons in the wilds of Wales, the real identity of the headless corpse over which Imogen weeps, Perdita's survival in Bohemia (and her relationship with Polixenes' son), and the parallel case in *The Tempest* (Ferdinand's safety and his discovery of Miranda).

Henry VIII, or All is True offers a model for this interplay of foreknowledge and ignorance. The original audiences knew the general outlines of the story before they entered the theatre, as do we, and many were probably more familiar than we with the episodes dramatized. Thus, the chief theatrical pleasure arises from the playwrights' manipulation of particular incidents within the ironic frame. Of the many such moments, one of the juiciest is Wolsey's confident sarcasm about his power to choose the king's new bride: "Anne Bullen? no; I'll no Anne Bullens for

---

[26] Wayne Booth, *The Rhetoric of Fiction* (Chicago: University of Chicago Press, 1961), p. 255.

[27] But not immediately. It is important that we do not learn about Sebastian's presence in Illyria until 2.1, immediately after Olivia has declared herself to be in love with the simulacrum of the young man. Directors who violate this withholding of information (as did Ian Judge in his 1994 production at Stratford) reduce the suspenseful pleasures of 1.5. "How will this fadge?" In 1.5. we do not know, and Olivia's confusion is the funnier for it; in 2.2, when Viola asks the question, we do know.

him, / There's more in't than fair visage. Bullen? / No, we'll no Bullens"
(3.2.87–89). This is perhaps a special case, since it depends upon historical
fact to frame and diminish the arrogant confidence of the deluded prelate,
but in this instance history offers what internal cues supply elsewhere. The
episode is characteristic of Shakespeare's exploitation of ironic effect
throughout his last phase. In *The Two Noble Kinsmen*, literary history
performs the same kind of service for the audience: the playwrights avail
themselves of the familiarity and popularity of Chaucer's original.

The brilliant early scene in *Cymbeline* involving the wicked Queen,
Doctor Cornelius, and Pisanio is an ironic extravaganza, as all three
characters step apart to impart private information to the audience. But
Shakespeare has multiplied the normal ironies by exaggerating the dis-
crepancies between what characters know and what they think they
know.[28] One who steps out of the fiction to confide in the spectator is
overridden by another whose information alters or contradicts the claims
of the first. For example, the Queen's smug confidence that she is playing
on Pisanio's stupidity and that the "cordial" for Imogen is in fact poison
has been preceded by the Doctor's revelation to the audience that the
"poison" is in fact a harmless sleeping drug. One of the most audacious
uses of irony in the entire canon is Imogen's awakening from "death" and
finding the headless corpse of the ridiculous Cloten, which she mistakes
for the body of Posthumus. Time after time Shakespeare amplifies the
effects of irony to cartoonish proportions, apparently playing with the
conventions of ironic distance and teasing the audience by augmenting its
perceptual advantage.

Despite the dominance of irony – or perhaps because of it – Shakespeare
also takes delight in surprising the privileged spectator. Nowhere do we
feel the rug removed more briskly than at the end of *The Winter's Tale*.
The oracle's words – "and the king shall live without an heir if that
which is lost be not found" – emphasize the return of Perdita, and we
are aware from the end of the third act, as Leontes is not, that his
daughter is alive and will serve as the means of his regeneration. But the
playwright does not tell the whole story, denying us knowledge of
Hermione's survival until the final moments of the last scene. This
combination of knowledge and ignorance is not a late discovery for
Shakespeare, of course: in *The Comedy of Errors*, having flattered us
with, and traded for laughter on, our awareness of the Antipholus twins,

---

[28] For a discussion of the centrality of this practice throughout Shakespeare's theatrical career, see
Bertrand Evans, *Shakespeare's Comedies* (Oxford: Oxford University Press, 1960), *passim*.

the twin Dromios, and the presence in Ephesus of Egeon, the play-wright shocks us with the Abbess's revelation of herself as the lost wife and mother. In performance, however, the tonal difference between that moment of recognition and Hermione's descent from the pedestal is immense. Although the two moments of revelation come from the same romance tradition, in the theatre one usually provokes laughter, the other tears.[29] The difference between the two endings indicates Shakespeare's ambition late in his career to provide a wider range of emotional effect. In both cases, however, he challenges our confidence in our superior understanding and thus transforms our comprehension of the world we thought we knew. This surprise would have especially jarred the first audiences, many of whom would have been familiar with Robert Greene's *Pandosto*, the prose fiction that is the principal source of the play. Watching the story unfold, they might well have been expecting Greene's ending, in which the grieving king, the model for Leontes, found himself sexually drawn to the beautiful princess and, on discovering her identify, "fell into a melancholy fit and . . . slew himself."[30] Knowledge of the original, the "old tale" first published a generation before but reprinted in 1607, must have amplified the powerful surprise of Shakespeare's twist.

Attention to these final revelations helps to define more precisely the relation between grammatical closure and narrative disclosure. The moment of recognition toward which the romance plot typically moves, the moment that Jameson sees as the naming of the Other, is enacted repeatedly at the level of the sentence. The listener finally reaches the moment of *cognitio*, the apprehension of the grammatical element – whether subject, predicate, or other essential unit – that gives order and clarity to the sentence. Once again, such a structure might be said to apply to every sentence in every play; but the syntactical arrangement of the sentence in the late plays magnifies the moment of cognition by making it difficult to reach: as Prince Hal puts it, "But when they seldom come, they wish'd for come" (*1 Henry IV*, 1.2.206). Likewise, in the romance narrative the moment of recognition or identification that serves to clarify the confusions and correct the false starts is given much greater emotional

---

[29] But this rule of thumb is not absolute: Tim Supple's RSC touring production of *The Comedy of Errors* (1996) took advantage of all the romance cues built into the play, and thanks to mysterious music, subtle lighting, and retarded pace, the spousal reunion was reverent and genuinely moving.
[30] *Pandosto, or The Triumph of Time*, in *An Anthology of Elizabethan Prose Fiction*, ed. Paul Salzman (Oxford: Oxford University Press, 1987), p. 204.

weight than the equivalent moment in, say, the earlier comedies. It is significant that romance narratives often complete themselves in an image of reanimation – the salvation of the mute Pericles, Hermione's statue coming to life. Such revivification corresponds to the cognitive epiphany that comes at the period of the completed sentence. As Terence Cave puts it, "the comedies and romances compose a complex structure of confusion – narrative, figurative, cognitive – in precisely the terms necessary for a final inversion delivering the maximum sense of coherence and rectification."[31]

As the statue scene makes clear, Shakespearean romance draws much of its emotional power from the fantasy of second chances. Such wish-fulfillment applies as well to the return of Perdita, of Cymbeline's sons, of Marina and Thaisa, of Ferdinand. The announced birth of the Princess Elizabeth at the end of *Henry VIII* takes advantage of this sense of renewal, of order recovered. The restoration of lost children provides the narrative release that the complex arrangement of the action has led the audience to desire; the reanimation of Hermione does so unexpectedly and (in the strict sense) wonderfully.[32] The reintegration of the sundered family or, more generally, of what had been dispersed – minus Mamillius – is to the narrative what the final clause is to the periodic sentence. The emotional release we feel at such a moment is captured in Puttenham's term for periodic constructions in poetry, the "long loose." The romances provide just such a "loose," completing the whole in a way that clarifies and makes tolerable all that has come before.

PERIODS, PERCEPTION, AND PERSPECTIVE

The arrangement of the verse sentence illuminates and shapes the audience's response to many of Shakespeare's preoccupations at the end of his working life. The first of these is the problem of perception, particularly the intermingling of illusion and fact in human experience. Todorov, in commenting on James's uses of the supernatural, argues that

the fantastic text is not characterized by the simple presence of supernatural phenomena or beings, but by the hesitation which is established in the reader's perception of the events represented. Throughout the tale, the reader wonders (in the same way that a character often does, within the work) if the facts

---

[31] Terence Cave, *Recognitions: A Study in Poetics* (Oxford: Clarendon Press, 1988), p. 286.
[32] See Thomas Bishop, *Shakespeare and the Theatre of Wonder* (Cambridge: Cambridge University Press, 1996), chapter 5.

reported are to be explained by a natural or a supernatural cause, if they are illusions or realities.[33]

The subtleties of the Jamesian style, then, particularly the "hesitation" attendant upon the famous hypotactic patterns, contribute to the reader's bewilderment, and it seems clear that something similar occurs to those who witness or, in seventeenth-century parlance, "hear" a performance of one of Shakespeare's last plays. The playwright has devised a poetic style that not only engages us in the activity of perception – all dramatic styles do so – but makes us conscious of the difficulties of accurate understanding and our liability to error.

This problem of interpretation surfaces repeatedly in the diction that the characters employ to comprehend and explain the extraordinary events that occur in the magical world of romance. In *The Winter's Tale*, the agon arises from Leontes' "Fancies," or, as Paulina calls it more specifically, his "weak-hing'd fancy" (2.3.118), and in the statue scene she plays with the problem of illusion in her warning to the bewildered king: "No longer shall you gaze on't, lest your fancy / May think anon it moves" (5.3.60–61). When, following the Folio stage direction, "*Hermione comes down*," we "perceive she stirs" (5.3.103) but are uncertain about how to interpret and thus take possession of this perception. Doctor Cornelius in *Cymbeline*, carrying his fake poison, assures the audience that the queen is "fool'd / With a most false effect" (1.6.42–43). The "unsettled fancy" of the mariners in *The Tempest* must be settled by means of music before Prospero can explain the subtleties of the isle. Anne Barton has persuasively shown that "efforts to distinguish the fictional from the 'real,' art from life, tales from truth, come in the Romances to replace the older, moral concern with identifying hypocrisy and deceit. It is not easy for characters to make these distinctions – nor, in some cases, for the theatre audience."[34] The syntactical challenges that Shakespeare poses in these plays engage the audience in the struggle to make such distinctions. The combination of hypotaxis and parataxis, the violent rhythms, false endings, and withholding of syntactical and referential satisfaction confuse us, forcing us to make adjustments, to see things differently, to change our minds about the sense of a word, the direction of a clause, the function of a phrase. What the world does to Pericles, the style does to the audience.

---

[33] "The Secret of Narrative," p. 156.
[34] "Leontes and the Spider: Language and Speaker in Shakespeare's Last Plays," in *Essays, Mainly Shakespearean* (Cambridge: Cambridge University Press, 1994), p. 178

Perception is related to point of view, of course, and thus to Shakespeare's late fascination with perspective. As a dramatist concerned with framing actions, with displaying human behavior in a meaningful shape, Shakespeare has always been sensitive to the relation between viewer and scene, or to the effect of contrasting episodes, or to other aspects of how persons and actions appear in relation to other persons and actions. But later in the career the philosophical applications of this problem begin to exert a powerful impact upon his thematic explorations of human action. A proof text for this concern is the "Dover Cliff" scene in *King Lear* (4.6), when the disguised Edgar attempts to cure his father's despair by arranging his apparent salvation, a "miracle" after a fall from the heights. Edgar hopes to teach his father patience: as he insists in their final scene together, "Men must endure / Their going hence, even as their coming hither" (5.2.9–10). Thus, the great speech in which he depicts the fearful – and fictional – vista of the sea below is essentially an exercise in perspectival description. From where they stand, objects that are actually enormous appear to be tiny, and smaller objects all but vanish:

> The fishermen, that walk upon the beach,
> Appear like mice; and yond tall anchoring bark,
> Diminished to her cock; her cock, a buoy
> Almost too small for sight.   (4.6.17–20)

Such images press home the truth that vision depends on viewpoint, and Edgar employs the principle of perspective to teach his father to contextualize his pain, to see through to the end of his sufferings.

This principle is one of the keys to understanding the ontology of the romances. Shakespeare's manipulation of time and place and his virtuosic treatment of theatrical illusion attest to his belief in the therapeutic effect of proper perspective. In the first act of *Cymbeline*, responding to Pisanio's account of his master's shipboard departure, Imogen argues that she would have watched "till the diminution / Of space had pointed him sharp as my needle," or "till he had melted from / The smallness of a gnat, to air" (1.4.18–19; 20–21). This description of spatial manipulation is relevant to the romance world in which *Cymbeline* is set: Imogen's experience is temporarily diminished and recontextualized as the action of the play moves from Lud's Town to Rome to Milford Haven to, momentarily at least, the heavenly realm of Jupiter. Throughout these plays, an event the characters regard as a disaster may in fact be the prelude to unexpected joy. For the mariners in *The Tempest*, the storm that interferes with their journey is catastrophic, the island a dead end, but as soon as the second scene opens, the theatre audience understands the storm, in the grammatical terms I have been using, as nothing more than an introductory element, a subordinate clause leading to heightened understanding and fulfillment.

The need for temporal perspective, the importance of seeing beyond the moment, is probably the most pervasive manifestation of this topic in the late plays, and a sophisticated statement of it links the first and second halves of *The Winter's Tale*. Time, the Chorus, not only declares himself the cause and the corrector of error but also announces his influence over fashion and feeling.

> it is in my power
> To o'erthrow law, and in one self-born hour
> To plant and o'erwhelm custom. Let me pass
> The same I am, ere ancient'st order was,   10
> Or what is now receiv'd. I witness to
> The times that brought them in; so shall I do
> To th' freshest things now reigning, and make stale
> The glistering of this present, as my tale
> Now seems to it.   15
>
>   (4.1.7–15)

To a sensitive auditor, at least, the speech must have had a chilling effect when delivered from the stage of the Blackfriars Playhouse to a "glistering" crowd of Jacobean aristocrats and fashion victims. The moment of youth and wealth is a brief one: to those who come after you, your power and beauty will appear as quaint and old-fashioned as the creaky old story you are watching now strikes you. It is tempting to unpack the subtle poetic means by which the contrast between past, present, and future is achieved – the elisions that permit the speaker to move quickly (to take less time), the delicate music of the rhyming tetrameter, the punning opposition of fresh and foul water ("reigning" and "stale"). But what is important for present purposes is the speech's emphasis on inevitable change and the value of the long view.

Recognition of the need for patience and perspective in the face of temporal depredation is especially pertinent to Shakespeare's manipulation of the diachronic potentialities of the poetic sentence or speech. Pericles' sufferings seem inexplicable and intolerable as they occur, but they are assuaged and almost effaced by the satisfactions of his end. Such relief is granted even when the miseries are largely self-inflicted, as with Leontes or Posthumus. The audience, attentive not only to the assurances provided by Gower, Time, Jupiter, Prospero, and other choric or theophanic figures but also to the formal pointers of the mode of romance, is given cause to expect a positive resolution. The words of Paulina's namesake are pertinent in this context: "we see through a glass, darkly" (1 Corinthians, 13). Moreover, the values of faith and patience are strongly implied as listeners negotiate their way through the syntactical seas of the late verse. Clauses and sentences can be trying, even incomprehensible, while one is lost in their midst; but they finally cohere into a pleasing and meaningful pattern.

The grammatical delays and obstacles that momentarily obscure meaning in the middle of a protracted sentence are parts of a larger whole that will eventually be elucidated.

JACH.   Had I this cheek
   To bathe my lips upon: this hand, whose touch   100
   (Whose every touch) would force the feeder's soul
   To th'oath of loyalty: this object, which
   Takes prisoner the wild motion of mine eye,
   Firing it only here; should I (damn'd then)
   Slaver with lips as common as the stairs   105
   That mount the Capitol: join gripes, with hands
   Made hard with hourly falsehood (falsehood, as
   With labour): then by-peeping in an eye
   Base and illustrous as the smoky light
   That's fed with stinking tallow: it were fit   110
   That all the plagues of hell should at one time
   Encounter such revolt.
                (*Cymbeline* 1.7.99–112)

To follow the speaker through such a labyrinth is to experience grammatically the arc described by the action of Shakespearean romance. The one massive period divides into three parts: (1) if I had such a creature as Imogen for my own, and (2) if I had behaved as badly as Posthumus has, (3) then I would deserve the worst possible punishment. But the meaning does not resolve itself for thirteen lines, through which the listener is made to suffer both the refusal to come to an end and the odious content. Jachimo is torturing Imogen theatrically, suspending her in a painful syntactical maze, and the theatre audience suffers with her as it makes its way to the promised end. Patricia Parker, writing of Adam's privileged view of human history at the end of *Paradise Lost*, points out that he must nonetheless wait for his eternal rest: "This suspended period of waiting, or of patience in its root sense, is part of the discipline of the creaturely perspective."[35] In sentence after sentence, Shakespeare employs grammatical and syntactical means to enforce that discipline upon the audience.

The emphasis on the end of the sentence brings us to Shakespeare's conscious obsession with endings in the romances. Romance fiction is notorious for its refusal to stop. Perhaps it is for this reason that the playwright has contrived such memorable conclusions for these plays, as if an immensely powerful authorial intervention were needed to halt the potential infinitude of the narrative. The endings of Shakespeare's romances are both predictable and surprising, fulfilling a pattern that we have come to expect, but doing so in an unconventional fashion. They are also about endings. According to Judiana Lawrence, "Iachimo's garrulity, which forces from Cymbeline the impatient 'I stand on fire: / Come to the matter' (168–69) and 'Nay, nay, to th' purpose' (l. 178), is a miniature version of the romance form's penchant for cliff-hangers."[36] In a play like *Cymbeline*, the final scene is to the narrative that precedes it as the last clause is to an extravagant periodic sentence. That festival of discoveries and recognitions is as long and complex as it is so as to afford the audience a release commensurate with the foregoing confusion and frustration. So it is with the statue scene in *The Winter's Tale*, where we expect the homecoming of Perdita to be the climax of the play and find ourselves surprised with an even greater miracle. Each of these scenes offers a theatrical instance of Mandelbrot's "fractal," a case of self-similarity in which a distinctive shape is visible on both a tiny and a grand scale.

What seems especially pertinent to the stylistic analysis I have been attempting is that Shakespeare makes his dramatic endings about his audience's desire for happy endings. He takes advantage of our wish for meaningful closure by providing conclusions that seem, if anything, too meaningful. In other words, the blatant fictionality of his endings calls attention to their impossibility – the multiple reunions at the end of *Cymbeline*, Hermione's mysterious return, Ferdinand's rescue, Marina's encounter with Pericles in the harbor at Mytilene.[37] The asymmetry

---

[35] *Inescapable Romance*, p. 152.

[36] Judiana Lawrence, "Natural Bonds and Artistic Coherence in the Ending of *Cymbeline*," *Shakespeare Quarterly*, 35 (1984), 458.

[37] Cf. Anne Barton: "*The Winter's Tale* admits something that Shakespeare's Elizabethan comedies had tried to deny: happy endings are a fiction . . . Shakespeare not only does not try to conceal, he positively emphasizes the fact that his material is the archetypal stuff of legend and fairy-tale. That we respond to it as something far more powerful and engaging than 'Cinderella' or 'Beauty and the Beast' testifies to the subtlety with which Shakespeare has adjusted his language and dramatic art to the demands of a new mode" ("Leontes and the Spider," pp. 180–81).

between the world we see staged and the world we inhabit stimulates a subtle and contradictory response: we recognize that such idealized resolutions do not occur in our own world, and yet we are allowed those consolations in the theatrical world, the "waking dreams" that Hazlitt found in Spenser. This commitment to unreality bespeaks Shakespeare's new and positive view of illusion, his re-dedication of himself to the power of fantasy and frank theatricality. And the extravagantly periodic style is both a sign of that conviction and one of his major instruments for imparting that commitment to the audience. Finally, without falling into a sentimental reverie about the playwright as Prospero, it seems legitimate to speculate on whether this embrace of the fictional has something to do with Shakespeare's awareness of, or disappointment at, or celebration of, his own professional end.

CHAPTER 5

Repetition

Happiness is longing for repetition.
                    Milan Kundera, *The Unbearable Lightness of Being*

The late plays feel almost obsessively reiterative. A conspicuous source of this impression is the reappearance of many of the stories, character types, and ideas that had occupied Shakespeare's imagination from the early 1590s. A long-time Jacobean playgoer attending the first performances of the romances would have recognized the playwright's abiding concerns: the separated family, the fraternal struggle for power, the slandered heroine, political usurpation and its consequences, the Virgilian concern with dynasty, an interest in familial reproduction, the destructive and redemptive sea, the restoration of that which was lost. In modern critical treatments, such structural and thematic repetition is a commonplace. Equally prominent, however, are the reiterative qualities of the poetry from which these familiar topoi emerge. The aural repetition characteristic of the late style creates a complex, artificial surface that gives these plays a distinctive sonic texture, one that delights the ear and excites the mind. To listen carefully to the reiterative patterns that resound everywhere in these late texts is to perceive one of the primary sources of their poetic power. The insistent repetition of vowels and consonants, words, phrases, syntactical forms, and other verbal effects makes the dramatic texts uncommonly musical. These sounds also witness to an exceptional self-consciousness consistent with Shakespeare's turn from the representational to the presentational.

I begin with an elementary demonstration of some musical effects contributed by auditory combinations. Such a potentially redundant emphasis on patterns of formal particulars – alliteration, assonance, and lexical repetition – is justified first by the extraordinary extent of the repeated sounds in the verse of this phase, and, second, by years of comparative inattention. The current privileging of what is seen over what is heard threatens to produce a critical culture deaf to the value of poetic properties. In this chapter, then, a liberally illustrated survey of basic forms of repetition is followed by an articulation of some of their benefits. These include the general functions of providing a musical or melodic line, of affording a sense of cohesion in the midst of disorder, of suggesting the presence of an authority figure accountable for clarity and satisfaction, and of creating the delights of auditory identification. Finally, I propose some benefits that such a poetic texture confers upon the last plays particularly.

The world of Shakespearean romance would be substantially poorer, theatrically and poetically speaking, without the abundantly reiterative verse to which Shakespeare devotes himself from 1607 forward. He has imagined an enchanted aural atmosphere consistent with the settings and stories of the romances, a world of sound in which repetition serves to tantalize the listener: apparently meaningful sounds generate expectations of illumination and fixity but never entirely satisfy those desires. Such poetic echoes operate in concert with the open-endedness of the romance form and with the reappearance of a host of familiar Shakespearean topics. Verbal and semantic patterns entice the audience by promising and withholding illumination, creating an atmosphere of hermeneutic instability. The effect of the poetry is to promote *un*certainty and to insist on ambiguity, and renewed attention to the verse not only helps to extend and complicate the favored topics of recent political criticism but also reminds us of aural pleasures and effects unavailable elsewhere.

ALLITERATION AND ASSONANCE

Alliteration is one of the first properties readers of poetry learn about and one of the last they talk about. As a consequence, anyone who undertakes to discuss the repetition of literal sounds in poetry will find few models for this kind of analysis. In 1589 George Puttenham, defining the trope he called "*parimion*, or the figure of the like letter," argued that by doubling of the initial consonant "you do notably affect th' eare."[1] This doesn't tell us much, and few critics since then have had much to say about alliteration. Those who have been most helpful are S. T. Coleridge, William Hazlitt, Kenneth Burke, and Stephen Booth. These days notice of consonance and assonance rarely occurs outside the precincts of

---

[1] *The Arte of English Poesie*, a facsimile reproduction ed. Edward Arber, with an Introduction by Baxter Hathaway (Athens, Ohio: Kent State University Press, 1988), p. 185.

Sophomore Literature (Poetry Unit), where the aim is usually to identify and label the specimen and then put it in a box until such time as it is needed for the reinforcement of meaning. From time to time a student, in response to an uncomfortable pause while the instructor stays for an answer, will hesitantly propose that the insistent repetition of initial consonants gives the poem or passage "a more poetic quality." We are told it helps the verse – I here revert to the infinitive of choice among beginning and insecure poetry students – "to flow." Having diffidently suggested this general effect, the respondent is usually encouraged to look beneath the surface and admonished specifically to connect the sound and sense, as with the serpentine "s" sounds in certain sections of *Paradise Lost* or – once again – Pope's "swift Camilla."

Shakespeare the novice, like most of his contemporaries, made abundant use of alliterated phrases, but within a very few years he had begun to suppress the practice, apparently considering it potentially ridiculous, appropriate mainly for pedants and poetic wannabees. We might think immediately of Pyramus's "O dainty duck! O dear!" or, in the roughly contemporaneous *Love's Labour's Lost*, of the pedantic Holofernes, declaring that he "will something affect the letter, as it argues facility," and reciting his "extemporal epitaph on the death of the deer": "The preyful Princess pierc'd and prick'd a pretty pleasing pricket." As Shakespeare gains experience at writing verse, literal repetition comes to seem mannered or affected, and even though *Richard II* and *Romeo and Juliet* contain abundant patterning and vocalic echo, by the middle of the 1590s he has mostly subordinated the practice, employing assonance and consonance delicately and without permitting literal repetition to call attention to itself.

So things continue for over a decade, until near the end of the tragic sequence, where one's ears perceive a shift of emphasis, as indicated in the discussion of *Macbeth* in Chapter 1. Repetition sounds most memorably in the tetrameter couplets of the witches ("Double, double, toil and trouble"), but Macbeth and other characters also speak in such schemes, and do so in decidedly serious passages. Such echoing of witch language may signify Macbeth's demonic affiliations, and it is also possible to argue that the verbal repetitions of the play at large constitute a poetic instrument for conveying its central theme – "consequence," that which follows upon. But the densely repetitive texture also reflects Shakespeare's changing attitude toward the representation of dramatic speech, his gradual commitment to ever more artificial poetic structures that will result in the stylistic extravagance of the last plays. Phrases such as "shakes so my single state of man," "will I with wine and wassail so convince" and "there shall be done a deed of dreadful note" create a reiterative aural fabric that sometimes functions meaningfully, but more important than any thematic significance is that Shakespeare is beginning to indulge in such formal extravagance with greater frequency and enthusiasm. In the romances he exhibits an almost self-indulgent attraction to assonance and consonance, allowing the ordering properties of the verse to assert themselves in ways not heard in *Hamlet* or *Othello* or in the earlier work generally.

It quickly becomes apparent that the mature poet has increased the intensity and frequency of these devices to the point of apparent immaturity, as if he cannot help himself.

> **Where** is Posthumus? **What** is in thy mind
> **That** makes thee stare thus? **Where**fore breaks that sigh　　　　5
> From **th'** inward of **thee? O**ne but painted **thus**
> **W**ould be interpreted a **thing perplex'd**
> Beyond self-explication. **Put thyself**
> Into a havior of **less** fear, ere wildness
> Vanquish my staider senses. **What's** the matter?　　　　10
> **Why** tender'st thou that paper to me with
> A look untender?　　　　　　(*Cymbeline* 3.4.4–12)

An initial *w* sound begins each of the first three sentences, and the pronoun "One" that opens the fourth effectively mimics the *w*. Eight instances of "th" occur between the last foot of line four and the end of line six. This assertive pattern of alliterated initial consonants is augmented by further repetitions: the pairing of initial consonants, as in "thy mind / That makes," or "thee stare . . . that sigh"; the repetition of internal consonants, such as the *r* sounds in "stare . . . Wherefore . . . breaks" (5), and the assonantal and consonantal rhyming of "thy mind" (4) and "makes . . . breaks" (5). Further, in addition to the *p* sounds that decorate lines six through eight, the appearance of a pattern is underscored by the interlocking use of "be," "er," and "ex" in "be interpreted a thing perplex'd / Beyond self-explication."

The alternation of initial consonants, audible in "thy mind that makes" (as in "Hung be the heavens with black") is known as "cross-alliteration," a device related to the Welsh *cynghanedd*, in which the alliterated pairs form a pattern of *abab*. Other examples include Paulina's "to *p*urge *h*im of that humour / That *p*resses *h*im from sleep" (2.3.38–39) or Iachimo's "How *b*ravely *th*ou *b*ecom'st *th*y *b*ed" (2.2.15). Sometimes *cynghanedd* is complicated so that the consonants sound chiastically, *abba*. Such highly patterned phrases can be found throughout the canon – one of the most remarkable is Cassius's trebled repetition, "*Th*ere *w*as a *Br*utus once *th*at *w*ould have *br*ooked" (*Julius Caesar*, 1.2.159) – but in the romances they sound more frequently and more strikingly, owing to the dense aural texture from which they emerge:

> And that most venerable man, which I
> Did call my father, *w*as I *kn*ow *n*ot *wh*ere
> *Wh*en I *w*as stamped. (*Cymbeline* 2.4.155–57)

This excerpt demonstrates the cooperation of a figure and its aural context: the underlined chiastic *cynghanedd* is then followed by two additional *w* sounds, and the impression of echo is further consolidated by the chiastic treatment of "was I / I was" in the last two lines.

As these passages show, a distinctive aural feature of the late verse is the interlocking of consonants and vowels in a poetic fabric that recalls the etymology of *text* in weaving. Initial alliteration, moreover, is supplemented by an abundance of internally repeated consonants. In a phrase such as "There's nothing ill can dwell in such a temple" (*The Tempest*, 1.2.458), "ill" is glanced at in "dwell," then both are altered with the repetition of the *e* and *l* in "temple," and these harmonies are grounded in the reiteration of the *th* and *n* sounds. Such interweavings are audible in lines that seem merely declarative, such as Prospero's "For thou must now know farther," as well as in the insistently musical "Wound the loud winds, or with bemocked-at stabs / Kill the still-closing waters."

They also dominate Prospero's recitation of Ariel's history:

> within which rift
> Imprison'd thou didst painfully remain
> A dozen years; within which space she died,
> And left thee there, where thou didst vent thy groans   280
> As fast as mill-wheels strike. Then was this island
> (Save for the son that she did litter here,
> A freckled whelp, hag-born) not honor'd with
> A human shape.   (*The Tempest* 1.2.277–84)

To begin with the smallest units, a series of vowel sounds spin themselves out to almost absurd lengths ("within which rift / Imprisoned thou didst painfully remain"); pairs of long vowels alternate with short ("she did litter here"); consonants are repeated independently and then combined and split apart (in "hast put thyself / Upon this island as a spy" (1.2.455–56), the *p, s,* and *i* sounds establish themselves separately and then coalesce in "spy"). This practice of joining and splitting phonemes creates

what Stephen Booth has called "pulsating alliteration," a sensation of expansion and contraction that implies density and activity, making the text effectively "poetic" even when it may not sound conventionally so.[2]
Let me offer some additional examples without detailed analysis:

> The *q*ueen of *c*urds and *c*ream.
> (*The Winter's Tale* 4.4.161)

> Here's a *f*ew *f*lowers; but 'bout midnight more:
> (*Cymbeline* 4.2.283)

> how *f*ar o*ff*, how near,
> Which way to be prevented, i*f* to be;
> I*f* not, how best to bear it.
> (*The Winter's Tale* 1.2.399–401)

> Ah, but some natural notes about her body
> Above ten thousand meaner moveables
> Would testify, t'enrich mine inventory.
> (*Cymbeline* 2.2.28–30)

> O *s*acred, *s*hadowy, cold, and constant queen,
> Abandoner of revel*s*, mute, contemplative,
> *S*weet, *s*olitary, white a*s* cha*s*te, and pure
> A*s* wind-fann'd *s*now, who to thy female knight*s*
> Allow'*s*t no more blood than will make a blush,
> Which is their order'*s* robe: I here, thy priest,
> Am humbled 'fore thine altar.
> (*Two Noble Kinsmen* 5.1.137–43)

Most of these are, relatively speaking, unremarkable passages, speeches that are not inordinately lyrical or in which the character is not under particular emotional stress. Predictably, in the great arias such basic poetic effects are multiplied.

When the emotional temperature does rise, we should not be surprised at a corresponding increase in the poetic pressure, as in the great recognition scene between Pericles and Marina (5.1). This is the most powerful exchange in the play, indeed one of the most moving scenes in any play. It is typical, in its poetic and emotional force, of the great scenes of discovery and reunion that make the romances so distinctively moving. The passion for duplicated sounds represents one of its most effective, if least

---

[2] Stephen Booth, *An Essay on Shakespeare's Sonnets* (New Haven: Yale University Press, 1969), pp. 87–88. Booth's comments on how poetic effects function in individual sonnets are extremely stimulating and applicable beyond their immediate subject. See also the essay by Kenneth Burke, "On Musicality in Verse," in which he demonstrates the complex effects of assonance and consonance in some poems of Coleridge: *The Philosophy of Literary Form* (New York: Random House, 1941), pp. 296–304.

remarked, poetic elements, the key to the music of the encounter, and the workings of literal repetition can be demonstrated efficiently in a few representative passages.

> If **I** sh*ould* tell my history, it w*ould* seem
> Like lies **d**isdain'd in the reporting.
> (118–19)

>   Thou **l**ookest
> Like one I **l**oved indeed.
>   (124–25)

>   **W**hat were **th**y friends?
> **H**ow lost **th**ou them? **Th**y **n**ame, **m**y **m**ost kind virgin?
>   (139–40)

> **M**y **n**ame is **M**a*r*in*a*.
>   O, I **am** mock'd.
>   (142)

>   tell m*e* if thou canst,
> **W**hat **th**is maid is, or **wh**at is like to b*e*,
> **Th**at **th**us hath made m*e* w*ee*p.   (183–85)

Even in that simplest and most touching of declaratives, "My name is Marina," the intensity of the plain truth is augmented by the musical syllables in which it is packaged. Here, repeated letters determine the beguiling sounds of the short sentence, obviously the echoing of the initial *m*s, but also the *n* in "name" and "Marina," the chiastic reversal of the *m* and *n,* and the vocalic repetition of the vowel sounds in the proper name. The hypnotic and transcendent power of the reunion resides to a large extent in the echoes that evoke an apparent pattern and thus seem to promise significance.

The play's most famous passage is similarly interlaced, studded with pairs and triplets of letters.

> O Helicanus, strike *me,* honored sir,   190
> Give *me* a gash, put *me* to present pain,
> Lest this great *s*ea of joys rushing upon *me*
> O'*er*bear the sh*or*es of my m*or*tality,
> And dr*ow*n me with their sweetness. O, come hither,
> Th*ou* that <u>beget'st</u> him that did thee <u>beget</u>;   195
> Th*ou* that wast born <u>at sea</u>, buried at Tharsus,
> And f*ou*nd <u>at sea</u> again! O Helicanus,
> D*ow*n on thy knees, thank the holy gods as l*ou*d
> A*s* thunder **th**reatens us. Th*is* *is* Marina.
>   (*Pericles,* 5.1.190–99)

The configuration of repeated vowels and consonants is immediately audible even to a casual listener, although it is worth pointing out that the number of combinations is always greater than one thinks.

The starting point for comment on the musicality of this passage is the alliteration of the second line, where the *g* and *p* sounds might serve as a textbook example. But the line is even more complicated than it seems for, as Kenneth Burke pointed out long ago, *b* and *p* sounds are closely related phonetically to *m* and constitute what he calls "*concealed* alliteration." He discerns another triad of such "cognates" in *d, t,* and *n,* a group whose relations are clearly audible in the last line quoted.[3] In addition to obvious and submerged instances of consonance, we should remark the sibilants in the first and third lines, and particularly the complex music of the fourth, in which the consonant of "O'er" is repeated in "bear" and then sounded again with the repeated vowel in "shores"; and all these similar sounds exaggerate the shift to *m* in "my mortality," which glances again at "or" in the first syllable of the noun. At times the blizzard of reiterated sounds – this is a point to which I shall want to return – seems to reach almost Spenserian proportions.

WORDS, WORDS, WORDS

"The ears of men," says John Hoskins, introducing possible means of reiteration in his treatise of 1599, "are not only delighted with store and exchange of divers words but feel great delight in repetition of the same."[4] Close attention to the passages I have cited reveals that the initial pleasures of alliteration and assonance are enhanced by a high density of repeated words. The excerpt from *Pericles* just quoted ("O, Helicanus, strike me, honour'd sir") gains much of its musical power from the repetition of the pronominal "me" after three different imperative verbs, each of them monosyllables. And as the passage continues the recurrence of words and phrases intensifies into a kind of chant.

> O, come hither,
> Thou that beget'st him that did thee beget;
> Thou that wast born at sea, buried at Tharsus,
> And found at sea again.   (5.1.194–97)

---

[3] "On Musicality in Verse," pp. 296–97.
[4] John Hoskins, *Directions for Speech and Style,* ed. Hoyt H. Hudson (Princeton: Princeton University Press, 1935), p. 12.

Of course the emotional release of this climactic reunion accounts for the effect of these few lines, but the meaningful content of the speech is colored, made more vivid, by the rhythmic duplication of simple sounds, words, and phrases. In addition to the obvious reiteration of "Thou that" and "beget," the pattern of repetition is subtly extended by the parallel series of verbs and prepositions in the last two lines. Even articles do their part to create a sense of reverie and wonder.

Lexical repetition is largely responsible for the incantatory appeal of all the romances, each play offering multiple instances of this ordering tactic. As in Pericles' "Thou that beget'st him," the aural effect of the repeated words is often intensified by other forms of echo. Two instances from the same scene of *The Winter's Tale* illustrate the extremes to which Shakespeare has taken the reiteration of words.

> Come, **captain**,
> We must be neat; not neat, but cleanly, **captain**:
> And yet the steer, the heckfer, and the *calf*
> Are all call'd neat.—Still virginalling
> Upon his palm?—How now, you wanton *cal f*,
> Art thou my *cal f*? (1.2.122–27)

> Go play, boy, play. Thy mother plays, and I
> Play too, but so disgrac'd a part, whose issue
> Will hiss me to *my* grave; contempt and clamour
> Will be *my* knell. (1.2.185–87)

In the first speech to Mamillius, the several repeated words are also connected to each other and to other words by virtue of certain interlocking sounds: the opening "c" sounds sharpen the effect of the first and second lines, and the syllable "all" sounds both in and around "calf." This concentration on sounds should not, however, prevent us from noticing the semantic repetitions as Leontes puns on and otherwise amplifies the word "neat." In the second speech, in addition to the restatement of "play," "my," and "will," the sonic integuments of the speech are created by the chiming of "iss" in "issue" and "hiss"; by the consonantal reiteration of "s" sounds in "so disgraced," of "c" in "contempt and clamour," of "l" in "will" and "knell"; and by the assonance of "play," "-graced," and "grave." Finally, although our grasp of early modern pronunciation is limited, the "k" in "knell" may well have been sounded as a hard consonant, making the consonants of the last clause even fiercer.

One complementary example from *The Winter's Tale*, Florizel's lyrical confession to the disguised Polixenes, exhibits a similar degree of lexical reiteration in a different emotional key:

POL.   <u>And</u> **th**is my neighb**OR** too?   370
FLOR.   <u>And</u> he, <u>and</u> m**OR**e
       Than he, <u>and</u> men – **the** earth, **the** heavens, <u>and</u> all:
       That *were* I crown'd **the** most imperial monarch,
       Thereof most *w*o**r**thy, *were* I **the** fairest you**th**
       That *ever* made **eye** s*we*r*v*e, had f**OR**ce and knowledge
       M**OR**e **th**an was *ever* man's, I would not prize **them**   375
       Without h*er* love; f**or** h*er*, employ **them** all,
       <u>Commend</u> **them** and <u>condemn</u> **them** to h*er* se*r*vice,
       OR to **th**eir own *per*dition.
                                   (*The Winter's Tale* 4.4.370–78)

The number of repeated words and interlocking syllables is extraordinary, and yet many of the repeated words are pedestrian – notably the many pronouns – so that the poetic texture of the language derives from the interlacing of quite ordinary materials.

Repeated words were a part of Shakespeare's poetic arsenal from early in his career. Patricia Parker, drawing on the rhetorical models proposed by Quintilian, Angell Day, and Thomas Wilson, has demonstrated his exploitation of the figure known as geminatio, or "the Doublet" in *1 and 2 Henry IV*.[5] The sixteenth-century rhetoricians are useful in their illustration of these figures, but even more useful than their exempla are their prefatory or explanatory discussions of how the poet is able to use these figures affectively. Here is George Puttenham on patterned words:

For the eare is properly but an instrument or conueyance of the minde, to apprehend the sence by the sound. And our speech is made melodious or harmonicall, not onely by strayned tunes, as those of *Musick*, but also by choise of smoothe words: and thus, or thus, marshalling them in their comeliest construction and order, and aswell by sometimes sparing, sometimes spending them more or lesse liberally, and carrying or transporting of them farther off or neerer, setting them with sundry relations, and variable formes, in the ministery and vse of words, doe breede no little alteration in man . . . the mind is not

5 Patricia Parker, *Literary Fat Ladies: Rhetoric, Gender, Property* (London: Methuen, 1987): in the early comedies, for example, "*geminatio verborum* has its counterpart in the whole play on doubling, twinning, or duplicity in which one twin is so to speak the repetition or 'doublet' of the other"; and she sees "a link between rhetorical gemination, as a repetition with no intervening space between, and the whole problem of kingly succession which is the larger burden of the *Henriad*, as of the history plays as a whole" (pp. 70–71).

assailable unlesse it be by sensible approches, whereof the audible is of greatest force for instruction or discipline . . . Therefore the well tuning of your words and clauses to the delight of the eare, maketh your information no less plausible to the minde than to the eare: no though you filled them with never so much sence and sententiousnes.[6]

Puttenham's recognition of the hypnotic power of artfully disposed words and phrases is shared by Thomas Wilson, who speaks more pointedly to the repetition of a single word, arguing that the "the oft repeating of one word doth much stir the hearer and makes the word seem greater, as though a sword were oft digged and thrust twice or thrice in one place of the body."[7] Wilson, taking the role of the English Quintilian, is concerned with the business of rhetoric and composition rather than the delights of poetry, but his analysis is applicable beyond its immediate audience.

Much contemporary discussion of the value of repetition implies its capacity to beguile the listener by charming the senses, and Shakespeare harnesses that power in the late plays especially. The repetition of words is dramatically appropriate, indeed almost necessary, in dialogue involving questions and answers, notably in those recognition scenes towards which the late plays move and into which much of their emotional force is concentrated.

PER.   Where were you born,
   And wherefore call'd Marina?   155
MAR.   Call'd Marina
   For I was born at sea.
PER.   At sea! what mother?
MAR.   My mother was the daughter of a king;
   Who died the minute I was born . . .
                     (*Pericles* 5.1.154–58)

To some degree the repeated words and phrases that dominate this passage are a function of the deliberate simplicity required by Pericles' practically comatose state.[8] Their minimalism conveys the delicacy of the interrogation, but it also expresses the inverted familial relation, seen earlier in the reunion of Lear and Cordelia, as the knowing child instructs the child-like parent.

---

[6] *The Arte of English Poesie*, p. 207.
[7] Thomas Wilson, *The Art of Rhetoric*, ed. Peter E. Medine (University Park: Pennsylvania State University Press, 1994), p. 225.
[8] See Inga-Stina Ewbank, "'My name is Marina': The Language of Recognition," in *Shakespeare's Styles*, ed. Philip Edwards, Inga-Stina Ewbank, and G.K. Hunter (Cambridge University Press, 1980), pp. 111–30.

The effects of lexical repetition sound most frequently in *The Tempest*. Even in the prose of the opening shipwreck – "All lost! To prayers, to prayers! All lost!"; "We split, we split, we split!" – the confused shouts of desperation take a reiterative form that returns poetically in the early speeches of Prospero and then throughout the work.

PROS.   . . . Tell your piteous heart
    There's *no harm* done.
MIR.   O woe the day!
PROS.   *No harm.*   15
    I have done nothing but in care *of thee*
    (*Of thee, my* dear one, *thee, my* daughter), who
    Art ignorant of what thou *art*, nought knowing
    Of whence *I am*, nor that *I am* more better
    Than Prospero, master of a full poor cell,   20
    And thy no greater father.
                       (1.2.14–21)

In addition to the indicated repetitions, the passage echoes with phonetic duplication: "heart . . . harm," "O, woe," "my dear . . . my daughter," "daughter . . . nought," "nought knowing," "full . . . cell," and "greater father." (Again, uncertainty about pronunciation may limit but does not invalidate speculation about phonetic echoes.) The regularity of certain metrical patterns and the isocolonic arrangement of clauses intensify the music of the repeated words, notably "thee, my dear one, thee my daughter" and "Of whence I am, nor that I am." And threaded into the dialogue are all those negatives: "No," "no," "nothing," "nought," "knowing," "nor," "no."

To catch the reduplicative flavor of Prospero's narrative to Miranda is to learn how to hear the language of the late style generally.

    Which thou heardst cry, which thou saw'st sink. Sit down,
    For thou must now know farther.   (30–31)

    Twelve years since, Miranda, twelve years since (53)

    What <u>foul play</u> had **we** that **we** came from *thence*?
    Or **blessed** was't **we** did?
                 Both, both, my girl.
    By <u>foul play</u>, as thou sayst, were **we** heaved *thence*,
    But <u>**blessed**</u>ly holp hither.   (59–62)

                  <u>**how to**</u> grant suits,
    <u>**How to**</u> deny them, *who í*advance and <u>*who*</u>
    <u>*To*</u> trash for over-topping, new **created**

The **creatures** that were mine, I say – or changed _'em_,
Or else new f0rmed _'em_; having both the key
Of officer and **office.**   (79–84)

The melodic attractions are apparent enough, and my typographical
indications are designed to stand in for potentially redundant description
of poetic and rhetorical details, among them assonance, alliteration,
epanalepsis, isocolon, and several species of paronomasia (polyptoton,
syllepsis, antanaclasis). Besides furnishing the basic pleasure of echoing
sounds, the various kinds of verbal play impart energy and motion to
what is dramatically a notoriously static scene.

That such echoing patterns are not confined to the protasis or to the
protagonist but resound throughout the play can be established by a
glance at the temptation scene (2.1.204–311), in which Antonio seeks to
inveigle Sebastian into fratricide. The villain begins his scheme by
priming his partner with anaphoric and rhythmic restatement, "They
fell together all, as by consent; / They dropp'd, as by a thunder-stroke"
(2.1.208–9), and continues by arguing that Ferdinand's disappearance is Sebastian's good fortune, demonstrating the transformation
linguistically:

SEB.   I have <u>no hope</u>
          That he's undrowned.
ANT.   O, out of _that_ 'no hope'
          What <u>great hope</u> have you! No hope _that_ **way** is   245
          Another **way** <u>so high a hope</u> _that_ even
          Ambition cannot pierce a wink beyond,
          But doubt discovery there.
                         (2.1.243–48)

Apart from the obvious echoes, the passage rings with assonance and
consonance; in addition to the aural repetition, we also catch the relentless
negatives, often double negatives, characteristic of Shakespeare's villains; the
glance at sleep imagery ("wink") to which the dramatic atmosphere of the
scene and the island has acclimated us; and the self-conscious toying with
words that extends the game begun earlier, when the conspirators play on
the metaphor of "standing water" (226). As is often the case in *The Tempest*,
and in most of the other last plays, language emerges as a subject itself, as
speakers play with it, take pleasure in it, test its capacities, and misuse it
consciously and unconsciously, sometimes, as here, at the same time.[9]

---

[9] See Anne Barton, "Shakespeare and the Limits of Language," *Shakespeare Survey 24* (1971), 19–30,
reprinted in *Essays, Mainly Shakespearean* (Cambridge: Cambridge University Press, 1994), pp. 51–69.

Antonio's favorite trick is structural recapitulation, the stringing together of formally similar clauses, as in his appositional elaboration of
Sebastian's single-word speech, "Claribel":

> **She that** is Queen of Tunis; **she that** dwells
> Ten leagues beyond man's life; **she that** from Naples
> Can have no note – unless the sun were post –
> The man i' th' moon's too slow – till newborn chins
> Be rough and razorable; **she that** from whom　　　　　　255
> We all were sea-swallow'd, though some cast again –
> And by that destiny, to perform an act
> Whereof *what's past is* prologue, *what to* come
> In yours and my discharge.　　(*The Tempest* 2.1.251–59)

This skein of clauses – it is not even a sentence – is calculated to enchant
the auditor into rhythmic sympathy with and, finally, assent to the
speaker's proposal. Its seductive power depends on the reiterative disposition of phrases, specifically on the pattern known as *conduplicatio*,
the repetition of words in succeeding clauses. Antonio/Shakespeare
strives for hypnotic effect by simplifying the diction, at least in the first
half, where until "razorable" no word is longer than two syllables and
most are monosyllabic; with regular disruption of the normal metrical
structure, each of the "she that" phrases being a trochee substituted for
an iamb;[10] and with syntactical duplication. Even those qualifying
clauses that violate the pattern of "she that" develop their own rhythmic
echo: "unless the sun were post" and "The man in the moon's too slow"
are identical in length and regularity, similar in the reliance upon
consonance and assonance, and completed with the repeated "o" sound.
In these dramatic circumstances Antonio's periphrastic style – his "circumstance" – amounts to verbal overkill, as even the dull Sebastian
seems to perceive in his response to the "Claribel" speech: "What stuff
is this?" But the local effect is less important than the overriding
dramatic goal: Antonio and Sebastian are the agents of a playwright
seeking to seduce his audience with words.

So it goes through other scenes and with other speakers. Some of the
richest passages in *The Tempest* owe their appeal and their memorability
to such lexical and sonic echo. For example, one of the play's axiological
cruces, the complex relation between biology and culture, is set forth in an
aurally pleasing and complex frame:

---

[10] On the expressive possibilities of this tactic, see George T. Wright, *Shakespeare's Metrical Art*
(Berkeley: University of California Press, 1998), especially chapter 13, "Trochees."

A devil, **a** born **devil**, *on who*se <u>nature</u>
<u>Nurture</u> can <u>never</u> stick; *on who*m my p<u>ai</u>ns,
Huma*ne*ly take*n*, *all, all* **lost**, quite **lost**.
(4.1.188–90)

Similarly, the effect of the play's songs – "Full fathom five thy father lies," "Where the bee sucks, there suck I" – is at least partly attributable to various kinds of echo. The notorious mystery surrounding Gonzalo's "Widow Dido" has been examined in almost every conceivable context except, I think, that of aural identity, simple rhyme. Is it perhaps just another case of internal echo that sounds as if it ought to mean more than it does? Such density and concentration promote the sense of pregnancy upon which much of *The Tempest* and many moments in the other romances depend.

PATTERNS

Verbal patterns are congruent with and supported by networks of reiteration operating on a larger scale. Most of these are narrative and structural, although thematic parallels and variations also make an impact. Internal narrative repetition has been a staple of Shakespearean dramatic structure since the early 1590s, the double wooing of Katherine and Bianca in *The Taming of the Shrew* being one of the most illustrative early cases. But rarely are the parallels and parodic construction made so insistent – or so insistently the topic of comment – as in most of the last works. In *Pericles*, for example, the incest of Antiochus and his daughter serves as the negative model for a network of familial relationships both similar and crucially different: Simonides and his beloved Thaisa, Cleon and Dionysa and their "malkin" daughter, Pericles and Marina. The reiterative verbal patterns stimulate an audience's perception of those symmetries and asymmetries. For example, the echoing line that seals Pericles' reunion with Marina, "Thou that beget'st him / That did thee beget," captures aurally the ironic difference between the healthy and perverse filial relations represented. In *The Winter's Tale*, likewise, the narrative replications and parallels seem obvious and abundant: the two kings consider each other brothers; their sons are only a month apart in age; Leontes employs complementary courtiers, Camillo, faithful in being unfaithful, and Antigonus, unfaithful in being faithful; Florizel replaces Mamillius by returning with Perdita as his fiancée; Perdita resembles her "dead" mother in the last act; the repetition of nature in art is foregrounded not only in the flower debate of Act 4 but most powerfully in the statue scene. One more visual instance of replication, this one grotesque, is Cloten's imitation of Posthumus in the middle of *Cymbeline*. Duplicating his rival's appearance by taking his clothing, the would-be rapist initiates a vicious masquerade that leads ultimately to his own decaptitation, and in a bizarre variation on his earlier disguise plots, Shakespeare contrives for Imogen to mistake the headless trunk of Cloten for the body of her beloved.

The Tempest is famous for the density and congruity of its mirrored actions. To mention only those events associated with the familiar topic of usurpation: Antonio's prompting Sebastian to suicide and fratricide would repeat in Naples his own theft of power in Milan and re-enact Prospero's seizure of the island and enslavement of Caliban, and all are burlesqued in "that foul conspiracy / Of the beast Caliban and his confederates / Against [Prospero's] life" (4.2.239–41). This reticulum of stories contributes to a dramatic design that seems both familiar and wonderful. But the pattern of narrative and thematic recapitulation goes beyond this text in that *The Tempest* is flagrantly intertextual: again, the cluster of echoes is especially audible in the temptation scene. As commentators since Coleridge have noticed, both in general structure and particular details, the episode restages the scene between the Macbeths before the killing of Duncan – Antonio's hectoring Sebastian about "What thou shouldst be," the image of the crown, the sleep imagery implying failure to comprehend or act, the suppression of conscience, even the image of the hungry cat (although it is used differently).[11] Everywhere in this scene Shakespeare repeats himself, unashamedly gazing back over his entire oeuvre and summoning up scenes, persons, themes, metaphors, bits of vocabulary, and other minor theatrical strategies, so much so that the personal allegorists can hardly be blamed for the vigor of their investigations. The recreated actions and speeches function as all allusions do, giving pleasure by exercising the mind and flattering veteran spectators on their perspicacity; and this audacious sort of authorial self-cannibalism contributes another layer of complexity, another apparently meaningful pattern of familiar, rearranged material. It also enhances the extraordinary self-consciousness that informs this and the other romances.

---

[11] For an excellent treatment of the densely allusive quality of this scene, see Paul A. Cantor, "Shakespeare's *The Tempest*: The Wise Man as Hero," *Shakespeare Quarterly*, 31 (1980), 64–75.

Henry VIII is structured, as many readers have recognized, so as to emphasize the resemblances among its three major narrative episodes, the political falls of Buckingham, Katherine, and Wolsey. The formal parallels of the Chaucerian original make themselves felt in *The Two Noble Kinsmen* and may help to explain the attraction of the authors to that source in the first place: the three queens who halt the ceremonial procession in the first scene, the married and unmarried sisters, the two noble kinsmen (with all their parallel speeches and pleas), the rival goddesses, the dramatic criss-cross at the end of the action. To this list we might add the juxtaposition of the heroic tale and the story of the Jailer's daughter.

A final topic pertinent to the mechanics of verbal and dramatic repetition is the practice of semantic doubling. Unlike the obvious increase in poetic patterning, the wordplay in this phase does not seem significantly different, either in kind or in degree, from that in the earlier plays. Throughout the comedies, histories, and tragedies comic and serious equivocation serves to amuse and disturb, revealing the unreliability of speech and often enriching a particular strain of meaning: in *Macbeth*, as I have indicated, the problem of duplicity is kept before us as words shift their senses and amphibology becomes a structural principle.[12] When he came to write the romances, Shakespeare had certainly not lost his ear for the quibble, and he employs it frequently, especially for its implied critique of linguistic vulnerability. Simon Palfrey's attention to the implications of polysemy has shown how it complicates the political concerns of the romance narratives.[13] Stephen Booth describes its more general function of making the dramatic language "exciting to listening minds."[14]

Leontes' speeches, as they seem to do with so many other devices, overflow with examples: the multiple puns on "play" in "Go, play, boy, play" and the manic retreat from the bovine connotations of "neat" help to indicate the suddenness and force of Leontes' madness. Ferdinand makes a Latinate pun on Miranda's name ("O wonder"), and in *Henry VIII* embedded ironies emerge when Wolsey, the butcher's son made good, puns unknowingly on Bullen.

In the context of repetition, wordplay offers a kind of semantic supplement, combining with the aural doubling of letters, words, and phrases to

[12] See Steven Mullaney, *The Place of the Stage* (Chicago: University of Chicago Press, 1988), chapter 6, "Lying like Truth."

[13] Simon Palfrey, *Late Shakespeare: A New World of Words* (Oxford: Oxford University Press, 1997).

[14] Stephen Booth, "Shakespeare's Language and the Language of Shakespeare's Time," *Shakespeare Survey 50* (1997), p. 5.

create patterns of apparent significance. John Hoskins, in *Directions for Speech and Style*, considers the effects of alliteration and paronomasia under the same rubric, as if one grew from the other,[15] and modern critics have suggested ways in which the double entendre is part of the larger strategy of calling attention to the surface of language. Jonathan Culler, for example, sees the pun as

a structural, connecting device that delineates action or explores the world, helping the plays (and also the sonnets) to offer the mind a sense and experience of order that it does not master or comprehend. We do not know what is the relation between "guilt" and "gilding" [in Lady Macbeth's "I'll gild the faces of the grooms withal, / For it must seem their guilt"], or between the straining of exertion and of filtering [in Portia's "The quality of mercy is not strained. / It droppeth as the gentle rain from heaven"], but we are urged to conceive an order in which they go together. Insofar as this is the goal or achievement of art, the pun seems an exemplary agent.[16]

Culler's argument parallels the claim I have been making about repeated sounds. To recognize in Leontes' wordplay a connection between *play* as "diversion," as "sexual misconduct," and as "performing a role" is to sense the presence of a meaningful pattern, and this sensation offers not only the pleasure of identification but also the illusion of potential significance. The network of double meanings thus emphasizes the materiality of the poetic medium and reinforces the impression of self-consciousness and artificiality suggested by the other instances of verbal design.

The duplication which constitutes the primary source of pleasure, and which contains all the other patterns I have mentioned, is the mimetic troping by the play of the actual world: reality is represented on the stage. As Ruth Nevo writes about this metatheatrical device, "The embedding of play within play dissolves representational boundaries so that the audience is required to suspend its attention, to negotiate a constant interchange between fictional reality and fictional allusion."[17] The high degree of metadrama in the last plays, much greater than in the more representational tragedies and even more than in the major comedies, constantly reminds the spectator that the action presented on the stage duplicates the actual world and that the mimetic copy is unreal and all the more valuable for its unreality. This act of repetition is the most general instance of the aural illusion created by the language, whereby the relationship of play to

[15] *Directions for Speech and Style*, pp. 14–17.
[16] Jonathan Culler, "The Call of the Phoneme," *On Puns* (Oxford: Blackwell, 1988), p. 8.
[17] Ruth Nevo, *Shakespeare's Other Language* (London: Methuen, 1987), p. 136.

life would seem to amount to a meaningful pattern, and yet it is immensely difficult to articulate that meaning. As Stanley Wells puts it about *The Tempest*, "The enchanted island reverberates with sounds hinting at tunes that never appear fully formed."[18]

METRICS

Blank verse is arguably the most pervasive instrument of repetition in any Shakespeare play, in that the sub-structural sequence of iambic feet creates an inescapable rhythm to which the audience's ears become accustomed and upon which the dramatic poet performs multiple variations. So far I have devoted comparatively little space to meter because its positive, ubiquitous contribution to coherence and regularity can be assumed. Wordsworth identified the fundamental attraction of such repeated rhythm when he described

a principle which must be well known to those who have made any of the Arts the object of accurate reflection; namely, the pleasure which the mind derives from the perception of similitude in dissimilitude. This principle is the great spring of the activity of our minds, and their chief feeder. From this principle the direction of the sexual appetite, and all the passions connected with it, take their origin: it is the life of our ordinary conversation; and upon the accuracy with which similitude in dissimilitude, and dissimilitude in similitude are perceived, depend our taste and moral feelings.[19]

The tension between likeness and difference obtains in all manifestations of blank verse – the lines are the same and the lines are different. Each poet who employs it creates a distinctive relation between them: some of the Tudor dramatists, say Marlowe, emphasize similitude; some of the Stuarts, say Ford, admit a much higher degree of irregularity. Shakespeare moves during the course of his career from one pole to the other, enacting in his own poetic career the larger cultural shift. In the early 1590s, mimicking Marlowe, he makes his blank verse regular and mostly smooth. As he becomes practiced the verse comes to sound more various while remaining more or less regular: that balance is audible in plays such as *Twelfth Night* and *Othello*. By 1607 or so, his approach to the pentameter line is infinitely more flexible and original, even daring. What is distinctive about his approach in the late plays is that he exploits the verse

---

[18] Stanley Wells, "Shakespeare and Romance," in *Later Shakespeare*, ed. John Russell Brown and Bernard Harris (London: Edward Arnold, 1966), p. 75.
[19] "Preface" to *Lyrical Ballads* (London: Longman and Rees, 1800), p. xxii-iii.

rhythms as a tool for perturbation: what would normally be a guarantor of order has become a source of disruption.

The metrical patterns audible in the romances might therefore be called "sophisticated" in that they exhibit the hand of a craftsman who long ago mastered his medium and now delights in taking liberties with it, modifying its regularity and pushing the forces of metrical subversion to the limit. In other words, they both do and undo their ordering function. Blank verse is built upon an inherent tension between the regularity of the familiar decasyllabic line (the forces of similitude), and the idiosyncratic energies of the English sentences that have been shaped into verse (the forces of difference).[20] By the time Shakespeare comes to write the last acts of *Pericles* and the other romances, as I have indicated in Chapter 2, he has given far greater power to the sentence at the expense of rhythmic consistency. In the early dramatic poetry the semantic unit tends to coincide with the poetic segment; as he gains experience, however, he is increasingly willing to run the thought past the end of the line, regularly enjambing the verse so that clauses extend without pause over two or even more lines. To compare two texts of relatively equal length, one from the beginning and one from the end of the career, is to find that the late play will contain about one thousand extra syllables, sounds that must be delivered by the actor and integrated into the pattern of pentameter. Such additional syllables alter the music of the verse and transform the sound of the play as a whole.

The power of these hypermetrical, enjambed lines to create instability and uncertainty in the metrical frame is felt in Queen Katherine's courtroom speech from *Henry VIII*:

> Sir, I desire you do me right and justice,
> And to bestow your pity on me; for
> I am a most poor woman, and a stranger,   15
> Born out of your dominions; having here
> No judge indifferent, nor no more assurance
> Of equal friendship and proceeding. Alas, sir!
> In what have I offended you? What cause
> Hath my behavior given to your displeasure,   20
> That thus you should proceed to put me off,
> And take your good grace from me? Heaven witness,
> I have been to you a true and humble wife,
> At all times to your will conformable;

---

[20] See Wright, *Shakespeare's Metrical Art*, especially chapter 14, "The Play of Phrase and Line."

Ever in fear to kindle your dislike, 25
Yea, subject to your countenance – glad, or sorry,
As I saw it inclin'd. When was the hour
I ever contradicted your desire? (2.4.13–28)

Katherine's plea is typical of this phase in its abundance of metrical idiosyncrasies: the construction of the sentence repeatedly overrides the claims of the line. Line 13 contains eleven syllables, ending on the hypermetrical and therefore light "justice"; line 14, although possessing the normal ten syllables, requires a stop between the ninth and tenth, producing an oddly weighted line; line 18 contains twelve syllables. Moreover, several lines are enjambed, most obviously the long participle that begins "having here" (line 16) and runs through to "proceeding" (line 18).

The effect of these supplemental syllables on the metrical structure of the play is potent, especially in combination with the other forms of deviation. As with syllables, Shakespeare has become much more liberal and varied in his use of stops.[21] The caesura, the mid-line pause, has become a major source of aural variety. Unwilling to wait for the end of the line, Shakespeare arranges that his speakers stop early and stop often. In Katherine's speech just quoted, line 18, "Of equal friendship and proceeding. Alas, sir!" contains two internal stops, one of the sort known as a "grand caesura," in which the full stop ("proceeding. Alas") falls between two unaccented syllables and thus significantly disturbs the beat. Line 26, "Yea, subject to your countenance – glad, or sorry," demands three stops. An especially tricky development of this technique is the placement of the pause in mid-foot, a maneuver heavily employed in the late plays:

Why, he that wears her like her med*al, hang*ing
About his neck, Bohem*ia – who*. . .
(*The Winter's Tale* 1.2.306–7)

Is goads, thorns, net*tles, tails* of wasps
(*The Winter's Tale* 1.2.329)

Often these quirky hestitations are combined:

They're here with me alrea*dy; whis*p'ring, rounding:
"Sicilia is a so-forth." 'Tis far gone.
(*The Winter's Tale* 1.2.217–18)

---

[21] Much of the information in the following analysis is derived from the work of Ants Oras, *Pause Patterns in Elizabethan and Jacobean Drama: An Experiment in Prosody* (Gainesville: University of Florida Press, 1960), and Wright, *Shakespeare's Metrical Art.*

The number of such oddly placed pauses increases markedly towards the end of the career, combining with other minor violations to transform the rhythmic foundations of the verse.

As Shakespeare gains experience his placement of the pause tends to migrate from the middle towards the end of the line. Every pentametric unit offers the poet nine possibilities for internal stops, a position after each syllable except the terminal. Leontes' line just cited, "Why, he that wears her like her medal, hanging," contains pauses in positions one and nine: such placement is extremely rare early in the career, whereas it is not surprising in a late play. Statistical analysis clarifies Shakespeare's changing practice: in *The Taming of the Shrew*, the percentage of pauses in each position of the line is as follows:

1st	2nd	3rd	4th	5th	6th	7th	8th	9th
5.3	9.8	4.4	35.6	19.2	17.4	4.9	2.8	0.7

In other words, over half the pauses in the play are confined to the fourth and fifth positions, with very few at the end of the line. In *Cymbeline*, however, the percentages are strikingly different:

1st	2nd	3rd	4th	5th	6th	7th	8th	9th
2.0	5.1	3.3	15.8	12.5	25.6	15.2	14.3	6.2

The primary difference is that the pauses are distributed more evenly. Moreover, in the late play the last three positions account for more than a third of all the stops, whereas in *Shrew* those three positions contain less than nine percent.[22]

Such freedom with pauses is consistent with other characteristic metrical variations. The number of inverted feet, i.e. the substitution of trochees for iambs, increases noticeably:

> THAT which I shall report will bear no credit
> Were not the proof so nigh. PLEASE you, great sir,
> *(The Winter's Tale* 5.1.179–80)

> IF by your art, my dearest father, you have
> PUT the wild waters in this roar, allay them.
> *(The Tempest* 1.2.1–2)

---

[22] See Oras, *Pause Patterns*, p. 68.

LIE there, my art. WIPE thou thine eyes. Have comfort.
                                        (*The Tempest* 1.2.25)

TELL him, if he i' th' blood-siz'd field lay swoll'n,
SHOWing the sun his teeth, grinning at the moon,
What you would do.
                            (*The Two Noble Kinsmen* 1.1.99–101)

Such inversions are especially potent when they occur at the beginning of
the line:

GOOD queen, my lord, GOOD queen, I say GOOD queen.
                                        (*The Winter's Tale* 2.3.60)

Finally, the late verse also displays an exceptional number of spondees, as
in Leontes' sarcastic command to Camillo: "Make that thy question, and
GO ROT!" (1.2.324)

Such irregularity helps to make the experience of listening to the lines
unstable and rewarding. The rhythmic variety is far more sophisticated
than the pleasurable thumping of the pentameters in *3 Henry VI*, for
example. Florizel's valentine to Perdita seems to capture, in its mercurial
shifts and other rhythmic pleasures, the exceptional, awe-struck quality of
his feelings:

> What you do   135
> Still betters what is done. When you speak, sweet,
> I'd have you do it ever; when you sing,
> I'd have you buy and sell so; so give alms,
> Pray so; and for the ord'ring your affairs,
> To sing them too. When you do dance, I wish you   140
> A wave o' th' sea, that you might ever do
> Nothing but that; move still, still so,
> And own no other function. Each your doing
> (So singular in each particular)
> Crowns what you are doing in the present deeds,   145
> That all your acts are queens.
>   (*The Winter's Tale* 4.4.135–46)

Audible throughout are the mutual effects of disjunction and conjunction, of chaos and order. The forces of deviation are potent: every line
except 10 and 12 is broken with commas and colons and other forms of
stop, some of the lines more than once. The rhythm, in other words, is
choppy and irregular, the pace alternately slow and rapid. Numerous
breaks divide the two halves of an iambic foot: "speak, sweet" (136), "ever:
when" (137), "so, so" (138), and "function. Each" (142). Concentration is

achieved mainly by means of elision or omission: for example, "ord'ring" becomes two syllables instead of three, and "of the" becomes a single soft beat.

Metrical violations notwithstanding, the fundamental rhythm is still audible, and other agents of cohesion, the tactics of poetic repetition and identification, oppose the instruments of disorder. First we hear the abundance of identical words and phrases: "When you" (136, 137, 140); "I'd have you" (137, 138), along with "what you" (135, 145), and "wish you" and "that you" (140, 141); "still, still" (142) and "so; so" (138), along with the other "so"s (139, 142, 144). Alliteration is present without being aggressive, as with all the n's in line nine: "And own no other function. Each your doing." There is assonance, or internal rhyme, in "sweet" and "speak" (136); again in "for the ord'ring" (139); and the oozing of line 140: "to, too, you, do, you." Five of the eleven syllables contain the same vowel sound. Finally, there is the chiming of the aural parallels of line 144: "so singular in each particular."

Florizel's praise of Perdita expresses a wish that she could remain always in the attitude of dance, and his metaphor for imagining her is as a wave of the sea, constantly in stationary motion, always changing and yet always the same. Without being too fallacious, we can say that clauses seem to come in waves, falling into distinct metrical units that follow one another metrically and rhythmically – note the rocking motion of "move still, still so" – until the final clause of the sentence smoothly ends the cycle. But once again the contribution of metrics here is not mainly situational. There is mimicry in this passage, an identifiable relation between sound and sense, but it is fleeting and, given the length and complexity of the play, relatively rare.

The metrical freedom Shakespeare displays in these late plays is part of his instinctive attraction to competing poetic impulses and pressures. Blank verse would normally be considered an instrument of cohesion, a foundational source of repetitive sound providing aural satisfaction and welcome regularity. But in the romances the forces of disequilibrium are so potent as to threaten the normal rhythms, and thus a normal source of normalcy works against itself. If the tendency in plots and in other formal features is towards a greater degree of artifice, this is distinctly not the case with the blank verse, which tends to sound more "natural," less obviously "poetic" than in the earlier plays. At the same time, however, the other forces of repetition are consistent with the self-conscious delight in artifice.

Just as these last works are emotionally draining, they are also rhythmically demanding, and the mental and emotional exercise proceeds from a conflict between the forces of coherence and chaos, good and evil, tragedy and comedy, long and short, or whatever names we happen to give to the antitheses Shakespeare exploits. In the penultimate scene of *The Winter's Tale*, considerable talk is heard about the intermingling of sorrow and joy. "There might you have beheld one joy crown another, so and in such manner that it seemed sorrow wept to take leave of them, for their joy waded in tears" (5.2.43–46). Metrically, we participate in a competition between the demands of unbroken rhythm, the iambic framework on which the verse is founded, and the counteractive forces of energy and deviation. Meter functions as a symbolic system, a sonic world that mimes in a general way the living, changing world of the play, which mirrors in a general way the living, changing world that we inhabit. Wright believes that the interlocking sounds represent a "system of internal obligations [that] mirrors the intensity of relations within and between people and between people and the divine order . . . Not only the normal iambic pentameter line but all its departures and deviations help to imply a world-view of continuing reciprocal engagement and mutual responsibility. No syllable, no foot, no phrase, no line, no sentence, no speech, no scene is an island entire to itself."[23]

The subtlety of that metrical system in the late plays corresponds to the complex understanding of experience represented on the stage. The delicate emotional balance achieved at the end of *The Winter's Tale* requires the audience to experience conflicting feelings at the same time: joy at the recovery of Perdita and sorrow at the loss of Mamillius; regret at the loss of Antigonus and pleasure at the marriage of Paulina and Camillo; delight at the bumpkins' social elevation and scorn at their misunderstandings. Sometimes the emotions are even mutually exclusive: our satisfaction at the reunion of Leontes and Hermione is mitigated by our unresolved contempt for his having destroyed his wife and his family's happiness. It can be argued that Leontes is able to accept the return of his wife only because she has finally been cleansed, because she is no longer a sexual being.[24] And yet it can be argued that she, as we have done, has forgiven him. The inescapable pain and the bitter ironies of the preceding acts do mitigate the joy and harmony of the reunion; and yet at the same time the joy and harmony of the reunion mitigate the inescapable pain and bitter ironies of the previous acts. Recent productions, notably

---

[23] *Shakespeare's Metrical Art*, pp. 259–60.
[24] For a more thorough discussion of gender and its influence on Shakespeare's late practice, see Chapter 6, below.

Edward Hall's 2005 version for Propellor, have tended to emphasize the awkwardness rather than the joy of the reunion. But both strains are present to modify and enrich the other. So it is with the meter: the regularity of the beat controls the rhythmic adventurism of the verse. Even in its sound patterns, the Shakespearean system of values implies its own opposites.[25]

SOME USES OF REPETITION

According to Hoskins in *Directions for Speech and Style*, "as no man is sick in thought upon one thing but for some vehemency or distress, so in speech there is no repetition without importance."[26] But what is the "importance" of the repetitions in both the verbal style and dramatic structure of the late work? What does this figure import through the text to the audience? What is its function? As with most of the other poetic strategies, I normally decline to assign specific semantic functions to repeated sounds. There is small profit in seeking thematic "meaning" in Arviragus's "**th**ou shalt not *lack* / **Th**e flower **th**at's *like* **th**y face, pale primrose" (*Cym.* 4.2.221–22), or any other such reiterative line. Nevertheless, certain aural configurations occasionally accomplish certain small chores. To take an example not hitherto cited, the circularity of Caliban's exultant "Freedom, high-day! High-day, freedom! Freedom, high-day, freedom!" ironically records his personal entrapment, the exchange of one master for another. Similar instances of meaningful repetition arise in all the romances. But for the most part these and other such examples of functional echo constitute special cases.

The repeated sounds heard throughout the romances offer satisfactions that usually do not pertain directly to meaning, or at least not to paraphrasable meanings. In Freud's well-known formulation, "Repetition, the re-experiencing of something identical, is clearly in itself a source of pleasure."[27] Assonance and consonance employed in such profusion, the doubling of words, the rhythmic recapitulation of phrases, the outbreaks of rhyme, the complex metrical schemes – all these devices offer the listener the pleasure of arrangement. These poetic contrivances also serve to separate the poetic sign and its denotative referent: returning to the etymology of "trope," we can say that such

---

[25] See Wright, *Shakespeare's Metrical Art*, p. 261.   [26] *Directions for Speech and Style*, p. 12.
[27] *Beyond the Pleasure Principle*, quoted in Bruce F. Kawin, *Telling it Again and Again: Repetition in Literature and Film* (Ithaca: Cornell University Press, 1971), p. 1

figures *turn* the reader's consciousness momentarily away from the thing signified and enforce a fleeting concentration on the surface of language. Pleasing patterns, in other words, call attention to themselves and in doing so press the claim of words as words, promoting ornamental value, their color and weight and arrangement. Sigurd Burckhardt puts it this way:

> the nature and primary function of the most important poetic devices – especially rhyme, meter, and metaphor – is to release words in some measure from their bondage to meaning, their purely referential role, and to give or restore to them the corporeality which a true medium needs. To attain the position of creative sovereignty over matter, the poet must first of all reduce language to something resembling a material. He can never do so completely, only proximately. But he can – and this is his first task – drive a wedge between words and their meanings, lessen as much as possible their designatory force and thereby inhibit our all too ready flight from them to the things they point to. Briefly put, the function of poetic devices is dissociative, or divestive.[28]

We may need to be reminded these days about the value of surfaces. Burckhardt's reference to "our too ready flight from [words] to the things they point to" supplies an apt description of literary criticism at the beginning of the twenty-first century.

Arrangement implies order, and the perception of order is pleasing to the human mind. The specific form of pleasure supplied by such extravagant repetition as that found in the romances is musical. Coleridge, in a lecture delivered in 1818, praised Spenser for the "indescribable sweetness and fluent projection of his verse" and went on to identify specifically the elaborate patterning of consonants in *The Faerie Queene*, declaring Spenser "particularly given to alternate alliteration, which is, perhaps, when well used, a great secret in melody."[29] To modern ears Coleridge's reference to "melody" may be slightly puzzling, in that our understanding of the noun is mostly restricted to its use as a synonym for "tune," as "a series of single notes arranged in a musically expressive or distinctive sequence" (*OED*, 3.a.). But an earlier meaning of "melody" (related to the Latin etymology in *mel*, "honey" or "sweetness") encompasses various forms of lyricism, particularly that associated with poetry, "beauty of sound in the arrangement of words, esp. in poetic composition" (*OED 1.c.*). Where we would normally distinguish between melody and rhythm,

---

[28] Sigurd Burckhardt, *Shakespearean Meanings* (Princeton: Princeton University Press, 1968), p. 24.
[29] Thomas Middleton Raysor, ed., *Coleridge's Miscellaneous Criticism* (Cambridge: Harvard University Press, 1936), p. 34 (Lecture 3 of 1818).

for example, Puttenham in the *Arte* speaks of "the pleasant melody of our English meeter."[30] In other words, "melody" in the sense that Coleridge employs it means more or less the same as "music." And in addition to sweetness, the smoothness (Coleridge's "fluency") of the verse depends upon the absence of obstacles.

The repetition of letters serves to streamline the poetic phrase, increasing the velocity of the line sometimes even when the letter itself is aurally harsh. In simple alliteration, the duplication of a consonant recently sounded generates in the listener a moment of delight, a brief instance of pleasing return. Musical composers, of course, use such reiterative patterns as the basis of melodic arrangement; in large compositions, such reiteration also accounts for the key signature of a piece. In poetry, alternation and chiasmus intensify the melodic and harmonic effect by complicating and varying the patterns of aural likeness. The musical analogy is even more evident in complex forms of literal patterning, such as the kind of "alternate alliteration" that Coleridge praises in Spenser, or the chiastic forms already demonstrated.[31] Virgil Thompson, wearing his music critic's hat, is helpful on this point: "I see no reason to deny that the constants of music, which begin with rhythm and meter and go on to cover all the possible combinations within any harmonic series, are not only structural elements for aiding memory but expressive vocabularies as well. Not dictionaries of emotion, not at all, but repertories of devices for provoking feelings without defining them."[32] This emphasis on indeterminacy is essential to an understanding of Shakespeare's practice generally, and particularly in the late poetry.

Music implies a musician, at whatever remove: although Ferdinand in *The Tempest* cannot see the maker of the enchanting sounds he hears, the audience can. The elaborate schemes of repetition that characterize the late style attest to the presence of a maker, or, to use a term deriving from the Greek for "maker," a poet. Our awareness of such a presence is a result of the self-conscious artifice. The production of coherence stimulates security, a confidence that the apparent chaos of the dramatic realm is opposed by forces of order. E. K. Brown, in his book about Forster, Proust, and other modernist fiction writers, describes the paradoxical

[30] *Arte of English Poesie*, p. 141.
[31] As Burke puts it, "this reversal . . . is quite common in music (where the artist quite regularly varies the sequence of notes in his theme by repeating it upside down or backwards)" ("On Musicality in Verse," p. 372).
[32] Virgil Thompson, "Music Does Not Flow," *New York Review of Books*, 17 December 1981, p. 49.

operation of stylistic echo: "Repetition is the strongest assurance an author can give of order; the extraordinary complexity of the variations is the reminder that the order is so involute that it must remain a mystery."[33] Such unseen security is one of the effects of Shakespeare's poetic textures. The tendency of literal repetition to bind words together, to establish and reconfirm sonic connections among syllables and phrases and lines, is just one of the multiple forms of rhythm at work in all the romances, and rhythm serves the poet, and the audience, as a defense against disorder.[34] Each play, in its narrative structure, embodies a struggle between chaos and order, or energy and control, to which the various poetic contests contribute.

Metrical patterning can serve as a model for other kinds of verbal arrangement. The aggregative effect of repeated consonants and vowels generates an aural security analogous to that supplied by the echoing rhythm of the iambic line. The poetic energies at work in these texts are powerful: they manifest themselves in lengthy sentences, elliptical constructions, confused and divagatory syntax, and irregular metrics, and they create a potentially anarchic aural climate. The conflict between emotional expressivity and the controlling influence of repeated sounds mimics the larger opposition between, for example, ellipsis and expansion. Audiences often have difficulty making immediate sense of the concentrated speech of a Pericles or Leontes, and yet the presence of insistent sonic echoes suggests a pattern. This design in turn implies a designer or some authorial figure responsible for arranging and controlling the aural world and the fictional world it mediates. As E. H. Gombrich reminds us, our recognition of such patterns not only delights the mind but also leads us to "form the preliminary hypothesis that we are confronted with a lawful assembly."[35]

Consonance and assonance, rhyme, and the repetition of words and phrases afford the pleasure – it is fundamentally a dramatic pleasure – of recognition. We like what we know, and the musical rewards of the text are intensified by the repetition of familiar letters and combinations of letters in proximate positions. Etymologically, the word "like" comes into

---

[33] E. K. Brown, *Rhythm in the Novel* (Toronto: University of Toronto Press, 1950), p. 105.

[34] Peter Brooks, speaking of the contribution of repetition in a novel like *Great Expectations*, offers a relevant analysis: "Repetition is clearly a major operative principle . . . shaping energy, giving it perceptible form, form that the text and the reader can work with in the construction of thematic wholes and narrative orders." *Reading for the Plot: Design and Intention in Narrative* (New York: Alfred A. Knopf, 1984), p. 123.

[35] E. H. Gombrich, *The Sense of Order: A Study in the Psychology of Decorative Art* (New York: Phaidon, 1979), p. 151.

Middle English from Old English and its related Teutonic languages, and the origins of its adjectival and its verbal uses are identical. In other words, we like things that are alike. The uncertainties of the random, crowded, and potentially dangerous realm of the play intensifies our satisfaction in perceiving the aural kinship I have been illustrating. Such pleasing resemblance goes a long way towards explaining the value of alliteration as a poetic instrument. This principle is demonstrated in Pericles' "O, come hither, / Thou that beget'st him that did thee beget," where the liquidity of the lines is fostered most obviously by the repetition of *th*, a sound that reappears five times in nine syllables. These repeated and related sounds aurally intensify the semantic resonance that attends the completion of this paradoxical sentence. Such instances of consonance and assonance infuse the scene with the effect of familiarity, habituating the ear to a pattern of likeness and difference, creating musical harmonies that add another layer to the fundamental rhythms of the iambic beat. The return to a strong consonant after an intervening letter or word generates the sort of auditory comfort we perceive when a tone is repeated in a musical line or a particular shape replicated in a decorative pattern. It is not such a long leap from Shakespeare's alliterative prodigality to some powerful examples of visual serialization: a Warholian group of Marilyn Monroes, a rank of columns on a Greek temple, a Parisian wall plastered with twenty copies of the same movie poster, a line of extended forearms, hands, and fingers in the *corps de ballet*.

What specifically do these various benefits contribute to Shakespeare's last plays? The first function has to do with mood or tone, and the touchstone for such treatment is that most alliterative of major poets, Edmund Spenser. The poet's poet unashamedly insists on the superficial glitter of his lines, delighting Elizabethan readers with those patterns they found invariably delightful.

> **Th**ey pass **th**e bitter **w**aves of Acheron
> **Wh**ere many **s**ouls **s**it **w**ailing **w**oefully,
> And come to **f**iery **f**lood of **Ph**legethon,
> **Wh**ereas the da**m**ned ghosts in torment fry,
> And with **sh**arp **sh**rilling **sh**rieks d*o* b*oo*tless cry,
> Cursing high Jove, **th**e which **th**em **th**ither sent.
>   (*The Faerie Queene* I.v.33)

These patterns are Elizabethan, to be sure, but they are more extreme than those found in the work of Spenser's contemporaries, a difference attributable to the central role of repetition in his poetic scheme. Alliteration takes its place with his archaism, manipulated forms of spelling, and the distinctive rhyming patterns of his original stanza as a poetic instrument calculated to inveigle his reader into an ideal imaginative domain. Moreover, the patterns have to do not only with his linguistic agenda but also with his conception of the patterned nature of reality.

Coleridge gestures towards the semantic function of literal repetition when he argues that Spenser "uses it with great effect in doubling the impression of an image," and cites the passage just quoted as an instance of such reinforcement: a doublet such as "wailing woefully" serves to enforce the semantic content of the phrase.[36] But its underscoring is general, not particular to the semantic content. Even more important is the accumulation of such doublets and triplets. Spenser's passion for consonance and assonance creates a surface of unreality, an intricate and complex system of parallels, duplications, and sonic repetitions. Hazlitt is right in his claim that Spenser, delighting in the succession of his distinctive poetic stanzas, "has invented not only a language, but a music of his own . . . The undulations are infinite, like those of the waves of the sea: but the effect is still the same, lulling our senses into a deep oblivion of the jarring noises of the world, from which we have no wish to be ever recalled."[37]

The operation of these acoustic and lexical echoes creates a poetic counterpoint that challenges and exhilarates the audience. When Jan Kott refers to *The Tempest* as a fugue, his perception invites both thematic and formal application: he accurately identifies the polyphonic texture perceptible throughout the last phase.[38] These musical effects induce aurally in the audience a sense of wonder corresponding to the aims and effects of the romantic or tragicomic mode. The verbal music supports the enchanted atmosphere that attends and complicates the action of Shakespeare's late romantic forms: it promises much but never wholly delivers the profundity implied. It is just this dynamic that makes the late plays seem so uncommonly rich and mysterious. The operation of the verbal patterns is thus paradoxical, their greatest significance being precisely an ostensible significance combined with a refusal to signify. The effect is dreamlike.[39]

[36] Coleridge, Lecture 3, p. 34.

[37] William Hazlitt, *Lectures on the English Poets* (London, 1818), p. 85.

[38] Jan Knott, "*The Tempest*, or Repetition," in *The Bottom Translation: Marlowe and Shakespeare and the Carnival Tradition*, tr. Daniela Miedzyrzecka and Lillian Vallee (Evanston: Northwestern University Press, 1987), p. 97.

[39] Of the many studies of the oneiric qualities of *The Tempest* and the other late plays, see particularly Nevo's *Shakespeare's Other Language*, pp. 136–43, and Marjorie Garber, *Dream in Shakespeare: From Metaphor to Metamorphosis* (London: Methuen, 1974).

The insistent poetic reiterations interact with the elliptical syntax to mystify the audience about a function that never manifests itself. Many passages, especially in *The Tempest*, encourage the audience to expect significance from the linguistic and structural patterns, but they stoutly refuse to yield those meanings entirely. Eager to satisfy the desire for comprehension, listeners find themselves both stimulated and frustrated. On the one hand, the repeated sounds or phrases in a brief and complex passage offer harmony, a richness of texture that stimulates desire for fulfillment. On the other, the text frustrates those expectations of clarity which the discovery of such patterns engenders: in the rapid flow of dialogue the repetitions themselves are succeeded by more repetitions which seem equally promising and equally unyielding. Such a method tantalizes the audience with the hope of clarification and fixity that art seems to promise, but it also demonstrates the difficulty and perhaps, finally, the impossibility of attaining them. Since order and comprehension seem always available but never thoroughly realized, the audience participates directly in an atmosphere of evanescence characteristic of all these late works.

Shakespeare may be said to be addressing himself directly to the problem of language and meaning, about which he maintains grave doubts. Denied or delayed communication becomes a minor but explicit motif: Pericles' refusal to speak until coaxed by Marina, the letters carried by Jachimo and Pisanio in *Cymbeline*, Antonio's and Sebastian's interruption of Gonzalo's utopian vision, the weeping queens in *The Two Noble Kinsmen*. Numerous acts of communication (a speech, a song, a banquet, a masque) are broken off or delayed or redirected. Our position is rather like that described by Caliban in his most memorable speech:

> Be not afeard, the isle is full of noises, 135
> Sounds, and sweet airs, that give delight and hurt not.
> Sometimes a thousand twangling instruments
> Will hum about mine ears; and sometimes voices,
> That if I then had wak'd after long sleep,
> Will make me sleep again, and then in dreaming, 140
> The clouds methought would open, and show riches
> Ready to drop upon me, that when I wak'd
> I cried to dream again. (*The Tempest* 3.2.135–43)

Often cited as evidence of natural sensitivity or of the magical atmosphere of the setting, these lines are most helpful as a statement of how the music of the repetitive style impresses an audience. In *The Tempest*, as Robert Graves pointed out long ago, the confusion of tenses contributes to a feeling of arrested time; lovely sounds "hum" about our ears; we seem to be about the receive riches of significance which remain forever elusive. The desired unity and gratification are contradicted by the brevity and compression of the text, and thus we find ourselves in what A. D. Nuttall has called an "atmosphere of ontological suspension" that pervades *The Tempest*, a region midway between promise and fulfillment.[40] This state of expectancy is also the source of constant pleasure, as we are told elsewhere: "For ever shalt thou love, and she be fair."

The presence of such poetic tantalization attests to Shakespeare's playful attitude towards his material, in that one of the principal effects of the new mode of romance or tragicomedy is to tease the audience. The structure of many of these dramas reinforces the fundamental erotic appeal of the verse by protracting but withholding the imminent resolution. Peter Brooks, commenting on an essay of Freud's, "Creative Writers and Day-Dreaming," writes about the aesthetic values of literary form, specifically what Freud calls "forepleasure."

The equation of the effects of literary form with forepleasure in this well-known passage is perhaps less trivial than it at first appears. If *Lust* and *Unlust* don't take us very far in the analysis of literary texture, *Vorlust* – forepleasure – tropes on pleasure and thus seems more promising. Forepleasure is indeed a curious concept, suggesting a whole rhetoric of advance toward and retreat from the goal or the end, a formal zone of play (I take it that forepleasure somehow implicates foreplay) that is both harnessed to the end and yet autonomous, capable of deviations and recursive movements. When we begin to unpack the components of forepleasure, we may find a whole erotics of form, which is perhaps what we most need if we are to make formalism serve an understanding of the human functions of literature. Forepleasure would include the notion of both delay and advance in the textual dynamic, the creation of that 'dilatory space' which Roland Barthes, in *S/Z*, claimed to be the essence of the textual middle. We seek to advance through this space toward the discharge of the end, yet all the while we are perversely delaying, returning backward in order to put off the promised end and perhaps to assure its greater significance.[41]

This suggestive paragraph helps to illuminate the way the late style functions in, and in concert with, the new dramatic mode. A seventeeth-century equivalent of this process of narrative tease is found in William Cartwright's prefatory verses in the 1647 Beaumont and Fletcher Folio.

---

[40] Robert Graves, *The White Goddess* (London: Farrar, 1948), p. 425; A. D. Nuttall, *Two Concepts of Allegory: A Study of Shakespeare's "The Tempest" and the Logic of Allegorical Expression* (New York: Barnes and Noble, 1967), p. 158.

[41] Peter Brooks, "The Idea of a Psychoanalytic Literary Criticism," *Critical Inquiry*, 13 (1987), 339.

> None can prevent the fancy, and see through
> At the first opening; all stand wondering how
> The thing will be, until it is; which hence
> With fresh delight still cheats, still takes the sense;
> The whole design, the shadow, the lights such
> That none can say he shews or hides too much.

The titillating diction of Cartwright's description is given special meaning in light of Brooks's plea for a textual erotics, for both capture the gamesome, self-conscious appeal of romance or tragicomedy.

Narrative progress towards the satisfactions of complete understanding, or closure, is indirect and irregular, and the chief pleasure rests in the delay and the circuitousness of the journey. Romance depends upon suspense, secrets, surprises, discoveries, peripeties, awakenings, revelations. Thus it automatically raises questions of epistemology but almost always leaves them open. It is a knowing form, a self-conscious mode reliant upon the audience's familiarity with conventions of comic and tragic storytelling and a willingness to be teased by the playwright's manipulation of generic signals. Romance ironically flatters the audience with privileged information, yet it deals in double ironies when it betrays this cozy relationship by a sudden reversal or surprise. Suspense and irony constitute only one pair of several antitheses inherent in tragicomic form (and implicit in its name); these have been described by Philip Edwards as "the pleasure of being kept out of the secret and the pleasure of being let into the secret."[42] Brooks's account of formal erotics is especially pertinent to the gestural narrative style of the late plays and of romance generally.[43] The formal divagations of plays like *Cymbeline* and *The Winter's Tale* recapitulate on a larger stage the sense of promise and profundity fostered by the texture of the verse.

ALLITERATIVE TALES

Hazlitt's perception about the undulation of the verse transports us conveniently into the world of Shakespearean romance, dominated as it

---

[42] Philip Edwards, "The Danger not the Death: The Art of John Fletcher," in *Jacobean Theatre*, ed. John Russell Brown and Bernard Harris (London: Edward Arnold, 1960), p. 164.

[43] Patricia Parker develops some of the same ideas as Brooks: "The suspensions which for Barthes become part of an erotics of the text recall not only the constant divagations of romance and its resistance to the demands of closure, but also the frustration in Ariosto of what Barthes calls the teleological form of vulgar readerly pleasure – the desire to penetrate the veil of meaning or to hasten the narrative's gradual striptease – by a continual postponement of revelation which leaves the reader suspended, or even erotically 'hung up'." *Inescapable Romance: Studies in the Poetics of a Mode* (Princeton: Princeton University Press, 1979), pp. 220–21.

is by the Mediterranean, dependent on marine imagery ("My name is Marina"), and structurally indebted to the undulations of narrative and of language. The literal repetitions on which so much of the verse depends enact the pattern of the waves, with identical sounds following one another in the ocean of text. The sea and its tempests are ambiguous forces in the late plays, serving initially to divide and destroy but finally helping to reunite the family. This poetic contention between the potential chaos of language and the comforting order of repeated sounds aurally conveys the fundamental narrative conflict in all the late plays. The structure of romance involves a journey or quest punctuated by stops along the way, and the similarity and difference of each of these temporary stations comprise a kind of skeleton for the story of the hero. In *Pericles* the parallels among the various stops on the hero's journey are contrived to establish and refract the centrality of the father–daughter relationship. This series of episodes, similar and dissimilar, might be described as a type of narrative alliteration, or perhaps anaphora: a consonance of stories designed to illustrate the human need for the profound comforts of proper familial relations. A pattern of expectation is proposed, frustrated, and ultimately fulfilled. As C. L. Barber and others have pointed out, the dramatic action of the romances is constructed to sever and then to re-establish *relation* of various kinds, specifically the relation of husband to wife, of father to daughter (less often, of father to son), and of human beings to a mysterious cosmic order. The perverse intercourse of Antiochus and his daughter epitomizes the contaminated, illegitimate form of connection from which Pericles must flee and which will be transformed into the recovered harmonious relations of husband, wife, and daughter in Ephesus.

Shakespeare's extravagant patterns of consonance and assonance work together with other ordering impulses, especially forms of narrative repetition, to create an imaginative realm of coherence and fixity. All the conventional definitions of "alliteration" and "assonance" are useful in clarifying this function, for in calling attention to the condition of proximity, dictionaries and guidebooks use terms such as "neighboring" words or syllables, speak of letters from the same phonetic "family," and emphasize the creation of sonic "agreement" or "harmony." These specific terms suggest that the literal relations responsible for the distinctive sound of the last plays help physically to constitute Shakespeare's representation of the familial bond and its indisputable value in human experience. The repetition of consonants and vowels creates ligatures between words that generate a sonic atmosphere of familial security. "Familiarity" is what is lacking, and what is needed, in the chaotic world of adventure. The return of familiar sounds in the repetition of letters reassures us poetically in the same way that the return of lost characters does in the action. Literal reiteration thus serves as the most particular example of Shakespeare's larger artistic aim in the romances, as revenge against the predatory forces of time.

All the late plays depend emotionally and theatrically on the restoration of the lost – "if that which is lost be not found" – and the major instance of this restoration is in the narrative reconstruction of the family. As early as *The Comedy of Errors* Shakespeare splits and rejoins families for dramatic purposes. In the histories and tragedies, he emphasizes separation, in the comedies and romances, reunion, and division of the family is part of the larger dynamic of splitting and reuniting, of chaos and order. Romance is by definition an extravagant form, the word "extravagant" capturing etymologically (again, Latin *vagare*, to stray) the vagrancy and uncertainty of the characters' experience. Thus the audience's wish for closure and reunion, a desire stimulated by the errancy and obstacles of the plot, makes it respond with especial warmth to the intimation of patterns and to other efforts at ordering and aggregation. If the use of consonance and assonance to intensify, to give shape and force to a particular verbal phrase, is one of its principal functions in any kind of poetry, that feature assumes an even greater role in plays that move so relentlessly toward relation and re-creation. The reunion of Pericles and Marina, of Cymbeline's family, of Leontes and Hermione, repeats in a new and sanctified form what has been lost or defeated by the forces of confusion and estrangement.

An epitome of how the sound palette informs the meaning of the action is found in the recognition scene in *Pericles*: in addition to its inescapable schemes of repeated letters and phrases, the encounter exhibits in its diction a compulsive devotion to the establishment of likeness. Throughout the exchange Shakespeare insists explicitly on the effect of resemblance and equivalence:

> She speaks,
> My lord, that hath endur'd a grief
> Might equal yours, if both were justly weigh'd.
> (*Pericles* 5.1.86–88)

The verb "equal" is repeated twice more, and Marina's ancestors ("My derivation") are said to have "stood equivalent with mighty kings." The progress of the dialogue depends noticeably on simile: "as wand-like straight," "Modest as justice." Pericles recognizes, of course, the physical resemblance to the lost Thaisa: "You're like something that . . ." (102), "My dearest wife was like this maid" (107), "Thou lookest / Like one I lov'd indeed" (124–25). The main business of the scene is the confirmation of familial resemblance, the identification of relation and kinship, the restoration of bonds, and that effort at identification is carried forward in language replete with equivalent sounds and identical letters that forge harmonious ties between words and lines. Reestablished relations ultimately serve to promote a sense of divine justice, and the miniature balances that an audience perceives in alliterated doublets feed a hunger for equity and compensation stimulated by the hazards and misfortunes of the plot. As letters resound again and again, in different combinations, the poetry establishes the personal and familial and even cosmic harmonies depicted in the action. Marina's recital of her history is itself a "relation" (123), indeed a relation of a relation, an act of communication connecting "points that seem impossible" (124).

If there is something mildly embarrassing about the reiterative arrangement of vowels and consonants, something apparently naive and child-like, much the same thing might be said of the plots on which the last plays are founded. Every narrative turn seems, as the gentleman reporter puts it in *The Winter's Tale*, "like an old tale still" (5.2.61). We seem to have heard these stories before, and the role of ancient Gower as theatrical mediator in *Pericles* makes explicit the reminiscent quality of Shakespearean romance: "To sing a song that old was sung, / From ashes ancient Gower is come" (1.1.1–2). It is hardly surprising that such a self-conscious recognitive device as alliteration or assonance should appear so prominently in dramas concerned so vitally with the reunion of divided families, with questions of identity, and with the compensatory uses of artifice. Such a fundamental use of rhetorical patterning is analogous to the way metaphor functions in Shakespearean comedy, as described by Terence Cave.

The accidents that fragment the world and then put it together again in *Twelfth Night* or *The Comedy of Errors* are closely linked with recurrent metaphors and figures of speech, and the ultimate sense of coherence they yield is that of an analogy restored or revealed, *as if* by chance (it being a more or less explicit assumption of such plays that chance is itself subsumed in the higher hidden order of analogy).[44]

---

[44] Terence Cave, *Recognitions: A Study in Poetics* (Oxford: Clarendon Press, 1988), p. 281.

The innumerable moments of aural recognition replicate in miniature, and thus create a sonic context for, the larger acts of reconciliation and anagnorisis on which the plots depend.

In the romances, the artificiality of these ostentatious aural figures declares the playwright's commitment to the alternative reality of the stage, his creation of, and invitation to the audience to inhabit temporarily, a world arranged and patterned. The realm of *Pericles* and *The Winter's Tale* affords its characters – and the theatregoers who watch and listen – the joys of reunion and rediscovery, and this movement towards coherence and satisfaction is to some degree a function of the old-fashioned nature of the romance form. Shakespeare's new and virtually unalloyed pleasure in sounds also attests to a faith in the power of language, a development that signals a major change in his view of his medium. The elaborate surface of the verse in the romances implies that Shakespeare has committed himself without apology, although not without self-scrutiny, to the value of surfaces generally. But these topics are sufficiently important to require a chapter of their own.

CHAPTER 6

Style and the making of meaning

Style is, in its roots, the language of instinct, and its workings are by
nature no less real than the rational purposes of positivist reality.

Richard Lanham[1]

This final chapter is devoted to answering the following question: how
does a detailed acquaintance with the technical features of Shakespeare's
late style help us to comprehend the plays, both collectively and individu-
ally? If the stylistic analysis developed in the foregoing chapters is to
amount to more than a dry accounting of poetic devices, metrical eccentricities, and sentence shapes, then it ought to elucidate those larger topics
of meaning and purpose with which criticism, despite the quantity of
work devoted to these texts, has continued to struggle. Therefore this
chapter necessarily reviews some well-known critical themes: for example,
the reader will find discussion of theatrical self-consciousness, the relation
of art and nature, the pain of loss and joy of reconciliation. Although
much of this material will be familiar, most treatments of those ideas
neglect the contribution of the poetry. My aim is to demonstrate how the
distinctive late verse joins with the dramatic mode to articulate and
modify these themes. I hope that we have now acquired a more comprehensive understanding of these plays' "formal grammar and poetic
idiom," to repeat the quotation from Kiernan Ryan cited in the Introduction, and that this understanding might give us a better chance at learning
"how to read them."[2]

Another way of forecasting what follows is to say that the chapter seeks
to elucidate what Frank Kermode has called the exceptional "imaginative
coherence" in Shakespeare's last creative phase.[3] The sophisticated verse,

---

[1] Richard Lanham, *The Motives of Eloquence: Literary Rhetoric in the Renaissance* (New Haven: Yale
University Press, 1976), pp. 214–15.
[2] Kiernan Ryan, *Shakespeare: The Last Plays* (London: Longman, 1999), p. 18.
[3] Frank Kermode, *Shakespeare: The Final Plays*, British Writers and their Work (London: Longmans,
Green, 1963), p. 16. In this respect Kermode and I follow Hazlitt: "the use he makes of the principle

like the romance form and the interest in reconciliation and artifice, is the product of an altered, complex understanding of human experience, and the poetic technique comprises audible traces of that thinking. The verse is new because the way of thinking is new. Most of the tragedies immediately preceding the final phase – especially *King Lear, Timon of Athens, Macbeth,* and *Coriolanus,* all fiercely anti-romantic – advance a profound critique of masculinity and present the most negative, even grotesque portrayals of female sexuality in the entire canon. Shakespeare's rejection of tragedy for romance is accompanied by an imaginative recuperation of the female and a concentration on the redemptive associations of femininity. The late verse is intimately related to this revised point of view. His embrace of the delights of romance and cultivation of an appropriate poetic style declare a conversion to new values, ideals often coded by his culture as feminine and secondary: art, stories, ornament, pleasure, fantasy, patience, forgiveness. The re-conception of his poetic medium bespeaks a renewed commitment to the compensatory power of illusion, a new theatrical realm that cheerfully confesses its status as a rhetorical construction. We have long been aware of an affirmative turn in Shakespeare's thinking after the tragedies. This chapter locates evidence for that transformation in the particular properties of the verse.

RETROSPECTION AND ROMANCE

Distaste for Victorian sentimentality about the aging artist's personal nostalgia should not prevent us from recognizing that around 1607 Shakespeare (consciously or not) entered upon a significant retrospective evaluation of his earlier work. In fact he was never not engaged in such a revisionary process, re-writing, for example, *Romeo and Juliet* in *A Midsummer Night's Dream,* or vice-versa. The professional self-scrutiny that commences about the time of *Macbeth,* however, represents a difference in kind. It is a commonplace that Shakespeare often borrows from himself, although he never repeats himself exactly: in this last period he recycles even more aggressively, reviewing his oeuvre and plundering the earlier plays for characters and narrative ideas. For example, the three

of analogy to reconcile the greatest diversities of character and to maintain a continuity of feeling throughout, has not been sufficiently attended to." Hazlitt goes on to speak of "the force of natural association, a particular train of feeling suggesting different inflections of the same predominant principle, melting into, and strengthening one another, like chords in music." *Characters of Shakespear's Plays* (London: C. H. Reynell, 1817), pp. 9–10.

mirroring usurpation plots in *The Tempest* are obviously lifted from *Hamlet, Macbeth,* and the earlier histories. As I indicated in Chapter 5, the language of the temptation scene (2.1), when Antonio wheedles Sebastian into attempting to murder his brother, borrows directly from the earlier verbal exchanges between the Macbeths. Even the names of the Italian conspirators, Antonio and Sebastian, echo those of the ship-wrecked comrades from *Twelfth Night.* Indeed, the shipwreck itself is a well-used Shakespearean beginning, not only for *The Tempest* and *Twelfth Night* but also the very early *Comedy of Errors. Cymbeline* repeats the stratagem of the heroine disguised as a boy, and the jealousy plots of *Cymbeline* and *The Winter's Tale* look back not only to *Othello* but also to *Much Ado About Nothing.*

The most palpable symptom of this retrospective mood appears in the characterization of Prospero, whose reflections on his political career have invited comparison with Shakespeare's own backward look at his profes-sional life. Even those critics suspicious of nineteenth-century readings of *The Tempest* acknowledge the inescapable parallel between mage and playwright: "The protagonist of *The Tempest* is a prince and a powerful magician, but he is also unmistakably a great playwright – manipulating characters, contriving to set them up in relation to one another, forging memorable scenes . . . The central preoccupations of almost all his plays are there in *The Tempest.*"[4] To acknowledge such retrospection, however, is not necessarily to place the dramatist "on the heights," gazing back lovingly at what he must leave ere long. It is simply to recognize that as he moved in a new artistic direction he returned to some tested formulae, always refitting those episodes and personae to the new kind of work he had begun to do and the fresh effects he sought.

If his own earlier plays served Shakespeare as an inventory for charac-ters and situations, another body of material stimulated him to retrospec-tion of another sort. A rekindled attraction to some of the great imaginative works of the Elizabethan era, a phenomenon referred to occasionally in the earlier chapters, now warrants more thorough atten-tion. The place to start, however, is in the culture at large: Shakespeare was not the only Jacobean Englishman looking backwards. Most literary historians see evidence of an important cultural revival of romance and chivalry not more than three or four years after the death of Elizabeth and accession of James, although they debate its breadth, its duration, its

[4] Stephen Greenblatt, *Will in the World: How Shakespeare Became Shakespeare* (New York: Norton, 2004), pp. 372 and 378.

significance.[5] Frances Yates, in studying the cultural rootedness of ideas in the last plays, finds in the "early Jacobean period a movement which might be called an Elizabethan revival," a nostalgia associated specifically with Prince Henry and articulated clearly in "Prince Henry's Barriers" and "Oberon."[6] She contends that the Jacobean spectator would have identified this fictional realm as the world of "Sidneyan Protestantism" and that Shakespeare would surely have heard in such theatrical enterprises echoes of his poetic predecessors. *Henry VIII* might be considered the King's Men's entry in this festival of reminiscence. Other revivals were less abstract: *Mucedorus*, newly amplified with additions, was performed at court shortly before the composition of *Pericles*, and Shakespeare could not have failed to notice its expression of cruder, or at least simpler, tastes – and its immense popularity.[7]

The last plays are shot through with characters, episodes, language, and themes from the works of Sidney, Greene, Spenser, Lyly, Marlowe, and some of the Spanish and Italian romance writers whose tales were popular in the sixteenth century, not to mention Gower and Chaucer. Shakespeare seems to have been drawn especially to fictions that must have given him pleasure in his twenties. Significantly, in composing *The Winter's Tale* he used the original 1588 edition of *Pandosto*, even though the novella was reprinted in 1607: this detail implies physical contact with some of his favorite books from an earlier age. It may also be relevant that *Shakespeare's Sonnets* appeared in quarto in 1609. Not only do the poems look back to a form that reached its apogee in the 1580s and 90s, but the extreme formality of the sub-genre of lyric seems consistent with the poet's rediscovered pleasure in artifice and verbal delights.

The sources of his borrowing suggest a conscious return to springs of fascination and pleasure from earlier days. Katherine Duncan-Jones believes that "Shakespeare in *The Winter's Tale* was consciously revisiting the life and works of Robert Greene, not merely appropriating some of the useful plot material of *Pandosto*."[8] For his depiction of Autolycus, for example, he took material from one of Greene's cony-catching pamphlets.

[5] See R. S. White, *Let Wonder Seem Familiar* (London: Athlone Press, 1985), p. 113.

[6] Frances A. Yates, *Shakespeare's Last Plays: A New Approach* (London: Routledge & Kegan Paul, 1975), p. 19. "Thus the theme of the revival of chivalry in the new generation – in the fairy prince, son of Arthur-James – is again set in the form of figures of romance emerging from rocks or caves" (p. 25).

[7] See Suzanne Gossett, Introduction to *Pericles* (London: Thomson Learning, 2004), pp. 72–73.

[8] Katherine Duncan-Jones, *Ungentle Shakespeare: Scenes from His Life* (London: Thomson Learning, 1997), p. 229.

He may also have remembered Greene in constructing the network of explanations and identifications that make up the last scene of *Cymbeline*, this time the closing episode of *James IV*, in which Sir Cuthbert Anderson and Queen Dorothea present and solve a riddle involving a lion's whelp.[9] Other highlights of Elizabethan drama seem to have remained active in his imagination: Prospero's connection to the spirit world in *The Tempest* is sometimes thought to represent Shakespeare's re-writing of *Doctor Faustus*. Certainly his acquaintance with Spenser helps to account for the pastoral qualities that, to some greater or lesser degree, mark all the late works. Frank Kermode points out that the Sir Tristram episode in Canto 2 of the *Booke of Courtesy*, lying behind the Jachimo–Imogen scenes in *Cymbeline*, probably shaped Shakespeare's adaptation of *Frederick of Jennyn*, and while Kermode may exaggerate slightly in asserting that Shakespeare knew *The Faerie Queene* as well as he knew any book, he is right to insist that we have neglected this major source, particularly the spirit of Book VI.[10]

Sidney's work seems to have exerted the most potent influence. *The Arcadia* and *Astrophil and Stella* supply Shakespeare abundantly throughout his career, from the sonnets and the narrative poems through to the very last works. But around 1605 he seems to have taken another careful look. Not only is the episode of the Paphlagonian king the basis for the Gloucester plot in *King Lear*, but the story may have shaped his dramatic alteration of his source material for the main plot.[11] Katherine Duncan-Jones sees *Pericles* as a "transmutation and compression of Arcadian romance" and identifies a number of Sidneyan elements: she believes the episode in which Pericles miraculously finds his father's rusty armor in the sea recalls the discovery of Amphialus's armor, "hacked in some places," and draws persuasive parallels between some of Sidney's and Shakespeare's heroines and villainesses.[12] Some of these resemblances had been suggested by George Steevens, who mentions, for example, the similarity of the names Pericles and Pyrocles (which may have been

---

[9] Juliana Lawrence, "Natural Bonds and Artistic Coherence in the Ending of *Cymbeline*," *Shakespeare Quarterly*, 35 (1984): in her study of the complex tone of that scene, Lawrence contends that "Shakespeare imitates Greene's naïve technique of effecting a sense of clarification – first by obscuring events in a riddle, and then by solving the riddle to the eminent satisfaction of all concerned" (p. 451).

[10] Kermode, *Shakespeare: The Final Plays*, p. 21n.

[11] Katherine Duncan-Jones reminds us that in Sidney's tale, after the old king is restored to his throne, the romancer's diction in depicting his death suggests the mixture of joy and despair that we see dramatized in Gloucester's end. "Liquid Prisoners: Shakespeare's re-writings of Sidney," *Sidney Journal Newsletter*, 15:4 (Fall 1997), 13–15.

[12] *Ibid.*, 17–20.

pronounced "Pïrocles").[13] Other characters and types may have been lifted from Sidney's romance: R. S. White proposes, for example, that the wicked Cecropia be considered the model for Dionyza in *Pericles* and the villainous Queen in *Cymbeline*.[14]

The nature of Sidney's influence is more abstract and far-reaching than as a supplier of characters, however. More significant is his exploitation of the multiple modes that combine to give *The Arcadia* its generic and philosophical layering. Stephen Greenblatt describes that original mixture:

> like many Renaissance artists, Sidney seemed instinctively to feel that for the world he wished to portray, there could be no unified, pure form with a single style, a uniform set of characters, and a fixed perspective. A single genre as conceived by Scaliger, Minturno, or any of the other theorists available to Sidney could not contain the world pictured in *Arcadia*, where life is a series of illogical reversals, coincidences and sudden revelations, where a resolution solemnly made one moment is broken in the next, where the qualities that seemed to ennoble the possessor lead him to treasonous acts, where tenderness turns to cruelty and suffering to pleasure.[15]

I quote at such length because the passage might, with very little adjustment, serve as a description of Shakespeare's generic freebooting in the romances. And the most meaningful resemblance is visible in the irresolutions and multiple ironies of Shakespeare's endings. As Greenblatt goes on to say about the uncertainty prevalent in *The Arcadia*, "in the mixed mode, to resolve is to lie."[16]

In *Cymbeline* Imogen's male disguise is reminiscent of Shakespeare's own earlier romantic comedies, of course, but the device seems also *au courant*, pointing as it does to his connection to Beaumont and Fletcher. They, too, had been borrowing from Sidney, taking advantage of the Elizabethan revival of which he seems to have been the focus. Not only was *The Arcadia* reprinted in 1605, but Gervase Markham's continuation of it, *The English Arcadia*, was published in 1607, and other adaptations appeared as well.[17] *Cupid's Revenge* (*c.* 1608), which may be the first

---

[13] *The Plays of William Shakespeare, Accurately printed from the Text of the corrected Copy left by the late George Steevens, Esq., with a selection of Explanatory and Historical Notes*, 9 vols. (London, 1811), VIII: 237–38.

[14] White, *Let Wonder Seem Familiar*, p. 142.

[15] Stephen Greenblatt, "Sidney's *Arcadia* and the Mixed Mode," *Studies in Philology*, 70 (1973), 272–73.

[16] *Ibid.*, p. 278.

[17] For a detailed look at this fashion for Sidney two decades after his death, see Lee Bliss, *Francis Beaumont* (Boston: Twayne, 1987), pp. 57–59.

full-scale collaboration between Beaumont and Fletcher, takes both its plots from *The Arcadia*: what is pertinent here is the character of Urania, a figure borrowed from Sidney's story of the disguised Zelmane in Book Two. In *Philaster* (c. 1609), the subplot involving the disguised Bellario also makes use of the heroine in male disguise.[18] Scholars have debated at length the question of whether *Philaster* preceded *Cymbeline* or vice-versa; only recently has much been said about the Shakespearean relevance of *Cupid's Revenge*.[19] But priority and exact influences are less significant than all three dramatists' interest in Sidney, in pastoral drama, and in stretching the boundaries of dramatic form in the direction of tragicomedy and romance.

Whether Shakespeare's re-reading of old favorites helped to prompt the romantic turn in 1607–8 or whether a change in his thinking then sent him back to sources of past pleasure, his re-discovery of old favorites apparently shaped his creative energies during the last phase of his professional life. In returning to the books of his youth, he seems to have reminded himself of the fundamental appeal of old-fashioned stories. It is important to recognize, however, that most of these Elizabethan originals, from *The Arcadia* to *Mucedorus*, are not as nostalgically simple or as naive as we might be inclined to think. Most are so thoroughly mixed in genre and tone that they offer the potential for ironic and romantic response.[20] And Shakespeare, in returning to them, seems to have thought about them in both ways. Such retrospection coincides with the playwright's revised way of thinking about his art and its relation to experience: his rediscovery of the pleasures of fiction, his refreshed attitude towards language, his renewed faith in theatrical illusion. Shakespeare would certainly have been conscious of how drastically literary tastes and styles

---

[18] See Bliss, *Francis Beaumont*, pp. 58–61, and Duncan-Jones, *Ungentle Shakespeare*, p. 231. Yates emphasizes the pastoral connection: "the style and themes of *Philaster* constantly recall Sidney's romance, *Arcadia*. The characters wander through pastoral landscapes exhibiting their romantic passions and their adherence to a Sidneian code of chivalric Puritanism" (*Shakespeare's Last Plays*, p. 30).

[19] See especially Arthur C. Kirsch, "*Cymbeline* and Coterie Dramaturgy," *ELH*, 34 (1967), 285–306.

[20] According to Simon Palfrey, "in turning to the romance mode Shakespeare not only invokes *The Arcadia*, but pays a type of homage to popular Elizabethan plays such as *The Rare Triumphs of Love and Fortune*, *Sir Clyomon and Sir Clamydes*, *Mucedorus*, *The Thracian Wonder*, and *Locrine*. These works tirelessly invoke chivalrous motif and sentiment but, as if faithful to their demotic franchise, remain strangely disobedient beasts. They share audience and orientation with old tales and ballads, possessing a tabloid topicality, a capacity to satirize, and an instinct toward allegory; they draw similarly upon fables, a genre rooted in the self-preservation and emotional democratizing of 'proletarian' communities. Improbable tales are not always the mollifying slave either of escapism or hegemony." *Late Shakespeare: A New World of Words* (Oxford: Oxford University Press, 1997), pp. 37–38.

had changed. The extreme artifice in Lyly's court comedies (not to mention in practically every sentence of *Euphues*), or the poetic formality and prodigal ornamentation of *The Faerie Queene*, or the narrative patterns of *The Arcadia* – each of these represents aspects of a style he and his Jacobean contemporaries had left behind. It also seems clear that he was fascinated by the self-conscious artfulness of these texts, and it was his particular gift to recognize the pleasurable patterns on which they depend, to appropriate and play with those patterns, and thus to convert them into a "modern," sophisticated kind of artifice.

RETROSPECTION AND PERSPECTIVE

This process of retrospection also coincides with Shakespeare's commitment to the beneficial effects of perspective. The topic seems to have been much on his mind at this moment, for reasons that we can guess at but never be sure of. In 1607 Shakespeare was forty-three years old: some take this as proof that he was getting old and knew it, others that he was in the fullness of middle age and would not have felt threatened by mortality or retirement or creative failure. Whether at age forty-three he was feeling weary of the world, simply weary of work, frightened by the death of his younger brother Edmund, threatened by the popularity of his youthful dramatic rivals and the shifts in public taste, pressured by his fellow shareholders to satisfy those changing tastes, or obliged to refresh his professional direction – for whatever biographical or commercial or other reasons, Shakespeare was exercising perspective on his own career at about this time. The importance of looking beyond one's immediate state, especially beyond present misery, is one of the major links, and contrasts, between his tragedies and romances. As I have indicated, Edgar's speech describing the perspectival relation between objects visible from the Dover cliffs is the seedbed for the theme as developed in the romances: literally and metaphorically, what one sees depends upon where one stands, a point ironically complicated by the blinded Gloucester's inability to see at all and by Edgar's imaginative invention of the perspectival scene. *King Lear* leads its audience to doubt and perhaps even to reject Edgar's efforts to hearten his desperate parent by giving him a sense of philosophical scope. But all the romances insist on the value of proper perspective, on the dangers of solipsism and hubris, on the inevitable limitations of our understanding.

Time the Chorus's remarks about temporal perspective, considered in Chapter 4, are seconded by another major statement from the same play:

Paulina's response to the arrival of Perdita and Florizel at the Sicilian court in 5.1. When the servant describes the alighting foreign princess as "the most peerless piece of earth, I think, / That e're the sun shone bright on," Paulina lashes out at his limited scope by apostrophizing her ideal of perfection.

> O Hermione,
> As every present time doth boast itself
> Above a better gone, so must thy grave
> Give way to what's seen now.
>   (5.1.94–98)

This critique of partial comprehension, of the tendency to privilege one's own point of view, is implicit in the action of all the late plays, and *The Winter's Tale* especially takes advantage of a particular strain of meaning associated with romance fiction, promoting as it does, by means of its temporal range, the virtues of the long view. Again, that theme is the burden of the speech by Time the Chorus, which telescopes generations and threatens the representatives of brave modernity with eventual decay and outmodedness. Lack of perspective is a product of solipsism, an inability to relate our own experience to that of other times, the equivalent of the failure to connect to those around us. A tragic figure such as Lear can be seen as a spectacular example of this error, and the opportunity to remedy self-absorption signifies one of the central distinctions between romance and tragedy. Yet recognizing our own limited understanding may be insufficient because the assumption that we have succeeded in achieving a balanced perspective may be fallacious: even Paulina, as she deplores the limited vision of the present, is herself declaring a partiality that another age might deny. Virtually every claim, even the wisest and most capacious, is undercut.

The need to maintain perspective governs our reception of the poetic style, particularly the syntactical constructions described in Chapters 3 and 4. The disjunction between the apparently simple romantic stories and the difficult verse sentences spoken by the characters is typical of the playwright's taste for paradoxical effects. *Cymbeline*, for example, opens with the fairy-tale trope of the princess whose choice of a husband displeases her father, and yet the opening lines are about as far from "once upon a time" as can be.

I GENT. You do not meet a man but frowns. Our bloods
         No more obey the heavens than our courtiers'
         Still seem as does the King's.

>   (1.1.1–3)

The circumlocution, negatives, asymmetrical comparison, and withheld words ([courtiers'] "faces" and [King's] "face") perplex rather than assist the listener, and even when the Gentlemen in their next several speeches provide details of the clandestine marriage – this is exposition, after all – the simple facts of the case are difficult to discern.[21] Throughout the romances such challenging syntactical threads direct the listener forward, toward expected comprehension. They point beyond themselves as well, the denotative line being a kind of semiotic system designed to represent meaning beyond the mere words.

Such a syntactical thicket promotes the importance of faith and the need for patience. The uncertainties of grammar and other unsettling syntactical moves simultaneously challenge the audience and place them in a state of dependency: we are encouraged to listen more carefully, to think harder, to seek beyond the words to the ideas that lie beyond them, and yet at the same time we are aware that comprehension depends on what might be called semantic providence. The relationship between listener and poet supervenes that between listener and speaker: we sense that the characters, like their words, are pointers to something beyond themselves. Such a dependent relationship is typical of the way that meaning is created in romantic narratives. Medieval courtly romance, for example, regularly includes a narrator who makes his presence felt and who frankly controls his narrative material.[22] Such a confidential relationship seems to be characteristic of consciously naive artistic forms.

Belief in perceptual guidance and confidence in an eventual happy outcome are markers of romance, and it is scarcely necessary to enumerate and illustrate the many injunctions to faith and hope scattered through Shakespeare's last plays. Patience is the temporal form of perspective, we might say, and in each of these texts the audience is required to wait. So are the characters, of course. The determining power of endings is exploited in *The Winter's Tale* in the familiar pun on "issue," both as outcome and progeny: the word appears, as both noun and verb, fourteen

---

[21] Frank Kermode comments helpfully on this disjunction in *Shakespeare: The Final Plays*: "The romance plot is not matched by an assumed simplicity of diction, but set off against tough late-Shakespearian verse; and this produces an effect almost of irony, so that several critics, among them Professor Danby, have tried to convey their sense that the dramatist is somehow *playing* with the play. I think this is true. For example, *Cymbeline* is the only play in the canon which has characters given to such tensely obscure ways of expressing themselves that not only the audience but the other characters find it hard to make out what they mean" (p. 22).

[22] Andrée Kahn Blumstein, *Misogyny and Idealization in the Courtly Romance* (Bonn: Bouvier Verlag Herbert Grundmann, 1977), p. 9. "The reader of the romance is made aware of the presence of a narrator who manipulates his material."

times (and again as "issueless"), a frequency almost twice as great as the nearest rival (*Richard III*, with eight, another play about progeny and heirs). On a sentence-by-sentence basis, the auditor must maintain faith in eventual satisfaction, specifically in semantic understanding. This grammatical maneuver replicates in miniature the larger effect of romance fiction, as Patricia Parker demonstrates in her reading of the structurally loose epics of Ariosto and Spenser.[23] To draw such a parallel between the operation of the larger narrative and the effect of the individual sentence, the latter effect repeated over and over again in the course of the dialogue, is to see with unusual clarity the way the poetic language has been calibrated to the kind of stories being staged. This is not merely an analogy: we are able to see how the poetic sentence makes meaning appropriate to its theatrical mode.

HYBRIDITY

The sophistication of the late style is to some extent a product of the widened perspective that the late plays commend, as if Shakespeare had rekked his own rede. In calling the style "sophisticated," I mean not only that it exhibits a self-consciousness about stories and ways of telling them, but also that it is characterized by inclusiveness, specifically a willingness to juxtapose and combine opposing styles and effects. Simon Palfrey calls this hybridity "contrapuntal" and gestures at its larger effects: "the romance 'world of words' proffers its own contingent, inherently contrapuntal laws of physics: within or around the hopeful verities of order and *telos*, it is an edgy universe of occluded origin and abrupt ellipses, of warps and falls and asymmetries, and of endings unresolved whatever the nostalgic pleadings."[24] Such thematic counterpoint is manifested stylistically in the smallest poetic combinations, as my earlier chapters have

---

[23] Patricia Parker, *Inescapable Romance: Studies in the Poetics of a Mode* (Princeton: Princeton University Press, 1979), pp. 35–36. The technique of "narrative *espacement*," she argues, "is also a kind of deferral in which the reader has the sense of time traversed because the reading itself is so time-consuming. The continual shifting from one story to another often provides what is virtually the cartography of a single moment, like the extended space of the Renaissance illustrations where the whole plot is revealed at once. The author alone can see the warp and woof of the 'cloth' he weaves (XIII.81.1–2), the sum of the frequent romance tapestries which reveal the form of an action before it happens and thus mediate between plot and person, the lofty authorial view and the character or reader still immersed in the process of time. The reader comes to this simultaneous perspective only in the act of interpreting what he has read, and the discovery of the shortness of actual elapsed time, when it had seemed so long, is truly a revelation."

[24] *Late Shakespeare*, p. viii.

indicated: almost every feature is accompanied by its opposite number, creating a verbal multiplicity that makes the verse difficult to describe accurately. To recall the most obvious example, the coexistence of elliptical and redundant constructions creates a dynamic of syntactic conflict, so that the listener is pushed and pulled in conflicting directions at once. This tendency to eliminate and to supplement, to do without certain words and to luxuriate in others, produces in the line those competing tonal effects that have animated the debate over genre. Palfrey's view is wider, describing as he does the binary oppositions in the narrative style: the tension between closure and digression, reticence and loquacity, suspense and surprise. As he points out, the "exploratory mode of discourse" devised for these late works "is at base level responsible to Shakespeare's 'generic task'."[25]

A widened professional perspective seems to account for Shakespeare's having been drawn to a hybrid theatrical form. For the working dramatist, perspective derived from and regenerated in him a process of retrospection. Looking back on the previous fifteen years, he seems to have been attracted to a theatrical genre that included modified forms of all three theatrical modes to which he had devoted himself up to this time: comedy, history, tragedy. The productive retrospection in which he engages broadens his own thinking about experience, a process which must be to some extent responsible for the change in mode. By this time in his career, the breadth of vision that Shakespeare brings to his work leads him to select a form that accommodates that long view. Also, in creating the new mode he apparently made use of his experience, as a company man, of the court masque. Romance is celebrated for its capacity to absorb various kinds of stories, for its range of tones, its flexibility and inclusiveness. And thus it is especially inviting to an artist whose vision seems to have broadened, who has gained sufficient perspective to want to explore a wide range of feelings and tones. This expanded attitude towards genre accounts not only for the critical debates over the form of the last four unaided plays, but also for the stretching of convention that results in the multiplicity of *Henry VIII* and *The Two Noble Kinsmen*. Having represented in various forms and to differing degrees the effects of comedy and tragedy, Shakespeare seems to want to include as many permutations of both forms as possible.

Although I have relied heavily on the term "romance," the tragicomic affiliations of these plays attest to Shakespeare's taste for variety. The pain

---

[25] *Ibid.*, p. viii.

arising from the malice and error in the tragedies is mitigated by the joys of salvation and reunion in the comedies, so that the audience experiences alternately and simultaneously the effects of tragedy and comedy. Reference to contemporary fashions in the Jacobean theatre may clarify Shakespeare's practice in creating such synoptic structures. His creation of theatrical romance coincides exactly with Beaumont and Fletcher's development of the tragicomic mode, the form that notoriously attempts just this tonal combination, and even those who insist on "romance" as the proper designation for Shakespeare's late plays confess the influence of the new Italianate form on Shakespeare. As Clifford Leech points out, however, Fletcher tended to generate such effects alternately, while Shakespeare preferred to mingle the responses associated with comedy and tragedy.[26] This distinction is not absolute, of course: *The Winter's Tale* divides broadly in half, the first largely tragic in spirit and the second mostly comic. But the emotionally overwhelming moments in the last plays are those which combine the two strains: the reunion of Pericles and Marina, for example, in which the joy of recognition is both qualified and magnified by consciousness of past sorrows; the same tonal complexity marks the coming together of Posthumus and Imogen in the final scene of *Cymbeline*. In fact, the moment of reunion that concludes all these plays, depending for its impact upon the tragic possibilities of division, offers the perfect mix of tragicomic effect.

The playfulness apparent in the poetry – its extravagance, its sudden dip into the homely, its knowing combination of effects – is of a piece with the inescapable self-consciousness of these texts. And one feature about which they are self-aware is the mixture of the modern and the old-fashioned, as Shakespeare both embraces and subverts such stereotypical associations. Gower's self-conscious depreciation of the story he presents as old-fashioned and trivial is a touchstone for the tonal mixture cultivated in this mode. It is a tale, he says, delivered

> To glad your ear and please your eyes.
> It hath been sung at festivals,
> On ember-eves and holy-ales,
> And lords and ladies in their lives
> Have read it for restoratives. (1 Chorus, 4–8)

---

[26] Shakespeare "was deeply conscious that a person, a situation, an idea could be simultaneously apprehended from two or more points of view . . . But in Fletcher's writing the double view of things depends on alternation rather than simultaneity of presentment." Clifford Leech, *The John Fletcher Plays* (London: Chatto and Windus, 1962), p. 147.

In short, this is the kind of story that, though it has a moral purpose, the modern world is inclined to disregard, a tale normally associated with frivolity and leisure: "in those latter times, / When wit's more ripe," he hopes that the listener will be willing to "accept [his] rhymes" (11–12). Whether Shakespeare himself wrote these couplets or whether they were written by his collaborator or predecessor, they are nonetheless wholly characteristic of his strategic mockery of his material in this phase.

Gower is the most thoroughly developed presenter, although the other texts depend upon similar mediators between stage and audience. In *The Winter's Tale* Time's dig at the hoary tale being dramatized is such a metatheatrical moment, as is the descent of Jupiter in *Cymbeline*. *The Tempest* ends with Prospero's ontologically uncertain epilogue, and *Henry VIII* and *The Two Noble Kinsmen* employ prologues and other evidence of authorial self-referentiality. These metadramatic intrusions emphasize the cultural devaluation of his material, as in Paulina's comment on the motion of the statue: "That she is living, / Were it but told you, should be hooted at / Like an old tale" (5.3.115–17). The ironic point, of course, is that we ourselves have hooted at the tabloid-style fictions Autolycus has been peddling to the Bohemian rustics, and yet we ourselves are emotionally engaged with and moved by the old story of the stone that came to life.

At the same time, however, Shakespeare invokes the frivolous, meaningless associations of such yarns to invest them with even greater artistic power. Paradoxically, he seems to say, the "mouldy tale" can carry greater significance than its reputation would seem to permit, can mean as much as the classically sanctioned forms such as tragedy and epic. This ambiguous stance towards his stories, his mocking their reputation and yet at the same time insisting on their value, is not an exclusively Shakespearean maneuver, however, but represents another glance backwards.[27] Sidney in *The Arcadia* and Spenser in *The Faerie Queene* both manipulated conventional expectations of frivolity and old-fashioned tales to develop ethical and even political themes.[28] This artistic dedication to frivolous stories is one of the principal manifestations of Shakespeare's revised conception of language, of poetry, and of the theatre.

---

[27] In thinking about the complexities of tone in romance generally I have profited from correspondence with Professor Clare Kinney of the University of Virginia.

[28] Howard Felperin writes with exceptional acuity about this maneuver, both in *Shakespearean Romance* (Princeton: Princeton University Press, 1972), and "Romance and Romanticism: Some Reflections on *The Tempest* and *Heart of Darkness*, Or When is Romance No Longer Romance?," in *Shakespeare's Romances Reconsidered*, ed. Carol McGinnis Kay and Henry Jacobs (Lincoln: University of Nebraska Press, 1978), pp. 60–76.

SOPHISTICATED STYLE

The verbal artifice that the sensitive ear discerns in the late style differs markedly from the obvious patterning in which the young Shakespeare delighted. In his devotion to the strictly symmetrical and the highly decorated, the novice playwright and poet – *Venus and Adonis* and *The Rape of Lucrece* come to mind – was satisfying the taste of the public. The formalized poetic structures of the first tetralogy, such as the keening contest between the grieving queens in 4.4 of *Richard III*, or some of the rhetorical showpieces of *Love's Labour's Lost*, or the extravagantly patterned speeches from a more mature (if still early) play such as *Richard II* – these passages are very much of their Elizabethan moment. In Richard II's extended deposition speech beginning "I give this heavy weight from off my head, / And this unwieldy sceptre from my hand" (4.1.203–21), the patterning advertises itself, inviting us to notice and to relish the repetitions, antitheses, rhymes, and other evidence of arrangement. Richard's speech is especially illuminating because, having had by this time some years' experience with such formulae, Shakespeare makes the verbal patterns inescapably part of the semantic significance. That Richard himself takes such delight in those same poetic schemes and verbal turns, that the expression seems as meaningful to him as the calamitous experience itself, is one of the keys to his political inadequacy, a significant historical determinant, and proof of Shakespeare's artistic growth.

The style of the late phase, however, is usually no less artificial than the verse of *Richard II* or *Romeo and Juliet*, even if the patterns are less obvious and the language less frankly "poetic." In fact, it might be said that the kind of artifice that passes itself off as more nearly "naturalistic" or "realistic" is fundamentally even more cunningly arranged than the assertive configurations of the early verse. The scare quotes around the two nouns in the previous sentence are meant to indicate their descriptive imprecision: Prospero and Paulina speak much less schematically and ornately than Richard III or Marcus in *Titus Andronicus*, but their verbal power is no less dependent on poetic patterns, deliberately and subtly concealed. Frank Kermode, citing Pericles' moving shipboard speech to the newborn Marina, the "terrible childbed" passage, puts the distinction this way: "This verse is certainly, if we can purge the pejorative sense of the word, artificial; what the poet seeks is certainly not to have Pericles speak as a man would in such a plight, but by every artifice to give grief a possible new music."[29] This analysis accords with the conclusions that emerge from examination of the technical features of the style. Although the late verse is more irregular and less obviously formal than most of the dramatist's earlier dramatic poetry, it is still highly wrought, still ornamented and self-conscious. As Kermode asserts, this is "music," lyrical, carefully composed, affective, but music of an exceptionally sophisticated kind. To press the analogy a bit, we might say that the melodic motifs and poetic phrases have been abbreviated, condensed to gestures or signals rather than set forth as fully articulated lyric strains.

Shakespeare seems to have recovered his Elizabethan enthusiasm for pattern but to have transmuted it into a poetic form so sophisticated that the verse seems both ornate and ordinary.[30] The complex lexical reiteration in *The Tempest* exhibits this kind of self-denying artifice: the repeated letters, words, and phrases are as abundant and as deliberately deployed as some of the earlier, obvious repetitions, but they are woven into the fabric of the play's language so subtly that they strike the ear as not quite so broad and insistent. Prospero's rant against Caliban depends upon such careful arrangement:

| ARI. | I go, I go. | *Exit.* |

PROS.   *A devil,* a born *devil,* <u>on whose</u> **nature**
          Nurture can **never** stick; <u>on whom</u> my **pain**s,
          Hum**an**ely taken, *all, all* <u>lost</u>, quite <u>lost</u>;
                                        (4.1.188–91)

This brief example exposes the way artifice both conceals and asserts itself. Prospero's denunciation employs the characteristic ellipsis: grammatically speaking, it is not a sentence, since it may be said to begin with an implied subject and verb ("Caliban is"). At the same time, however, the lines ring with repetition, from Ariel's unnecessarily duplicated exit line through the various identical repetitions and near echoes: "devil" and "devil"; "on whose" and "on whom"; "nature," "nurture," and "never"; the assonance

---

[29] *Shakespeare: The Later Plays,* p. 17. Kermode goes on to draw an explicit connection between Shakespeare's late and early verse: "That a poet is always, however he may change, one poet, is a reflection prompted by the recollection of Clarence's sub-marine fantasy in Richard III" (p. 17).

[30] George T. Wright summarizes this complex poetry as follows: "Changes in Shakespeare's verse style continued to the end of his career. In particular, the patterning of sound in his last plays becomes increasingly complex, with adventurous displays of repeated words and word elements (syllables, vowel and consonant sounds), rewordings of ideas, self-interruptions, stresses falling on minor words, and line endings that cut into grammatical phrases in surprising ways." "Shakespeare's Verse," in *Reading Shakespeare's Dramatic Language, a Guide,* ed. Lynne Magnusson, et al. (London: Thomson, 2001), p. 67.

of "pains," "Humanely," and "taken"; "all, all"; "lost" and "lost." Even subtler rhythmic variations can be discerned: for example, the first "A devil" is expanded and modified to become "a born devil," while two lines later "lost" is similarly expanded and modified to become "quite lost." A familiar trick is Shakespeare's juxtaposition of the aurally similar but semantically opposed "nature" and "Nurture," a conjunction of contradictory nouns that focuses a thematic antithesis.

This deliberate confounding of the realistic and the wrought, the conversational and the highly artificial, is a stylistic embodiment of one of the most important strains of meaning in the romances, the permeability of the world and the stage. In the early plays Shakespeare stressed the poetic pattern, differentiating it from everyday, actual speech, just as he stressed the difference between the realm of the play and the actual world. Such was the taste of the day. The patterns of the comic action in a play like *The Comedy of Errors* – two sets of twins, brothers marrying sisters, rediscovered mothers and fathers – make it vastly different from the world of lived experience, just as the artifice of the language in *The Comedy of Errors* divides the two spheres. In the late plays, however, Shakespeare has dissolved the boundary between illusion and reality, exploring instead the way the realms of the theatrical and the actual interpenetrate and are often mistaken for each other. So with the verse, which sometimes seems natural and sometimes highly ornate, just as real human speech may sometimes seem theatrical. Artifice is as great as in the early work but is often made to look as if it has disappeared.

THE GENDERING OF ROMANCE

The prominence of artifice in the late work – in style, in structure, in presentation – attests to a striking turn on Shakespeare's part, a devotion to ornament consistent with his passage from tragedy to romance. This commitment to surface and style is surprising given his verifiable movement away from the heavy patterning of the early plays. It also runs counter to a powerful cultural strain, fed by the burgeoning Puritan ideology and widespread anti-Catholicism, according to which decoration is wicked and likely to obscure the truth. Historically speaking, the noun "ornament" originally signified not merely decoration but "equipment" or "furnishings," adornments that were also functional, but its meaning had by this time shifted toward the more modern sense of embellishment, something applied and superficial. In an early intimation of the high modernist aesthetic, decoration came to be equated with deception, outward show with suspicion: as Bassanio puts it in considering Portia's caskets, "The world is still deceived with ornament" (*The Merchant of Venice*, 3.2.74). Decoration was identified with the external or inessential, clothing and cosmetics being the most familiar objects of censure.

One of the primary sources for these attacks was early modern religious polemic, deriving ultimately from the Pauline strictures against personal vanity. Taking material also from the writings of the church fathers, these religious writers often summoned up images of female adornment as a sign of iniquity. Juan Luis Vives's *Instruction of a Christian Woman*, commissioned by Catherine of Aragon for her daughter Mary and translated into English in 1557, provides an especially vivid statement:

Saint Ambrose speaketh of painting in this manner: Hereof (sayeth he) cometh those inflamings of vices, to paint their faces with colors, lest men should mislike them, and with the adultery of their face, they go about adultery of their body. What a madness is it, to change the natural image, and take a picture: and whiles they fear their husbands' judgment to utter their own. For she giveth first judgment of herself that would be other wise than she was born; and so while she goeth about to be liked of other, first of all she disliketh herself.[31]

Face-painting is condemned as an act of re-creation, of rejecting the natural or God-given in favor of the imagined visage. In deploring make-up as a prelude to adultery, Vives regards its use as "adulterating" or diluting the divine image: artifice adulterates the essence or integrity of the face. His association of women and artifice reappears not only in the writings of the Puritan ideologues but also in the work of the Elizabethan satirists. By the end of the century another target was the French, with their delight in display. Still another was Catholicism, especially its icons, symbolism, and ceremony. And all these evils occupied the same cultural space as the most familiar of the Puritan targets, the misrepresentation of the stage.

Such misogynistic attacks on decoration are part of a larger cultural fear, a suspicion of the imagination and all its expressive products.[32] Many of the anti-theatrical tracts issued throughout the 1580s and 1590s equate ornament and cosmetics with rhetoric (the "harlot rhetoric") and language, and most of these implicitly constitute an attack on women,

---

[31] Book Two, Chapter Eight, "Of raiments," tr. Richard Hyrde (London: 1557), p. xcvi. I have modernized the spelling.

[32] Madhavi Menon has discussed the equation of ornament and cosmetics with rhetoric and language in *Wanton Words: Rhetoric and Sexuality in English Renaissance Drama* (Toronto: University of Toronto Press, 2004), chapter 1. Her principal interest is the perils implicit in metaphoric figures.

specifically on the ills traditionally attributed to Eve. Frequently the polemicists, concerned as they are with cross-dressing and sexual license, direct their aim at the effeminizing effects of theatrical performance. A late example of this discourse, William Prynne's *Histrio-mastix* (1633) recapitulates at practically psychopathic length (the book runs to some 1000 pages) the misogynistic views of his predecessors. Prynne defends his range in the prologue, 'To the Christian Reader':

> *there are several passages in this Discourse, which prima facie may seeme heterogeneous to the present subject, as those concerning* Dancing, Musicke, Apparell, Effeminacy, Lascivious Songs, Laughter, Adultery, obscene Pictures, Bonefires, New-yeares gifts, Grand Christmasses, Health-drinking, Long haire, Lordsdayes, Dicing, with sundry Pagan customes *here refelled: but if you consider them, as they are here applied, you shall finde them all materially pertinent to the theame in question, they being either the concomitants of Stage-playes, or having such neare affinity with them, that the unlawfulnesse of the one are necessary mediums to evince the sinfulnesse of the other. Besides, though they differ in Specie, yet they are homogeniall in their genericall nature, one of them serving to illustrate the quality, the condition of the other.*[33]

Reaching back to Augustine and even the Greeks, Prynne avails himself of the traditional association of theatre, effeminacy, music, festivity, and other forms of imaginative pleasure. Throughout his screed the theatre is denounced not only because of its power to emasculate but also because its perversion of language for frivolous ends. Words misused in this way are equated with lewd apparel, laughter, and other profane uses of divine gifts.[34]

The extremity of Prynne's argumentative style may be unique, but his thinking typifies a pervasive strain in early modern English thought. He believes that "God's children . . . *must abandon all idle, fabulous unprofitable discourses; Because that for euery idle word that men shall speake they shall give account at the day of judgement:* so they must likewise *direct even all their actions, speeches, recreations to Gods glory, the edification of others, and their owne spiritual good.*"[35] Prynne, it should be noted, directs his aim at the perceived waste and effeminacy of the Caroline court, the realm that Annabel Patterson has characterized as organized around the "royal romance" of Charles I and Henrietta Maria. According to Patterson,

[33] William Prynne, "To the Christian Reader," in *Histrio-mastix, or The Player's Scourge* (London, 1633).
[34] Passages such as this one bring to mind some of the anti-feminist views considered in my treatment of *Coriolanus* in Chapter 1, notably Tertullian's claim that "with the word the garment entered" and the related association of men with numbers and deeds.
[35] *Histrio-mastix*, p. 128.

Prynne's trial for treason included the "subtle, unstated charge that he had challenged the Caroline culture at its heart, attacking as decadent and unchristian the genres in which the court read itself."[36] Wherever he strays, Prynne always returns to the iniquities of the stage, particularly its fictional pleasures: "the subject matter of our stage-Playes, is for the most part, *false and fabulous;* consarcinated [patched together] of sundry merry, ludicrous, officious artificial lies . . . But such is the subject matter of most Comicall, of many Tragicall Enterludes. Therefore they must needs be odious and unlawfull unto Christians."[37] Images, imagination, illusion, fictions, cosmetics, idleness, theatre – all these topics were vulnerable to charges of triviality and effeminacy; they are also fundamental elements of Shakespeare's late plays.

This list of vain pursuits should also include the pleasures of romance fiction. Rosalie Colie has referred to "the frippery of the mode's metaphor and attribute,"[38] and this is precisely the basis on which romances were condemned or satirized in the sixteenth and seventeenth centuries. Prynne certainly thought of published romances as frivolous and false, attacking "Arcadiaes, and fained Histories that are now so much in admiration."[39] Although dramatic romance did not exist as a distinct mode (even though any number of plays by various writers might have been so designated), romance fiction in general was a recognized and thriving enterprise, its conventions and themes well established, and one source of its success was its putative appeal to women.

The romances that appeared during Elizabeth's reign were probably read mostly by aristocratic women and men, although as the seventeenth century progressed it seems that gentlewomen and female servants also came to be seen as devotees of the mode. Barbara Lewalski describes James's daughter, Princess Elizabeth, as a kind of self-fashioned heroine, "constructing her life and times in terms of a romance narrative."[40] For her as well as for other women of her class, the virtue of such a fiction was

[36] Annabel Patterson, *Censorship and Interpretation* (Madison: University of Wisconsin Press, 1984), p. 167–68.

[37] *Histrio-mastix,* p. 106.

[38] Rosalie Colie, *Shakespeare's Living Art* (Princeton: Princeton University Press, 1974), p. 278.

[39] *Histrio-mastix,* p. 913.

[40] Barbara Lewalski, *Writing Women in Jacobean England* (Cambridge, Mass.: Harvard University Press, 1993), p. 45. Lewalski goes on: "Princess Elizabeth was accorded various epithets: Elizabeth Rediviva, Queen of Hearts, Winter Queen. They name romance roles pressed upon her from her happy childhood, through her fairytale wedding to her preferred suitor, to her short reign as Electress Palatine and Queen of Bohemia, to her long life in exile as figure of pathos, object of chivalric devotion, and symbol of Protestant resistance" (pp. 46–47).

its contribution to a fantasy of escape. "Romance was likely to be especially liberating for royal and noble women: in romance, though not often in life, they rule kingdoms, have exciting adventures, match with their true loves, display boldness and wit. And while they may suffer violence and dire catastrophe, they do so nobly, courageously, admirably."[41] In something like an early modern version of the trickle-down theory, romance fictions also seem to have been made available to female members of households, including servants. In this context, much has been made of Sir Thomas Overbury's satiric portrait of a chambermaid: "She reads *Greenes* workes over and over, but is so carried away with the *Myrrour of Knighthood*, she is many times resolv'd to run out of her selfe, and become a Lady Errant."[42] According to Lori Humphrey Newcomb, a chambermaid might easily have read Greene, since unmarried women of different classes sometimes entered service, but she points out that "far from being typical of Greene's readership, this female domestic servant probably represents the lower limit of its spread."[43] Near the upper limit we might find Jonson's Lady Would-be, who has cast herself in the role of romance heroine: as she hastily departs in pursuit of her husband, like Una in search of Redcross, she says to Mosca, "I pray you lend me your dwarfe" (*Volpone*, 3.5).[44]

By the end of the sixteenth century English culture had managed to "feminize the readership of romance."[45] Helen Hackett has demonstrated that at the end of the Elizabethan and beginning of the Jacobean era "some sort of connection was developing between women and romance which had less to do with actual women's reading habits than with cultural perceptions of romance as 'women's reading' and cultural constructions of romance as a feminine genre."[46] Publishers, writers, and translators all seem to have targeted women as likely clients for romance.

---

[41] *Ibid.*, p. 46.

[42] Sir Thomas Overbury, *Characters* (London: 1611), G$_{12}$. As Stanley Wells wryly puts it, "the scholars took over from the chambermaids in the eighteenth century." "Shakespeare and Romance," in *Later Shakespeare*, ed. John Russell Brown and Bernard Harris (London: Edward Arnold, 1966), p. 64.

[43] Lori Humphrey Newcomb, *Reading Popular Romance in Early Modern England* (New York: Columbia University Press, 2002), p. 90.

[44] On Jonson's linking of women and romance, see David Bergeron, "'Lend me your dwarf': Romance in *Volpone*," *Medieval and Renaissance Drama in England*, 3 (1986), 99–113.

[45] Lori Humphrey Newcomb, "Gendering Prose Romance in Renaissance England," in *A Companion to Romance, from Classical to Contemporary*, ed. Corinne Saunders (Oxford: Blackwell, 2004), p. 123.

[46] Helen Hackett, *Women and Romance Fiction in the English Renaissance* (Cambridge: Cambridge University Press, 2000), p. 10.

John Lyly, publishing *Euphues and His England* in 1580, included a prefatory message addressed "To the Ladies and Gentlewomen of England," and many other English romancers adopted this stratagem.[47] Lyly's preface contains the much-quoted observation that "*Euphues* had rather lye shut up in a Ladyes casket, then open in a Schollers studie,"[48] and in many other such introductory epistles and paratexts the authors of romance advertised their work as especially suitable for ladies. In Barnabe Rich's *Farewell to Militarie Profession*, the narrator announces his motive for fiction when he says "I see now it is lesse painfull to followe a Fiddle in a Gentlewomans chamber: then to marche after a Drumme in the feeld."[49]

The kinds of stories told by the romancers also led their fictions to be classified as feminine. Although such poems and tales offered adventure narratives involving shipwrecks, desert places, and other such exotic material, they almost always featured episodes of courtship, plots that moved towards conjugal harmony and familial reconciliation. Chastity – first threatened and ultimately preserved – was a cornerstone of such stories. Central, too, was the theme of heritage, a topic that generated tales of lost children and divided families. According to Hackett, "the subject matter of the romances foregrounds the feminine in several ways. The use of the family as a structuring principle of narrative, and the high value placed upon female chastity, give a high profile to the roles and virtues of daughters, wives, and mothers."[50] These stories, treating love and adventure, danger and rescue, and virtue imperiled but finally rewarded, were widely mocked as naive and old-fashioned. They were also exceedingly popular.

It would be misleading to imply that women were the primary consumers of romance fiction, especially given literacy rates and other conditions of the patriarchal system. Men were surely the main buyers and readers of literary romance and its producers knew that: *Euphues and His England*, like a number of other such works, also contains a preface addressed "To the Gentlemen Readers." Scholars have recently begun to

---

[47] According to Newcomb, "English Renaissance romances increasingly were framed by epistles to gentlewomen, or embedded remarks to 'ladies.' Indeed, the authorial appeal to female reader, collective or specific, became a signature feature of Elizabethan romance" ("Gendering Prose Romance in Renaissance England," p. 124).

[48] "To the Ladies and Gentlewomen of England," in *The Complete Works of John Lyly*, ed. R. Warwick Bond, vol. II (Oxford: Clarendon Press, 1902), p. 9.

[49] Barnabe Rich, *Farewell to Militarie Profession* (London, 1581), a. ii.

[50] Hackett, *Women and Romance Fiction*, p. 150.

suspect that their appeals to female readers were to some extent a coded message to males: "they clearly expected to have male readers to whom a flirtatious address to women readers would announce that titillating reading pleasures were to follow."[51] But the romancers were seeking to sell as many books as they could, and one of their marketing strategies was the direct appeal to women.

As Overbury's and Jonson's caricatures suggest, the staples of romance increasingly became a target for satire. Early in Elizabeth's reign the objections to romance tend to be earnest and morally based, as in Ascham's diatribe in Book I of *The Schoolemaster* against all things Italian (all except the Italian language per se). Seeking to protect young men from frivolous temptations, Ascham is especially contemptuous of the romantic fictions that were being translated with increasing frequency in the middle of the sixteenth century:

These be the enchantments of Circe, brought out of Italy to mar men's manners in England: much, by example of ill life, but more by precepts of fond books, of late translated out of Italian into English, sold in every shop in London, commended by honest titles, the sooner to corrupt honest manners, dedicated over boldly to virtuous and honorable personages, the easilier to beguile simple and innocent wits.[52]

The classical image of the lethal seductress reveals what Ascham thinks about the seductive pleasures of romance, and it is worth noting here that some of the Italian texts being translated in Ascham's day were the stories of Boccaccio, Brooke's version of *Romeus and Juliet*, and those contained in Painter's *Palace of Pleasure* – in short, some of Shakespeare's favorite stories.

As the satiric response to romance began to grow, two of the main objects of ridicule were the supposed femininity and undeniable popularity of the form. The young Thomas Nashe, writing apparently from Cambridge in the late 1580s, ridicules the "bable bookemungers," those who

endeuor but to repaire the ruinous wals of *Venus* Court, to restore to the worlde that forgotten Legendary licence of lying, to imitate a fresh the fantasticall dreames of those exiled Abbie-lubbers, from whose idle pens proceeded those worne out impressions of the feyned no where acts, of Arthur of the rounde table,

---

[51] *Ibid.*, p. 11.
[52] Roger Ascham, *The Schoolemaster*, ed. Lawrence V. Ryan (Ithaca: Cornell University Press, 1967), p. 67.

Arthur of little Brittaine, sir Tristram, Hewon of Burdeaux, the Squire of low degree, the foure sons of Amon, with infinite others.[53]

Nashe strikes out at multiple targets: his complaint appears in a longer passage deploring the way that modern poets pander to women, he ridicules the taste for trashy fantasy, and he even manages to connect romance with Rome ("exiled Abbie-lubbers"). Many other examples might be cited, from Francis Meres in 1598 to Thomas Underdowne in 1605 to Wye Saltonstall in 1631.[54] What is fascinating is that the attitude of the critics is rather like the attitude Shakespeare encourages us to take to Autolycus's ballads in the fourth act of *The Winter's Tale*.

The reader will have already noted an exception to these satirized texts: *The Countess of Pembroke's Arcadia*. Most of the literary figures who comment on romance – Francis Meres is a good example – praise Sidney's work and set it apart from the "low" status of romance generally. And yet the associations I have been exploring are pertinent to *The Arcadia*, Sidney himself having played upon the feminine and frivolous reputation of the form. He imagined his sister, Mary, as the primary and ideal reader of his "toyful book," a dedication expressed in the full title and developed in the introductory epistle: "you desired me to do it, and your desire to my heart is an absolute commandment. Now it is done only for you, only to you." Sidney urges her to "read it, then, at your idle times": such an injunction may suggest that the length and scope of many romance fictions were thought suitable for aristocratic women who had the leisure for such pursuits.

The feminine connection is further secured in Sidney's metaphor for what the Countess might expect to find in the narrative: she should be "looking for no better stuff than as in a haberdasher's shop, glasses or feathers."[55] Modesty trope or not, the shopping image allows Sidney to exploit the cultural condescension such writing provoked. Lyly adopts the same ironic stance towards his fiction:

You chuse cloth that will weare whitest, not that will last longest, coulours that looke freshest, not that endure soundest, and I would you woulde read bookes that have more shewe of pleasure, then ground of profit, then should *Euphues* be as often in your hands, being but a toy, as Lawn on your heads, being but trash,

[53] Thomas Nashe, *The Anatomie of Absurditie*, in *The Works of Thomas Nashe*, 4 vols., ed. Ronald B. McKerrow, vol. 1 (Oxford: Basil Blackwell, 1958), p. 11.

[54] Hackett offers an overview of these critiques, in *Women and Romance Fiction*, pp. 20–24.

[55] *The Countess of Pembroke's Arcadia*, edited with an introduction and notes by Maurice Evans (Harmondsworth: Penguin, 1977), p. 57.

the one will be scarce liked after once reading, and the other is worne out after the first washing.[56]

Sidney's and Lyly's playful ironies were not shared by the moralists, who seized on the notion of romance as "trash." Thomas Powell, in his guide to rearing productive children, *Tom of All Trades, or the Plaine Path-way to Preferment,* (1631) specifically proscribed the reading of romances for gentlemen's daughters. After recommending simple clothing and lessons in plain stitching, Powell continues: "In stead of Song and Musicke, let them learne Cookery and Laundrie. And in stead of reading Sir *Philip Sidneys Arcadia,* let them read the ground of good huswifery."[57] Powell seems to have known what was popular.

By the time Shakespeare made the shift from tragedy to the new form, romance had – to adapt Lyly's phrase – emerged from the lady's closet and made its way onto the public stage. Certain London theatres had for years offered performances of plays that could be classified as romances, or that contained elements in common with romance: magic, adventure, journeys, and other such narrative materials. The enduring popularity of these dramas is indicated by the appearance in 1607 of Beaumont's *The Knight of the Burning Pestle,* the text that registers better than any other the absurdities and excesses of a certain segment of popular taste. The popularity of romance with women is not of particular interest to Beaumont: Rafe, the apprentice, is the figure carried away with chivalric fantasy. The principal target is the vulgarity of public taste.

Another document relevant to this scenario is Thomas Shelton's English version of *Don Quixote,* published in 1612 but written, according to the translator, "some five or six years" earlier. Beaumont may have been influenced by Shelton's translation,[58] and it is a good bet that Shakespeare knew it, although when he read it is uncertain. The preface takes the form of a fictionalized conversation between the translator and a friend, one who urges Shelton to make his long-completed rendering of Cervantes' ironic novel available to the English-speaking reader: "In conclusion let thy project be to overthrow the ill compiled *Machina* and bulke of those Knightly Bookes, abhorred by many, but applauded by more."[59] The subtlety of Cervantes' take on the fictions of chivalry and adventure, a

[56] "To the Ladies and Gentlewomen of England," pp. 9–10.
[57] (London, 1631), p. 47.
[58] See Bliss, *Francis Beaumont,* pp. 39–42.
[59] *The History of the Valorous and Wittie Knight-Errant, Don-Quixote of the Mancha, Translated out of the Spanish* (London: Ed. Blount and W. Rarret, 1612), "The Author to the Reader," A₃.

sophisticated combination of irony, fascination, and even a form of respect, must have been appealing to Shakespeare's equally sophisticated and ambivalent intelligence.[60] The rapid appearance of Cervantes in English, the first translation into another language, speaks to the popularity of its targets: romance was both a topic of public comment and a lightning rod for artistic mockery. This is the cultural climate in which Shakespeare moved as he scouted for new theatrical material around 1607–8.

WENCH-LIKE WORDS

The feminine reputation of romance is a vital context for understanding Shakespeare's adoption of the form and his late representation of women. Critics have recently begun to observe how the last plays exhibit – indeed how their effect and meaning depend upon – Shakespeare's reconception of the feminine, particularly his revised understanding of female sexuality. Barber and Wheeler write that the tragic "fear of femininity" underlying *King Lear* and *Coriolanus* seems to have been overcome, and that the romances depend upon the recovery of "benign relationship to feminine presences, accomplished by going through an experience of separation and loss that culminates in reunion."[61] The viciousness of the Gonerils and other witches of the tragedies have yielded to the salutary influence of such women as Marina, Imogen, Hermione, and Paulina. Female monstrosity is not exorcised entirely, of course, but it remains controlled or disempowered in such figures as Dionyza, the wicked queen in *Cymbeline*, and the absent Sycorax in *The Tempest*. Cleopatra, that most remarkable figure of extravagance and imagination, serves as the hinge that permits Shakespeare to move from tragedy to romance.

Cleopatra serves also as a pointer to the way that Shakespeare's verse has been converted into an instrument suitable for romance, and for the values and ideas with which the form is associated. Doctor Johnson's observation that the "quibble was to him the fatal Cleopatra for which he lost the world, and was content to lose it" is more than a dubious

---

[60] As Richard Lanham puts it, speaking of Cervantes' "contempt for romances" and "his fondness for them," "The two views oscillate with the same kind of complexity we have found incarnated in *The Courtier*, and lend to *Don Quixote* that characteristic epistemological richness subsequent prose fiction was so often to lack" (*The Motives of Eloquence*, p. 217).

[61] C. L. Barber and Richard Wheeler, *The Whole Journey: Shakespeare's Power of Development* (Berkeley: University of California Press, 1986), p. 298.

comment about the prominence of the pun.[62] The character, and especially her extravagant speech, embodies an attitude towards language and
its uses that is pertinent to the stylistic complexity of the late verse.
A modern statement of the historical conception I have described appears
in William Empson's censorious remarks – rather surprising, coming
from the author of *Seven Types of Ambiguity* – about Shakespeare's
attachment to wordplay. "It shows lack of decision and will-power, a
feminine pleasure in yielding to the mesmerism of language, in getting
one's way, if at all, by deceit and flattery, for a poet to be so fearfully
susceptible to puns. Many of us could wish the Bard had been more
manly in his literary habits."[63] This is Doctor Johnson in modern dress,
although, as with Johnson, the negative evaluation and the misogynistic
vocabulary do not cancel the accuracy of the insight. Shakespeare's
fondness for the seductive pleasures of the pun represents another link
between the feminine and the popular.

The mature Shakespeare seems not only "susceptible" to the pun but
positively to court it, as he does the pleasures of poetic extravagance
generally. Certain passages are flagrant and unapologetic in their ornamentation, and sometimes their language is described as specifically
feminine. In the fourth act of *Cymbeline*, as the kidnapped sons of the
king lament the apparent death of the boy Fidele, actually their sister
Imogen in disguise, Arviragus declares his intention to give the dead
youth a proper funeral:

> With fairest flowers
> Whilst summer lasts, and I live here, Fidele,
> I'll sweeten thy sad grave: thou shalt not lack
> The flower that's like thy face, pale primrose, nor
> The azur'd harebell, like thy veins: no, nor
> The leaf of eglantine, (4.2.218–23)

The florid mourner proceeds for six more lines before his brother Guiderius breaks in to silence him: "Prithee, have done, / And do not play in
wench-like words with that / Which is so serious" (4.2.229–31). This
exchange is an obvious but not atypical example of the ostentatious
auditory patterns devised for the late plays. Its excesses represent a form
of sophisticated play, a sporting with poetic effects consistent with the
outlandish stories chosen and with the self-consciously theatrical manner
in which they are staged.

---

[62] *The Works of Samuel Johnson*, ed. Arthur Sherbo (New Haven: Yale University Press, 1968), VII: 74.
[63] William Empson, *Seven Types of Ambiguity* (Harmondsworth: Penguin, 1973), pp. 110–11.

An outpouring of "wench-like words," Arviragus's lament is feminine, by Jacobean standards inherited from the misogynist tradition, because it is emotionally fluent, lengthy, repetitious, and replete with poetic – indeed "flowery" – imagery. One of the several minor ironies at work in this exchange is that Guiderius's plea for masculine restraint is as musically ornate as the speech he condemns. In fact such decorated passages are frequent and characteristic of the late work: Antonio's conspiratorial invitation to Sebastian, Pericles' outburst in the first recognition scene, Jachimo's rhapsody over the sleeping Imogen, some of Caliban's lyrical reflections, Palamon and Arcite's effusions. This late delight in poetic virtuosity signifies a reconsidered conception of poetic and fictional pleasure. It can also be seen as evidence that Shakespeare has consciously aligned himself with forms and ideas that his culture associated specifically with women. Simon Palfrey goes so far as to say that Shakespeare has created "an at least partially feminized theatre."[64] What is most significant for my purposes is that this imaginative recovery of the female is stylistically significant.

" Women are words, men deeds" – as much of the historical commentary I have cited indicates, language has often been identified with the female. Precedents for thinking about style and gender include Erasmus's well-known desire to create a "more masculine" style and the larger controversy, of which it is a part, over Ciceronian and Senecan forms of prose.[65] The complex syntax, digressive and roundabout, the ostentatiously repetitive verbal figures of *The Tempest*, the compromised metrical scheme audible throughout the last phase, the abundant equivocation that Palfrey treats – all these properties suggest an association of language with a kind of feminine creativity. That angle of vision is reinforced by the affirmative representation of the women in the last plays, and particularly the approval of the female voice.

Debate has arisen about the limits and the costs of this re-imagination of the feminine: the reunion of Hermione and Leontes is hedged with a sense of pain and lost time, and recurring themes in recent criticism include the desexualized nature of the restored family and the constraints

[64] Palfrey, *Late Shakespeare*, p. 197. The complete passage reads as follows: "The presence of many women in Shakespeare's audience may have demanded some kind of echoic satisfaction, an at least partially feminized theatre; one might identify an analogy with the popularity of romance tales among female readers. Such popularity might further suggest how putatively obedient closures need not disempower the female."

[65] *Ciceronianus*, cited in Patricia Parker, *Literary Fat Ladies* (London: Methuen, 1987), p. 14.

on female agency.[66] Alison Thorne, objecting to the "sentimental ideal-ism" implicit in "privileging the reparative relationship between fathers and daughters (based on the Lear–Cordelia model)", summarizes the work of recent feminist scholars:

Besides making the obvious point that such icons of female monstrosity as Dionyza, Sycorax and Cymbeline's evil queen are recognizably products of the same paranoid masculine imagination which gave birth to Regan, Goneril and Lady Macbeth, they note that even the treatment meted out to their virtuous counterparts continues to be dictated to a large extent by deep-seated anxieties over women's maternal functions, sexuality and autonomy.[67]

Directors have begun to take up these ideas, accentuating such anxieties. Edward Hall's production of *The Winter's Tale* for Propellor (2005) concludes with Leontes separated from the core group of Hermione, Perdita, Florizel, Polixenes; he wanders awkwardly on the margins of the stage, obviously now the uncomfortable outsider. Even when the endings are thus darkened by an emphasis on the pain inflicted by male tyranny and folly, however, the emotional curve of the narrative and the complex tone of the reunions do much to ameliorate the effects of this "paranoid" masculine imagination. Audiences still respond with relief and joy at the fact of reunion.[68] Whether or not we think of the women at the end of the romances as returned to the system of male domination, it is clear that Shakespeare's conception and representation of the feminine have changed since he wrote *King Lear* and *Macbeth*.

Sensitivity to the new style of poetry offers guidance in how we might think about this altered understanding. The late style, like the forms it projects, endorses qualities considered historically and culturally associ-ated with the feminine: ambiguity, mystery, artifice, pleasure. Simon Palfrey, in his effort to modify the view of the romances as unrelentingly patriarchal and dependent upon the marginalization of women, argues that "the 'traditional' male-gendered understanding of pastoral romance" is inadequate:

---

[66] See Janet Adelman, *Suffocating Mothers: Fantasies of Maternal Origin in Shakespeare's Plays, "Hamlet" to "The Tempest"* (London: Routledge, 1991), pp. 235–37, as well as Marilyn Williamson, "Doubling, Women's Anger, and Genre," *Women's Studies*, 9 (1982), 107–19, and Carol Thomas Neely, *Broken Nuptials in Shakespeare's Plays* (New Haven: Yale University Press, 1985).

[67] Alison Thorne, Introduction to *Shakespeare's Romances: Contemporary Critical Essays* (New York: Palgrave Macmillan, 2003), pp. 19–20.

[68] As Palfrey suggests, "to erase the marks of feminine agency because the framing plot is irredeem-ably patriarchal seems curiously unkind to an audience who, as the play proceeds, will have spent anxiety or approval upon just such defiance or self-definition" (*Late Shakespeare*, p. 197).

whereas each story's nominal teleology is patriarchal, emotional investment and often narrative organization are, almost as unremittingly, feminized. A foolish or venal male hegemony is altered and humanized by the incorporation, as a persuasive instrument of power and decision-making, of a "feminine principle" based not only in the faithfulness of chastity but the eloquence of the female tongue.[69]

He might have added that this feminization of tone and of narrative extends to the style as well.

Shakespeare's renewed affirmation of the feminine helps to account for his reconceived attitude towards language, his altered attraction to dramatic forms, and his view of the theatrical enterprise itself. Ornament, indirection, disguise, words, and fiction generally, which are usually regarded as potentially lethal in the sequence of great tragedies, no longer seem minatory. Rather, they are acknowledged and developed as sources of consolation and creativity. And the new prominence of repetition, rhyme, assonance and consonance, and other forms of auditory ornament embodies this changed attitude poetically: what had been considered meretricious, excessive, even embarrassing, becomes pleasing and unifying. It is surely meaningful that the dramatic experience of separation and recovery is dramatized in language characterized by aural harmony and coherence. The auditory atmosphere of concordant sounds intensifies the sense of relation and familial reordering that gives the romances their extraordinary emotional power. The recuperation of the female, in other words, is heard not only in the eloquence of the female tongue but also in the poetic consonance that constitutes the virtual realm.

ARTIFICE AND ILLUSION

The illusion here is not that art is an illusion, but that life is.
                                                Rosalie Colie[70]

The return to artifice and virtuosity heard in Shakespeare's late verse is a token of the playwright's reconceived attitude towards his art, the exchange of mimesis for poesis. No longer content merely to represent the conflicts of this world, he has instead imagined new ones. Embracing the metatheatrical conventions of presentational theatre, Shakespeare dissolves the conventions of representational drama that he had more or less observed in the tragedies. Now he toys with his theatrical instruments,

---

[69] *Late Shakespeare*, p. 196.
[70] *Shakespeare's Living Art*, p. 279.

frequently acknowledges the audience with choruses, narrators, epilogues, and abundant asides, mirrors his own dramatic actions in plays within plays, enriches his fictional world with gods and goddesses, dream landscapes, oracles and masques, and assumes the role of a player, a mediator, an "interpreter" in the strict sense of a go-between.[71] In a sense, the senior playwright of the King's Men begins to act again, not literally but virtually. One of the most telling signs of this reconsidered approach to drama is his new commitment to the delights of romance fiction. That he should have taken up romance at all, as Ben Jonson's notorious jibes at *Pericles* and *The Tempest* indicate, was something of a transgressive act, a discarding of a classically sanctioned form (Sidney's "high and excellent tragedy") for an old-fashioned popular mode associated with naïve audiences and with women in particular. For the Elizabethans and Jacobeans, tragedy, with its historical authority, was evidently masculine. This prejudice survives in the long-standing privileging of tragedy over comedy: love stories are merely pleasurable tales, useless fictions for and about women; real men read tragedies. These commonplaces form the backdrop against which Shakespeare exchanges what Janet Adelman has called the "end-stopped form" of tragedy for the more "open" form of romance.[72]

The late commitment to the pleasures of artifice also betokens a refreshed view of the affirmative capacities of language, an endorsement of words as a medium for constructing an alternative reality. Throughout the first years of the seventeenth century Shakespeare's estimation of language seems to have deteriorated. From *Hamlet* and *Othello* to *Timon* and *King Lear*, human speech seems predominantly an instrument of deception. Eloquence is what Cordelia refers to as a "glib and oily art," theatre an empty, misleading spectacle.[73] Implicit in all these tragedies is the positive understanding that the creator's way with words paradoxically exposes the danger of language misused: Iago's vicious gift for misrepresentation is finally inferior to his creator's talent for representing that misrepresentation. But Shakespearean tragedy rarely makes such artistic confidence explicit, and always the theme emerging from the narrative is

---

[71] This method is documented in the work of, among many others, Barbara A. Mowat, *The Dramaturgy of Shakespeare's Romances* (Athens: University of Georgia Press, 1976), Felperin, *Shakespearean Romance*, and James Calderwood, *Shakespearean Metadrama* (Amherst: University of Massachusetts Press, 1971).

[72] *Suffocating Mothers*, pp. 73–74, 190.

[73] For thoughtful commentary on these negative views, see Anne Barton, "Shakespeare and the Limits of Language," in *Essays, Mainly Shakespearean* (Cambridge: Cambridge University Press, 1994), pp. 51–69.

the capacity of language to destroy: in the hypocritical professions of Lear's daughters, the flattery of Timon's parasitical "friends," the duplicitous punning of the weird sisters in *Macbeth*. This is the side of communication that Coriolanus cannot bring himself to accommodate.

The shift from doubt to faith, or from mimesis to poesis, as I indicated in Chapter 1, takes place against the linguistic disputes of early modern England, specifically the conflict between Baconian skepticism about words and a Ciceronian enthusiasm for them. Shakespeare seems to oscillate between the two poles of thought in *Coriolanus* and *Antony and Cleopatra*. Bacon's was the "modern" position, Ascham's the old-fashioned, and the playwright once again seems to have looked backwards. If there is something of the skeptical Coriolanus and the dubious Octavius in Shakespeare, there is something of the extravagant Volumnia and Cleopatra as well: on the one hand, all the plays of this phase, especially *Macbeth*, exhibit a suspicion of language, its unreliability, its polysemic traps, its expressive inadequacies; on the other, they also admit an attraction to its material pleasures, creative ambiguity, and conciliatory power. The poetic victories of Volumnia and Cleopatra, although predicated on mortal defeat, clearly represent a triumph of the values of theatre and of voice, with all its vices. Accommodating his Baconian suspicions of language and its representational capacities, Shakespeare embraces the possibilities of ambiguity rather than fearing or seeking to control them. He commits himself to the vice of voice, accepting and making use of what has been called, in another context, "the gift of gap."[74] The space between the signifier and the signified, the territory that frightens both Coriolanus and the Renaissance Senecans, may indeed be treacherous. Gaps in tales may, in Puttenham's terms, "breed great confusion." But as his verb suggests, such a space is also generative, full of fanciful opportunity. At the end of the tragic sequence Shakespeare determines not to suppress but to exploit these possibilities.

The romantic turn attests to Shakespeare's devotion to the compensatory value of the word. His retrospective appreciation of Elizabethan fiction, his late re-engagement with Sidney, Spenser, Greene, and others, seems to have reminded him of the consolatory and diverting capacities of language. He invites the audience to relish the words themselves, not only for their power to illuminate but for their power to delight. In this respect the romances indicate finally a preference for Ciceronian over Senecan

---

[74] See R. A. Shoaf, "The Play of Puns in Late Middle English Poetry: Concerning Juxtology," in *On Puns: The Foundation of Letters*, ed. Jonathan Culler (London: Blackwell, 1988), p. 53.

values. Bacon, in admonishing the reader of *The Advancement of Learning* against "the first distemper of learning, when men studie words, and not matter," offers a symbol of that error: "It seemes to me that *Pigmalions* frenzie is a good embleme or portraiture of this vanitie: for wordes are but the Images of matter, and except they haue life of reason and inuention: to fall in loue with them, is all one, as to fall in loue with a Picture."[75] The emblematic use of Pygmalion is especially apt for understanding Shakespeare's thinking about his own role as a maker of art. *The Winter's Tale* famously blurs the distinction between the actual and the artistic by inviting us to fall in love with various forms of illusion, above all with Hermione's statue and, that which it represents, the play itself. For the mature Shakespeare, to fall in love with a picture is not self-evidently a fault: the artistic illusion, in the case of theatre a mingling of the verbal and the visual, is not a secondary endeavor, not an inferior form of experience. On the contrary, verbal illusion is a heightened form of human experience, even more vivid and no less valid than the illusion it copies and of which it is a legitimate part.[76]

When Jupiter rides into *Cymbeline* on his eagle he does so in Post-humus's dream, distanced from the audience and even from the reality of the play world. The deity's appearance is a form of illusion occurring within a play that is itself an illusion. So it is with Hermione's appearance to Antigonus in a dream. This distancing strategy discloses the implicit meanings associated with the mode of romance. By turning at the end of his career to stories of fantasy and magic, Shakespeare commits himself not only to the value of illusion but to the beneficent power of fiction in general. The tragedies record a profound abhorrence of the perils and deceits of illusion, a fear that exposes the playwright's serious doubt about his own profession. The turn to romance implies a reversal of this dubious view, an embrace of the illusory and the poetic. Shakespeare's professional doubts, if not dismissed, appear to have been at least allayed or balanced with renewed faith. Thus in the last plays the instances of spectacle tend to be affirmative rather than threatening, a point best demonstrated in the last scene of *The Winter's Tale*. The moving statue could be terrifying: as

---

[75] Francis Bacon, *The Advancement of Learning*, ed. Arthur Johnston (Oxford: Clarendon Press, 1974), pp. 17–18.

[76] As Philip Edwards puts it, "The argument that it is 'not life' has two answers: that it is as real a thing to contemplate this as to do anything else; and that if one looks elsewhere, like Bacon, for a true picture of 'reality' one has only fragments of suspicion, guesses and doubts, and the sense that 'we are such stuff as dreams are made on'." *Shakespeare and the Confines of Art* (London: Methuen, 1968), p. 153.

Paulina puts it, "you'll think / (Which I protest against) I am assisted / By wicked powers" (5.2.89–91). But instead of a demonic show, Paulina presents her audience with what amounts to a miracle – or a cheap trick. A work of art, an imitation of life, suddenly becomes "real," and this miracle occurs in a play which is itself an imitation of life, a fiction in which imaginary persons come to life for the pleasure of a credulous audience. Shakespeare relishes the indistinguishability of the illusory and the "actual." We are mocked with art, as the play puts it. We can't tell if the statue is an actor or a monument – audiences take pride in noting how still the actress is as she impersonates the statue – and we can't tell if the resurrection is a miracle or a gimmick. The artificiality of all experience, with Providence as the artist, the divine playwright, is the great theme of Shakespeare's last phase. Now is the moment for Prospero's revels speech.

Rather than quote it, however, I will conclude by denying the positive description I have just presented: the last plays are just as full of doubt, subversion, and ironic challenge as they are of affirmation and harmony. The poetic and generic hybridity I have been exploring is a stylistic manifestation of the ambivalence Shakespeare encourages his audience to consider and to relish. The end of *Cymbeline* is both a moving reconciliation and a dramatic carnival. Hermione's revival is both joyous and painful.[77] In *Henry VIII*, the rise of Anne Bullen must have struck its Jacobean audiences as joyful and minatory: the smutty puns on "emballing" and the knowledge of Anne's unhappy end color the celebration towards which the action moves, the birth of the Princess Elizabeth.[78] Probably the most complex interplay of affirmation and doubt occurs in *The Tempest*, a play whose insistence on questioning its own positivism seems incompatible with the Victorian image of the serene Shakespeare. The apparently frivolous genre secures its authority by mocking its own significance.

This recognition of a doubly ironic tone throughout the last plays should be extended to the style as well. Conflicting impulses govern Shakespeare's newly casual approach to poetic speech, specifically his

---

[77] What Anne Barton says about the ending of *The Winter's Tale* is true of the romances generally: it "admits something that Shakespeare's Elizabethan comedies had tried to deny: happy endings are a fiction. A fiction, but not quite a fairy tale." "Leontes and the Spider: Language and Speaker in Shakespeare's Last Plays," in *Essays, Mainly Shakespearean*, pp. 180–81. Also see Felperin, "Romance and Romanticism," pp. 67–68.

[78] According to Palfrey, "The very brittleness of Anne's precedent – the historical awareness that rhetorical idealism and popular applause could not in her case withstand the claims of flesh and realm – helps one give a political perspective to the tropes of celebratory, even redemptive, royal femininity" (*Late Shakespeare*, p. 200).

disregard for syntactical connection in the sentence, his tolerance for metrical irregularity, and his heterogeneous mixture of the artificial and the naturalistic. Thus the style helps to confirm and to validate these competing attitudes towards romance and teaches us to read the apparently antithetical conclusions that the action of the plays suggests.

Those readers who have felt that Shakespeare is reaching " beyond the words" are simply describing a phenomenon that audiences notice every time one of the romances is performed. Each of the last plays offers its audience the promise of something beyond. The tantalizing verbal configurations, particularly the echoing combinations that seem to promise profundity or hint at meaning that remains elusive, faithfully represent the fictional realms of Pericles' Mediterranean or the worlds of Sicilia and Bohemia. Some magical agency, some providential force seems to stand beyond the characters and their actions: there is something numinous about the world of Shakespearean romance. Caliban's intimations of beauty and fulfillment in the world of dreams may stand as an image of this realm, the thousand twangling instruments as a synecdoche for Shakespeare's late style.

LATE, NOT FINAL

The romances have been valued, sometimes thoughtlessly, for their affirmations, and usually such admiration undervalues the ironic or negative strain that also informs them. The wisdom associated with the complex vision of the romances is isolated and taken as evidence of Shakespeare's last thoughts, a version of the Victorian wish that our Shakespeare should end his career in the tonic key. But the career continues, and the balance seems to begin to shift once again.

The affirmations of the four principal romances, however qualified, seem less pertinent in thinking about *Henry VIII* and *The Two Noble Kinsmen*. Indeed, the failure of these plays to match the positive tones of the earlier four "last" plays is one of the reasons why a substantial number of critics have doubted the value of a distinct group or single designation for the plays from *Pericles* onwards, and why some earlier critics, lacking the bibliographic information we have, attempted to remove them from the canon altogether. The joyful climaxes of *The Winter's Tale* and *Cymbeline*, though tinged with doubt and pain, are not sustained through the whole sequence. *The Tempest* is a kind of pivot in this respect: the shadows have begun to loom larger; evidence of irresolution is too great to ignore. In *Henry VIII*, the birth of Elizabeth is the putative happy ending, of course, but an audience cannot forget how much suffering has been endured to reach that conclusion, how much blood has passed under the bridge. That blood cannot be dismissed, even by the joyful news of the birth of the great queen.[79] Similarly, *The Two Noble Kinsmen* is clouded with doubt, the last act marked by pain and death.[80]

In the main body of romances, strategies of subversion operate dialectically with complementary tactics of affirmation, and the effect is usually to amplify the sense of joy, to throw the weight upon the miracle of the happy ending. By the time of *Henry VIII* and *The Two Noble Kinsmen*, these deflationary strategies seem dominant, more potent than their beneficent complements. Such negative possibility is also encoded in the poetic style. To sense that there is something beyond the words does not mean that what lies beyond the words is necessarily reassuring. Shakespeare's style still seems elliptical, roundabout, crowded, and extravagant, but the sense of possibility no longer appears to obtain. He seems to be changing his mind again.

---

[79] For a balanced discussion of the conflicting generic signals encoded in the play, see Gordon McMullan's Introduction to his Arden3 edition (London: Thomson Learning, 2000), especially pp. III–15.

[80] Richard Proudfoot, in an important article written in the 1960s, distinguishes between this and the earlier romances: "*The Two Noble Kinsmen* is unlike these plays in that the winning of love and the death of Arcite are juxtaposed at the end so that the overwhelming impression is not so much of the value of love as its appalling cost. Not since *All's Well that Ends Well* had Shakespeare written a play whose conclusion leaves such a sense of unease. It is almost as if he was beginning once more to call in question the positive power of love." "Shakespeare and the New Dramatists of the King's Men," in *Later Shakespeare*, ed. John Russell Brown and Bernard Harris (London: Edward Arnold, 1966), p. 271.

Index